Recording Angels

Recording Angels

The Secret World of Women's Diaries

Sarah Gristwood

London

First published in Great Britain 1988
by HARRAP Ltd
19-23 Ludgate Hill, London EC4M 7PD

ISBN 0-245-54519-0

Designed by Jim Weaver

Phototypeset by Facet Film Composing Limited
Leigh-on-Sea, Essex

Printed and bound in Great Britain by
Mackays of Chatham, Kent.

Contents

Acknowledgements

Among the many to whom my thanks are due, two names come first: Marta Bruno, who made me a present of the idea for this book in a boat on Lake Maggiore, and Hazel West, who did an enormous amount of research in less scenic surroundings. I also owe a great deal to Valerie Grove who, as Valerie Jenkins eighteen years ago, began compiling material for a book of unpublished teenage diaries. This material she very kindly allowed me to see, and it formed an invaluable background for my own work.

I should like to thank the Museum of London for allowing me to see their unpublished suffragette material and all those friends and associates who have suggested names, books, or leads.

In assembling *Recording Angels*, I was greatly helped by Margaret Gaskin, and by Jackie Opie and Sue Skempton, who turned my illegible pages into a smoothly typed text.

Where possible, the date preceding each extract follows the style of the original source.

List of Sources

Abernon, Viscountess d', *Red Cross and Berlin Embassy 1915–1926.* John Murray, 1946.

Acton, J.E.E. (ed.): *Journals of George Eliot.* London, 1885.

(Anon): *Go Ask Alice.* Prentice Hall Inc, 1971; Avon Books, 1972.

Askwith, Betty: *A Victorian Young Lady.* Michael Russell Ltd., 1978.

Asquith, Lady Cynthia: *Diaries, 1915-18.* Hutchinson, 1968.

Bashkirtseff, Marie: The Journals of Maria Bashkirtseff. John Murray, 1974; Virago, 1985.

Bentley, Toni: *Winter Season—A Dancer's Journal.* Random House/Jill Norman, 1982.

Berridge, Elizabeth: *The Barretts at Hope End.* John Murray, 1974.

Bodichon, Barbara Leigh Smith: *An American Diary 1857-8.* Routledge Kegan Paul, 1972.

Brittain, Vera: *Chronicle of Friendship* and *Chronicle of Youth,* edited by Alan Bishop, Gollancz, 1981. Reproduced by permission of Victor Gollancz, the publishers, and McMaster University, Canada, the proprietors.

Brown, Michele and **O'Connor, Ann (compilers):** *Woman Talk: 2. A Woman's Book of Quotes.* Futura, 1985.

Burney, Fanny: *The Journals and Letters of Fanny Burney (Madame D'Arblay).* Clarendon Press, 10 vols, 1972 on.

Carrington, Dora: *Letters and Extracts from her Diaries,* ed. by David Garnett. Cape, 1970. Reprinted by permission of the David Garnett Estate, The Sophie Partridge Trust and Jonathan Cape Ltd.

Castle, Barbara: *The Castle Diaries.* Weidenfeld & Nicolson, 1984.

Cavendish, Lady Frederick: *The Diary of Lady Frederick Cavendish,* ed. by John Bailey. John Murray, 1927.

Chesnut, May Boykin. *A Diary from Dixie,* ed. by Ben Ames Williams. Harvard University Press, 1980.

Clifford, Lady Anne: *The Diary of the Lady Anne Clifford.* Heinemann, 1923.

Cooper, Jilly: *The Common Years*. Methuen, 1984.

Cullwick, Hannah: *The Diaries of Hannah Cullwick, Victorian Maidservant*, ed. by Liz Stanley. Virago, 1984.

Dessaulles, Henriette: Passages quoted are reprinted from *Hopes and Dreams: The Diary of Henriette Dessaulles 1874-81*. Copyright 1986. Translated by Liedewij Hawke. Reprinted with permission of the publisher, Hounslow Press, Toronto, Canada.

Dixon, Agnes M: *The Canteeners*. John Murray, 1917.

Duberley, Mrs Henry: *Journal Kept During the Russian War*. London, 1855.

Duras, Marguerite: *La Douleur*, trans. by Barbara Bray. Collins, 1986.

Eberhardt, Isabelle: *A Passionate Nomad*, translated by Alina de Voogd. Virago Press, 1987.

Fountaine, Margaret: *Love Among the Butterflies*, ed. by W. F. Cater. Collins, 1980, and *Butterflies and Late Loves*, ed. by W. F. Cater. Collins, 1986.

Frank, Anne: *The Diary of Anne Frank*. Translated by B. M. Mooyaart. Doubleday, 1952; Vallentine, Mitchell & Co. Ltd.; Pan Books Ltd., 1954.

Fremantle, Anne: *The Wynne Diaries* (3 vols; 1935, 1937, 1940). Reprinted by permission of Oxford University Press.

Froude, J.A: *Letters and Memorials of Jane Welsh Carlyle*. London, 1883.

Fry, Elizabeth: *A Memoir of the Life of Elizabeth Fry With Extracts from her Journals and Letters*, ed. by two of her daughters. London, Charles Gilpin, 1847.

Gawthern, Abigail: *Journal*. The Thornton Society, 1978–9.

Gladstone, May (Mrs Drew): *Diaries and Letters*, ed. by Lucy Masterman. Dutton (NY), 1930.

Hanff, Helene: *84, Charing Cross Road*. André Deutsch, 1971; Futura, 1981.

Hibbert, Christopher (ed.): *Queen Victoria in Her Letters and Journals*. John Murray, 1984.

Hillesum, Etty: *Etty: A Diary 1941-3*, trans. by Arnold J. Pomerans. Jonathan Cape, 1983; Triad Grafton, 1985.

Hoby, Lady M: *Diary of Lady Margaret Hoby 1599-1605*, ed. by Dorothy M. Meads. Routledge, 1930.

Irvine, Lucy: *Castaway*. Gollancz, 1983.

James, Alice: *The Diary of Alice James*, ed. by Leon Edel. Reprinted by permission of Dodd, Mead & Company, Inc. From *The Diary of Alice James*, edited by Leon Edel. Copyright © 1984 by Leon Edel.

Jameson, Anna Brownell: *Winter Studies and Summer Rambles in Canada*. McElelland & Stewart, 1923.

Jephson, Lady: *A War-Time Journal—Germany 1914 and Travel Notes*. Elkin Mathews, 1915.

Johnson, Lady Bird: *The White House Years*. Weidenfeld & Nicolson, 1979.

Keller, Helen: *The Journal of Helen Keller*. Michael Joseph, 1938.

'Lady X': *Diary of My Honeymoon*. John Long, 1910.

Langton, Anne: *A Gentlewoman in Upper Canada: The Journals of Anne Langton*. ed. H. H. Langton. Irwin Publishing Inc., 1964.

Last, Nella: *Nella Last's War—A Mother's Diary, 1939-45*, ed. by Richard Broad and Suzie Fleming. Falling Wall Press 1981; Sphere Books, 1983.

Lawrence, Honoria: *The Journals of Honoria Lawrence*. Hodder & Stoughton, 1980.

Lister, Anne: *I Know My Own Heart: The Diaries of Anne Lister (1791-1840)*, ed. by Helena Whitbread. Virago, 1980.

Llangollen, Ladies of: *A Year With the Ladies of Llangollen*, ed. by Elizabeth Mavor. Viking, 1984; Penguin, 1973.

Longfellow, Fanny Appleton: *Fanny Longfellow*. Peter Owen.

Mallon, Thomas: *A Book of One's Own, (People and Their Diaries)*. Ticknor & Fields, 1984; Penguin Books, 1986.

Mansfield, Katherine: *Journal of Katherine Mansfield*, ed. by J. Middleton Murray. Constable, 1954.

Milburn, Clara: *Mrs Milburn's Diaries: An Englishwoman's Day-to-day Reflections, 1939-45*, ed. by Peter Donnelly. Harrap, 1979.

Milner, Marion: *A Life of One's Own*. Chatto & Windus, 1934; Virago, 1986.

Mitchison, Naomi: *Among You Taking Notes*, ed. by Dorothy Sheridan. Gollancz, 1985.

Monkswell, Lady: *A Victorian Diarist—Extracts From The Journal of Mary, Lady Monkswell 1873-1895*, ed. by The Hon. E. C. F. Collier. John Murray, 1944.

Morley, Helena: *The Diary of Helena Morley*. Virago, 1981.

Newton, Ellen: *This Bed My Centre*. Virago Press, 1980.

Nin, Anaïs: *Henry and June*. W. H. Allen, 1987. *Journals: Vols. I-VIII*, ed. by Gunther Stuhlmann. Peter Owen/Quartet, 1966 on. *Journal of a Wife*. Peter Owen, 1984; Quartet, 1986.

Northumberland, Elizabeth, Duchess of: *The Diaries of a Duchess*, ed. by James Greig. London, 1926.

Partridge, Frances: *A Pacifist's War*. Hogarth Press, 1978, and *Everything to Lose: Diaries 1945-1960*. Gollancz, 1985.

Plath, S: *The Journals of Sylvia Plath*, ed. by Ted Hughes and Frances McCulloch. Ballantine Books (a division of Random House), 1982.

Pless, Princess D: *Daisy, Princess of Pless by Herself* and *From My Private Diary*, ed. by Major Desmond Chapman-Huston. John Murray, 1913-14.

Pollock, Linda: *A Lasting Relationship: Parents and Children Over Three Centuries*. Fourth Estate (Publishers) Ltd., 1987.

Ponsonby, Arthur: *More English Diaries*. Methuen, 1927.

Potter, Beatrix: *The Journal of Beatrix Potter from 1881 to 1897*, trans. by Leslie Linder. Frederick Warne & Co., 1966.

Pougy, Lione de: *My Blue Notebooks*, trans. by Diana Athill. André Deutsch, 1979. Reprinted by Century Hutchinson, 1986.

Pym, Barbara: *A Very Private Eye*. Macmillan, 1984. Reproduced by permission of Macmillan, London and Basingstoke.

Rittenhouse, Maud: *Maud*, ed. by Richard L. Strout. Macmillan, New York, 1939.

Roberts, Rachel: *No Bells on Sunday*, ed. by Alexander Walker, Pavilion Books, 1984; Sphere Books, 1985.

Sambourne, Marion: *A Victorian Household*, ed. by Shirley Nicholson. Barrie & Jenkins, 1988.

Sand, George: *The Intimate Journal*, ed. and trans. by Marie Jenny Howe. Academy Press, Chicago, 1977.

Sarton, May: *Journal of a Solitude*. Women's Press Ltd., 1985.

Schlissel, Lillian: *Women's Diaries of the Westward Journey*. Schocken Books, 1982.

Shelley, Mary: *The Journals of Mary Shelley*, ed. by Paula R.Feldman and Diana Scott Kilvert. The Clarendon Press, Oxford, 1987.

Sheridan, Betsy: *Betsy Sheridan's Journal*, ed. by William Lefanu. Oxford University Press, 1986.

Shippen, Nancy: *Her Journal Book*, ed. by Ethyl Armes. Lippincott Co., London & Philadelphia, 1935.

Shonagan, Sei: *The Pillow Book of Sei Shonagan*, trans. & ed. by Ivan Morris. Oxford University Press, 1967; Penguin, 1971.

Shore, Emily: *The Diary of Emily Shore*, from *More English Diaries* by Arthur Ponsonby. Methuen, 1927.

Simcoe, Mrs: *Mrs Simcoe's Diary*, ed. by Mary Quayle Innis. Macmillan, Canada, 1965.

Stark, Freya: *A Winter in Arabia*. John Murray, 1973.

Thompson, Tierl: *Dear Girl: The Diaries and Letters of Two Working Women 1897-1917*. The Women's Press, 1987.

Tolstoy, Sophia: *The Diaries of Sophia Tolstoy*, trans. by Cathy Porter. Random House, New York, 1985.

Truitt, Anne: *Daybook, The Journal of an Artist*. Pantheon Books, 1982; Penguin, 1984.

Victoria, Queen: *Queen Victoria In Her Letters and Journals*, ed. by Christopher Hibbert. John Murray, 1984.

Waddington, Mary King: *My War Diary*. John Murray, 1918.

Webb, Beatrice: *The Diaries of Beatrice Webb*. Virago Press, 1982-4.

Weeton, Miss: *Journal of A Governess 1811-25*, ed. by Edward Hall. Oxford University Press, 1939.

Williams, Eve: *Ladies Without Lamps*. Thomas Harmsworth Publishing, 1983.

Woodforde, Dorothy (ed): *Woodforde Papers and Diaries*. Peter Davies, 1932.

Woolf, Virginia: *The Diary of Virginia Woolf, A Writer's Diary*, [and main diaries], ed. by Leonard Woolf. Hogarth Press, 1977-84. Reproduced by permission of The Estate of Virginia Woolf and the Hogarth Press.

Wordsworth, Dorothy: *Journals of Dorothy Wordsworth*, ed. by Mary Moorman. Oxford University Press, 1971.

Wyndham, Joan: *Love Lessons, A Wartime Diary*, Heinemann, 1985; Flamingo, 1986; and *Love is Blue, A Wartime Diary*. Heinemann, 1986; Flamingo, 1987.

Foreword

'Many people blame me for not keeping a proper diary, a record of my life with Leo Nikolaevich,' wrote Sophy Tolstoy, the novelist's wife, almost exactly a century ago. 'But it is so hard to renounce my *personal* feelings about him, so hard to be impartial.' Thank God she didn't succeed. Diaries are the most personal, the most revealing and—as these pages show—often the most unexpected form of writing. That is just what makes them so compelling to read.

When the idea for a book on women's diaries was first suggested, it struck me at once as a good one. So good, in fact, that someone must surely have done it before... Not so. There have been several anthologies of diaries and diarists, but they have been very largely about men. That, of course, says something about the general neglect of women's history, women's work, women's experience. It also, from my point of view, offered a unique opportunity. How better to fill in some of the gaps, flesh out the skeletal picture of women's lives over the last centuries, than through their diaries, the 'silent friend' (Sophy Tolstoy again) who heard not only the details of their daily lives but the secrets of their inner ones?

Open the pages of a woman's diary, and you never know quite what you are going to find. Elizabeth Fry from the nineteenth century talks about how children interfere with her career; Barbara Castle from the twentieth talks about her hairdos. Nella Last, a middle-aged housewife in the Second World War, chronicles her personal voyage of female liberation. Barbara Pym can't keep her mind off food.... Florence Nightingale succumbs to despair. No one fits meekly into the boxes provided for them. After the first few months of research on this book, I felt as if I had reached out to stroke a pet cat, and found I'd caught a tiger by the tail.

Slowly, the secret world of women's diaries is beginning to see the light of day. For many years, novelists and scriptwriters have cashed in on the peek-a-boo pleasure offered by the diary form. The Pooters, E. M. Delafield's 'Provincial Lady', Mrs Dale. (No fictional diarists are included in this book—truth was so strange that fiction seemed superfluous and their inclusion would, in any case, have compromised the validity of any conclusions that might be drawn.) But every other month now, it seems, another newly rediscovered diary reaches the bookshop shelves and I for one am glad of it. It eases what you might call my anthologist's conscience.

In compiling edited extracts from the diaries of a hundred or more women, one is most bitterly aware of how very much has to be left out. Many of the diaries referred to here are long out of print, unavailable in this country or to be found only in university libraries or the British Museum. Some have never been published at all; others are, in their complete form, uninviting if not actually unreadable. But all the same, I should like to begin this book not only with a celebration of women diarists, but with an apology to them, for casting what is of necessity such a flickering light over their private lives. Or perhaps for casting any light at all... 'it's my soul that holds the pen', wrote Henriette Dessaulles, on refusing the request of an inquisitive friend to read her diary; '... it is impossible to let her read my soul'.

Tread softly, seems to be the message—for you tread on my dreams.

Sarah Gristwood
April, 1988

Part I
A Mental
Looking-glass

- Journalizing
- On Youth and Age
- Looks

Chapter 1
Journalizing

'*Let diaries, therefore, be brought in use.*'—Frances Bacon

For Whose Eyes Only

The reading of diaries has often been almost as popular as the writing of them. There is undeniably a pleasurable element of peek-a-boo, of trespassing on to private ground. In that, though, the readers may be deluding themselves. Do diarists write for their own eyes only or for a yet unknown and maybe hoped for reader? Oscar Wilde's Cecily has the first—or maybe the last—word on that. No, Algernon may not see her diary itself, but she hopes he will order a copy later: 'You see, it is simply a very young girl's record of her own thoughts and impressions, and consequently meant for publication.'

Does Cecily have a point or not? In 1768 the young Fanny Burney, one of the best-known female diarists, began her journal like this:

Addressed to a Certain Miss Nobody
Poland Street, London, 27 March 1768
To have some account of my thoughts, manners, acquaintance and actions, when the hour arrives in which time is more nimble than memory, is the reason which induces me to keep a Journal. A Journal in which I must confess my *every* thought, must open my whole heart! But a thing of this kind ought to be addressed to somebody—I must imagion [sic] myself to be talking—talking to the most intimate of friends—to one in whom I should take delight in confiding, and remorse in concealment:—but who must—this friend be? to make choice of one in whom I can but *half* rely,

3

would be to frustrate entirely the intention of my plan. The only one I could wholly, totally confide in, lives in the same house with me, and not only never *has*, but never *will*, leave me one secret to tell her. To *whom*, then, *must* I dedicate my wonderful, surprising and interesting Adventures?—to *whom* dare I reveal my private opinion of my nearest relations? my secret thoughts of my dearest friends? my own hopes, fears, reflections, and dislikes!—Nobody!

To Nobody, then, will I write my Journal! since to Nobody can I be wholly unreserved—to Nobody can I reveal every thought, every wish of my heart, with the most unlimited confidence, the most unremitting sincerity to the end of my life! For what chance, what accident can end my connections with Nobody? No secret *can* I conceal from Nobody, and to Nobody can I be *ever* unreserved. Disagreement cannot stop our affection, Time itself has no power to end our friendship. The love, the esteem I entertain for Nobody, Nobody's self has not power to destroy. From Nobody I have nothing to fear, the secrets sacred to friendship Nobody will not reveal; when the affair is doubtful, Nobody will not look towards the side least favourable.

And Anne Frank, another famous young diarist, wrote:

Saturday, 20th June, 1942

I haven't written for a few days, because I wanted first of all to think about my diary. It's an odd idea for someone like me to keep a diary; not only because I have never done so before, but because it seems to me that neither I—nor for that matter anyone else—will be interested in the unbosomings of a thirteen-year-old schoolgirl. Still, what does that matter? I want to write, but more than that, I want to bring out all kinds of things that lie buried deep in my heart.

'Always keep a diary,' said Mae West. 'Someday it will keep you.' Hollywood's darling, Mary Astor, did keep one, and it almost broke her instead. After extracts were read out to the court in her scandalous divorce case, the jury had the whole book burnt as pornographic. It must have been the kind of thing Oscar Wilde was thinking of when he gave Gwendolen Fairfax her famous line: 'I never travel without my diary. One should always have something sensational to read in the train.'

In the same play, *The Importance of Being Earnest*, Wilde wrote something much truer than that. The governess, Miss Prism, asks the inexperienced Cecily why she bothers to keep a diary at all. Cecily replies: 'I keep a diary in order to enter the wonderful secrets of my life. If I didn't write them down, I should probably forget all about them.' Or not believe they existed at all, perhaps. To keep a diary is not just a way to hold on to our experiences. It is a way to validate them, to clarify them in our own minds... small wonder that the impulse to journalize is amazingly wide-spread.

The habit is more prevalent at some stages of life than at others and has been more popular in some centuries than in others. Keeping a diary has, for obvious reasons, been most popular among the leisured and literate upper and middle classes, though by no means confined to them. What can it have cost the eight hundred pioneer women, who made the wagon-train journey west to California, to have sat down day by day and recorded the chores, the happenings, the hopes and fears, the Indian raids and the bones along the trail? If the entries women make in their diaries vary from the stylish introspections of Virginia Woolf to the funny terseness of the Misses Wynne more than a century earlier, so too do the things they write about—the preoccupations, practical or precious, that become apparent through the standard formula of 'Today I...'

'No one will grasp what I'm talking about,' Anne Frank continues, 'if I begin my letters to Kitty [her name for her diary "friend"] just out of the blue so, albeit unwillingly, I will start by sketching in brief the story of my life.'

'Nobody' will know what she is talking about? Neither Anne Frank nor Fanny Burney could at the time of writing have been aware how many ears and eyes 'Nobody' was in future years to assume. But it looks as if they were both aware of the ambivalence at the heart of diary writing. Is the writer really talking to herself, or to an unknown, ideal, unattainable Other? Is it really the most private form of writing known to man—or woman—or a sneaky surfacing of the exhibitionist streak which lies at the heart of us all?

'... if I die,' wrote Katherine Bisshopp in 1817, 'I shall be much obliged to the first person into whose hands this Book may happen to fall, to destroy it instantly'... 'I have written much that I would show only to a very few,' wrote Emily Shore a few years later, 'and much that I would on no account submit to any human eye. Still even now I cannot entirely divest myself of an uncomfortable notion that the whole may some future day when I am in my grave be read by some individual, and this notion has without my being often aware of it, cramped me, I am sure.'

Beatrice Webb in her twenties vacillated as to whether her diaries should be burnt unread, shown to her father and then burnt, or sent to a friend. But in the course of a long life another option became more attractive, and the first work on typing and editing the diaries as for publication was done by Webb herself. 'What a blessing that I can write in this little book without fearing that anyone will read and

ridicule the nonsense and half-sense I scribble,' she wrote in 1882.
'That has been the attraction of a "diary-book" to me—one can talk
one's little thinkings out to a highly appreciative audience, dumb but
not deaf.' She is, in those despairing and lonely twenties, another who
cannot keep off the subject of journalizing, another who speculates:

> It would be curious to discover who it is to whom one writes in a diary.
> Possibly to some mysterious personification of one's own identity, to the
> Unknown, which lies below the constant change of matters and ideas,
> constituting the individual at any given moment.

And as for why:

> A diary is only the reflection of one's mind for one's own interest and
> amusement in after years: or, rather, it is, with me, an outlet for
> expression...

Of course there are other diarists who know, as a matter of fact, not of
metaphysical speculation, that they are writing for more than an
audience of one... Virginia Woolf's diary was to her a 'kindly
blank-faced old confidante', an authorial gymnasium where she
practised her writing effects and invented her novels, a repository of
memories for her future self, 'Old V.' ('How I envy her the task I am
preparing for her!') But she was under no illusions that the books would
never be read by anyone other than Old V.:

> *Saturday, March 20th*
> But what is to become of all these diaries, I asked myself yesterday. If I died,
> what would Leo make of them? He would be disinclined to burn them; he
> could not publish them. Well, he should make up a book from them, I think;
> and then burn the body. I daresay there is a little book in them; if the scraps
> and scratching were straightened out a little. God knows.

The journals of Anaïs Nin became the main body of her life's work.
Keeping a diary was, for her, about the 'quest for self'. But the
numerous volumes were also to be stored for safety in a Brooklyn bank
vault, lest accident should befall them and the world be deprived.

Other diarists wrote with a more limited audience just as firmly in
mind. Dorothy Wordsworth, the poet's sister, wrote in the hope that
she might 'give Wm. pleasure by it'. George Sand kept a wild journal
with the intention of sending it to Alfred de Musset, the lover who had
abandoned her. Honoria Lawrence and her husband Henry in
Victorian India wrote a journal 'to' each other; later she also wrote one
to their son in boarding-school at home. (While the dictionary shows
that there is no distinction of meaning between 'diary' and 'journal', it
looks as if, in earlier centuries, the distinction between 'journal' and
'letter' was rather blurred as well...)

Is the diary/journal the most authentic form of self-expression, the one least subject to censorship, to policy, to the need to get a specific message across? Well, yes—and no. As mentioned above, the possibility of the entries being read by someone else is always at the back of the diarist's mind.

The journal/letter remains an authentic record of day-to-day experience, a record of what in the fabric of daily life seemed important at the time. There is always the chance, moreover, that once the writing habit has started, a diary will claim its own. Take Mary Shelley, whose Journals were recently published. Volume I was written in tandem with her husband, the poet, and very dull it is too, at least when she has the composition of it—a terse record of journeys and books. Volume II resumes a few months after Shelley's death—and what a difference. Long outpourings, the agonized record of loss and despair—and of gradual rebirth into life again. It is as if, with the poet's drowning, a true diarist was born.

A Friend in Need

For the lonely, keeping a diary can be a source of comfort, a friend in need.

'Dear friend', is how Daisy, Princess of Pless, an Edwardian English girl who married a German aristocrat, addressed her diary, through the long years when she must sometimes have needed one. 'My dear precious friend,' said the American teenager Alice, more effusive in her need. 'I'm so scared and so cold and so alone,' she had written earlier. 'I have only you, Diary. You and me, what a pair.'

'This unknown one was once my only friend,' wrote Beatrice Webb, 'the being to whom I went for advice and consolation in all the small troubles of a child's life.' And Anne Frank, as already mentioned, addressed her thoughts to an imaginary friend:

> And now I come to root of the matter, the reason for my starting a diary: it is that I have no such real friend.
>
> Let me put it more clearly, since no one will believe that a girl of thirteen feels herself quite alone in the world, nor is it so. I have darling parents and a sister of sixteen. I know about thirty people whom one might call friends—I have strings of boy friends, anxious to catch a glimpse of me and who, failing that, peep at me through mirrors in class. I have relations, aunts, and uncles, who are darlings too, a good home, no—I don't seem to lack anything. But it's the same with all my friends, just fun and games, nothing more. I can never bring myself to talk of anything outside the common round. We don't seem to be able to get any closer, that is the root of

the trouble. Perhaps I lack confidence, but anyway, there it is, a stubborn fact and I don't seem to be able to do anything about it.

Hence, this diary. In order to enhance in my mind's eye the picture of the friend for whom I have waited so long, I don't want to set down a series of bald facts in a diary like most people do, but I want this diary itself to be my friend, and I shall call my friend Kitty.

'My diary has become a rather cumbersome friend whom I still love but no longer need,' wrote Canadian schoolgirl Henriette Dessaulles in 1876. Less ruthlessly cold-blooded, more women apologize to their diaries when they haven't written in them for some time. 'How shameful of me', 'So sorry for neglecting you', 'How could I?' . . . Sorry. Sorry. *Sorry.*

'I have no friend,' wrote Mary Shelley, explaining to herself her impulse to begin the journal again after Shelley's death.

Now I am alone—oh, how alone! The stars may behold my tears, and the winds drink my sighs; but my thoughts are a sealed treasure, which I can confess to none. But can I express all I feel?

Alice James, sister of the novelist Henry James, knew an impulse somewhat the same:

May 31st, 1889

I think that if I get into the habit of writing a bit about what happens, or rather doesn't happen, I may lose a little of the sense of loneliness and desolation which abides with me. My circumstances allowing of nothing but the ejaculation of one-syllabled reflections, a written monologue by that most interesting being, *myself,* may have its yet to be discovered consolations. I shall at least have it all my own way and it may bring relief as an outlet to that geyser of emotions, sensations, speculations and reflections which ferments perpetually within my poor old carcass for its sins; so here goes, my first Journal!

Release is implicit too in this passage from Etty Hillesum's diary:

Sunday, 9 March [1941].

Here goes, then. This is a painful and well-nigh insuperable step for me: yielding up so much that has been suppressed to a blank sheet of lined paper. The thoughts in my head are sometimes so clear and so sharp and my feelings so deep, but writing about them comes hard. The main difficulty, I think, is a sense of shame. So many inhibitions, so much fear of letting go, of allowing things to pour out of me, and yet that is what I must do if I am ever to give my life a reasonable and satisfactory purpose.

Some, of course, have been looking for more than relief from the intensity of their feelings when first they sat down to write a diary. Some have been looking for Answers, no less. In the 1970s American writer

May Sarton, sculptress Anne Truitt and dancer Toni Bentley were all looking for access to and deeper understanding of their artistic selves. Etty Hillesum, whose diary finished on the road to Auschwitz and whose life ended there soon after, hoped that the one would give the other a 'reasonable and satisfactory purpose', as she says in the extract quoted above. All diarists are explorers of the mind—some more consciously than others. And none more consciously than psychologist Marion Milner.

Her book, *A Life Of One's Own,* first published in 1934 under the pseudonym of Joanna Field, is 'the record of a seven years' study of living'. It was researched, almost as one might research a mystery, out of the diaries she had earlier kept as a way of answering the big, basic questions she asked herself. 'What will make me happy? What do I really want from life?':

> Was there not a way by which each person could find out for himself what he was like, not by reading what other people thought he ought to be, but directly, as directly as knowing the sky is blue and how an apple tastes , not needing anyone to tell him? Perhaps, then, if one could not write for other people one could write for oneself...

Even if the price, she warns, is often to find oneself more of a fool than one thought. She had her eyes opened a bit when, as a first step in her journey of self-discovery, she sat down to record what had been in her mind one ordinary working day:

> My main concern when I got up this morning was whether I'd be able to get my hair cut before going to work: and whether I wasn't looking pale and tired, and how limp I felt, almost unable to cope with going to see F. I was in the depths when I rang up the hairdresser and he couldn't see me.... I was cheered by finding the S. Street place would cut my hair: and having it done by a polite young man. At the office I hoped there'd be someone about to see how nicely my hair was cut, and how attractive it looked. On combing it I thought how plain I was. Then I lunched with F. and had no leisure for thinking of my looks, except when I knew I was flushed and had he noticed it. I left him in a glow of elation that all had gone so well, thinking what an intriguing person I was. After a bit of work, not very concentrated, and an attempt to find Miss P. and show her my new hair-cut, I chatted to her and thought how charming I had been. I went to the club and was delighted to hear M. say my hair looked charming. We played ping-pong and playing better than usual I thought I was a fine creature.... At supper... I wondered whether I was talking well, and when they mentioned M. I felt a slap in the face because he'd sent a p.c. to someone else: also sort of hurt because they said he wasn't strong and mightn't stand roughing it. I hated to think these people knew him. They might guess that I'd taken him

seriously, and knew that I was only one of many for him. But I think none of them really understood him and I did. I came home and sorted photos to put in a book, picking out those that were good of me. Good God!

Recording Angels

Sometimes women begin keeping a diary for less introspective reasons—to chronicle events of historical importance.

> I began talking my White House diary into a tape recorder at our home,
> The Elms, two or three days after November 22, 1963. Why did I record it?
> I think for the following reasons: I realized shortly after 22, that I stood in a
> unique position...

wrote Lady Bird Johnson. As wife to the President of the United States, and successor to Jacqueline Kennedy, she certainly did, and the event of 22 November with which the diary opens is an eye-witness account of President Kennedy's assassination. But she is far from the first, or the last, woman to begin a diary impelled by the need to pay tribute to some unique experience. It may be to chronicle a war or a journey—like the *Swiss Journal* kept, on behalf of the whole party, by a traveller on the first Cook's tour.

Sometimes the writers feel impelled to keep a tally as precise as that of the recording angel up above. Sometimes it is their own score-card they are keeping, as in the older diaries, like the one kept by Lady Margaret Hoby around 1600 for the purposes of religious discipline and improvement. Sometimes, it is the score-card of the world and the diarist becomes less a chronicler than a testifier, a bearer of witness. Vera Brittain goes into a long explanation not of why she wrote her diaries of the First World War years but of why she chose later to publish them:

> I belong to the few who believe in all sincerity that their own lives provide
> the answers to some of the many problems which puzzle humanity.

'It is hardly necessary to say,' writes Frances Partridge in the Preface to *A Pacifist's War:*

> ... that the following extracts from my diary of 1940-5 were not written with
> any idea of publication, but as a means of relieving the various emotions
> aroused by the Second World War, ranging from boredom to horror, fear
> and disgust. Why publish them? ... Perhaps my chief purpose is to testify to
> the pacifist beliefs I developed in my teens during the First World War, and
> which I shared with my husband Ralph.'

Sometimes, though, the testament is to oneself, the diarist bearing witness for an audience of one. 'I will endeavour to persevere in writing this as perhaps I may at some future time derive some pleasure in looking over even this deplorable remembrancer of my troubles,' wrote Katherine Bisshopp in 1817.'... it has become to me a valuable index of my mind, and has been the record of faults and follies which have made my cheek burn on the reperusal,' wrote Emily Shore a few years later. 'So often have I found strength in turning over the back pages of my life,' wrote Beatrice Webb in 1887. These three aren't in any way unusual. Nor—apart from a few variations of vocabulary—do they speak for their own century alone. To judge by internal evidence, re-readers among diarists are not the exception, but the rule. Remember Virginia Woolf preparing a treat for 'Old V.'... Gwendolen Fairfax, you are not alone!

D for Danger

Intimacy, honesty, the ability to put you in touch with your own feelings—all the qualities for which others have valued diary writing—are powerful enough to be potentially double-edged weapons, as Katherine Mansfield, ill with T.B. and living in exile abroad, admitted in a letter to Middleton Murray:

5 October 1920

.... The Journal—I have absolutely given up. I dare not keep a journal. I should always be trying to tell the truth. As a matter of fact I dare not tell the truth. I feel I *must* not. The only way to exist is to go on and try and lose oneself—to get as far as possible away from *this* moment. Once I can do that all will be well.

And Elizabeth Barrett (later-to-be Browning), still living under her father's domination when she began her year-long diary on 4 June 1831, spelt out the problem with frankness.

To write a diary, I have thought of very often at far & near distances of time: but how could I write a diary without throwing upon paper my thoughts, all my thoughts—the thoughts of my heart as well as of my head?—& then could I bear to look on *them* after they were written? Adam made fig leaves necessary for the mind, as well as for the body. And such a mind as I have! —So very exacting & exclusive & eager & headlong— & strong— & so very, very often wrong.

Diaries are dangerous, seems to be the message. They represent Pandora's Box, the can of worms. Open the door, lift the lid, and who knows what you might have unleashed on to the world.

In the 1941 film *Kathleen*, the teenaged Shirley Temple accuses her governess of prying in her diary. 'If you were a nice girl with a nice clean mind,' the governess replies, 'you wouldn't keep a diary'. Perhaps it is symbolic, and not just for fear of prying eyes, that those books aimed at young girls are often sold with locks...

Henriette Dessaulles, returning to her convent school in Canada almost a century earlier, had qualms of her own:

August 24 1876

... Now you have come to an end, poor old notebook. Such a lot of secrets I've scribbled in you! You'll go and join your brothers in my Swiss chest and when I'm older I'll burn you. But I'll reread you first and I'll probably squirm with embarrassment at my juvenile ravings. I'll buy a new notebook to take your place—but I doubt it will be safe from the nuns' prying eyes! Therefore, I haven't quite made up my mind whether I'll confide in it or not. If not, it will remain as unsullied as my life in the convent, which is going to be virtuous, innocent... and dull!

Her doubts proved justified:

January 23 1877

Diaries are in fashion and there's many a secret lying about. Augustine's and Emma's diaries have been seized. The nuns were indiscreet enough to read them, and carried their despotism to the point of burning them without consulting the unfortunate authors. People's rights receive short shrift on these holy premises. I'm not worried about *my* diary. I keep it in a safe place...

But if writing a diary is playing with fire, almost more of a surprise is the number of diarists who seem half inclined to use the match themselves.

Anaïs Nin in earlier years wrote of her diary as an opium addiction which she tried hard to break. Actress Rachel Roberts, in the opinion of her biographer Alexander Walker, wrote herself to the point where the only logical option was suicide. Cynthia Asquith, starting her diary in 1915, was wary

Thursday, 15th April

I have always thought it would be unwholesome for me to attempt to write a diary. I'm sure it will make me think my life drab and strain after sensation to make copy for my autobiography. I shall become morbidly self-conscious and a valetudinarian about my career, so I shall try not to be un-introspective, and confine myself to events and diagnoses of other people. In any case I am entirely devoid of the gift of sincerity, and could never write as though I were really convinced no other eye would ever see what I wrote. I am incurably self-conscious. This impromptu resolution sprung from an absurd compact I made with Duff Cooper that we would both begin a diary at the same moment, and bind each other over to keep it up. He has given me this lovely book—but instead of inspiring, it paralyses me and makes me feel my life will not be nearly sufficiently purple.

In 1947 novelist Jean Rhys began a diary to try and write herself out of a block. But was it wise? Was it *safe?* She conducts an inquisition within its pages and the inquisitor gets the italics:

> *You are aware of course that what you are writing is childish, has been said before. Also it is dangerous under the circumstances.*

> Yes, most of it is childish. But I have not written for so long that all I can force myself to do is to write, to write. I must trust that out of that will come the pattern, the clue that can be followed....

> *All right, but be damned careful not to leave this book about.*

Finis

Why do women write diaries? There are plenty of answers, as we have seen. But why do they *stop?* For some the journey's end comes fairly obviously... for the pioneer women, of course, it was literally at the journey's end. (For Florida Scott-Maxwell, it worked the other way around. Having begun a notebook-companion at the age of eighty-two she dropped it when she set off on her travels: 'What need of a notebook when one is out in the world?')

Elizabeth Barrett kept a diary for the last months of the family's life at their old home Hope End—and then stopped. George Sand wrote a journal in times of great emotional imbalance—and then turned back to her professional writing when (with the journal's help?) she began to recover. That is a chain of events we can all understand.

Deaf and blind Helen Keller began a diary in mid life and in great distress after the death of Annie Sullivan, the 'Teacher' who had opened up the world to her. 'This journal is a godsend,' she wrote. 'It is helping discipline my mind back to regular work.' Three and a half months later: 'Why, oh, why, did I start this diary, knowing how crowded my life had been for many years?' The diary in fact ended very shortly afterwards. Had the friend in need been a friend indeed? But again, there is at least one voice speaking out of a very different experience. The nineteenth-century actress Fanny Kemble, settling down into the early boredom of what proved to be a deeply unhappy marriage to a Southern American slave-owner, wrote: 'I do not keep a diary any more... I do not find chronicling my days helps me to live them.'

There is another cessation for the diary-keeping habit. How many of us kept a diary at some point in our teens, the time when we were most vividly aware of being in a 'unique position'—and then stopped as the awareness (and the doubts, the hopes, the fears) became less acute? Fifteen-year-old 'Alice's' signing off is a slightly distorted version of that natural decline, reflecting the distortion of her death three weeks (and some pages) later from a drug overdose;

September 21

I used to think I would get another diary after you are filled, or even that I would keep a diary or journal through my whole life. But now I don't really think I will. Diaries are great when you're young. In fact, you saved my sanity a hundred, thousand, million times. But I think when a person gets older she should be able to discuss her problems and thoughts with other people, instead of just with another part of herself as you have been to me. Don't you agree? I hope so, for you are my dearest friend and I shall thank you always for sharing my tears and heartaches and my struggles and strifes, and my joys and happinesses. It's all been good in its own special way, I guess.

See ya.

For Henriette Dessaulles, as for so many others, the signing-off point came on the verge of marriage: 'I don't feel the need to keep a diary any more, it's so much more enjoyable to confide in *him!*' Several nineteenth-century diaries, in fact, stop formally and tantalizingly on the wedding night. For Fanny Longfellow the *adieu* (or, as it proved to be, the *au revoir*) was no less formal, but came a little later along the line:

July 13, 1844

The anniversary of our wedding day. Celebrated it right joyfully by my first drive abroad with baby, Henry, nurse, and Tom, and our first dinner in the new dining-room. Hillard joined us. Charles provided a handsome bouquet and resurrected for the occasion some of our wedding-cake whose existence I knew not of. What a year this day completes! What a golden chain of months and days, and with this diamond clasp, born a month ago! I wonder if these old walls ever looked upon happier faces or through them down into happier hearts.

With this day my journal ends, for I have now a living one to keep faithfully, more faithfully than this.

Did she keep her word? Well, she made no more entries on her own activities, except for a few in a separate journal she kept on her religious experiences. But she started a whole new journal to chronicle the progress of the children (see p.204) ... Once it has bitten deep, the diary habit doesn't let go that easily.

Chapter 2
– On Youth and Age

'Nothing improves with age.'—Lauren Bacall

'Being seventy is not a sin.'—Golda Meir

'Old age,' said Ninon de l'Enclos, 'is a woman's hell.' There is a certain impulse, born of feminism and 'anti-ageism', to protest: why should it be hell for a woman if not for a man? Why should it be hell for either? Why should age matter?

In a sense, of course, it doesn't, in that calendar years are often an unnecessarily crude way of assessing someone's mental and emotional development, looks or situation in life. All the same, if you were reading a diary extract, out of context, isn't it quite likely that one of the first things you would need to know before responding to it is just that: the writer's age? If the extract were from a mother writing about her young child, you might take it on trust that the writer was somewhere between twenty and forty, without needing to enquire much further—unless she proved to be sixteen or forty-six . . . More usually, though, we can expect the question of age to be implicit in our response. Sometimes, indeed, it is very difficult to get away from. Take the large number of diaries written in the teenage years. *We* need to know that the writers are thirteen or fifteen or seventeen. *They* can hardly refrain from commenting on it. When Sue Townsend titled her wonderfully accurate book so precisely *The Secret Diaries of Adrian Mole Aged 13¾,* she knew exactly what she was doing.

Early Promise

On age—or rather, on youth:

> *Sunday, April 19th, 1795*
>
> This was a day that made me reflect very seriously as I accomplished my
> seventeenth year and I must own I think it prodigiously old as it is not far
> from twenty. This made me spend a very dull birthday as at the bottom of
> my heart I was very sad to think I was beginning the eighteenth year of my
> life and that till now I had wasted my time in a very foolish way but I took
> resolutions to begin to be more applied to things that will be of more use to
> me in future and to enjoy life as it is very short. I was quite Philosophical
> and mean to remain it.

So wrote Betsey Wynne, who with her sister Eugenia, kept a diary from
1789–1820 as their family toured the Continent. Betsey Wynne was not
a young lady unduly given to philosophical speculation under normal
circumstances. And for the sake of the readability of the rest of her
diary, it is nice to be able to record that her determination to put
frivolous things behind her was doomed to fail.

Queen (then Princess) Victoria's voice, sonorous with the
consciousness of future responsibility, strikes an even stronger
moral note:

> *24 May 1837*
>
> Today is my 18th birthday! How old: and yet how far I am from being what
> I should be. I shall from this day take the firm resolution to study with
> renewed assiduity, to keep my attention always well fixed on what I am
> about, and to strive to become every day less trifling and more fit for what, if
> Heaven wills it, I'm some day to be!...

They speak, both of them, in terms of self-improvement. And if Betsey's
tone at least sounds as if the original Eve has not been anything like
subdued in her yet, that is all the more reason to put their good
resolutions down to the moral training of earlier days.

Yet, only thirty-five years or so after Victoria was writing, a Miss
Julia Newberry, a young American whose family seem to have been as
constantly on the move as were the Wynnes, sat down to celebrate her
seventeenth birthday in the South of France. She was already less
concerned with the future than with past achievement. She was, in fact,
adding up the score:

> I have been twice to Florida, & three times to Europe. I have been to two
> boarding schools & gained a great many friends in different ways. Have
> been run away with twice, & had my portrait painted. I have learned how
> to faint, & have inherited a fortune. Have been through a long illness, &
> had a terrible sorrow! And I might have been married if I had chosen.

On the other hand I have never had on a long dress, or been into society as a young lady; Nor in the conventional form, have I been to my first ball.—I have never given my photograph to a young man, or any other souvenir either, nor have I made my hair uneven by distributing locks among my friends. I have never waved my handkerchief to a male biped on the other side of the street, or appointed a rendezvous on my way to school.—I have never sworn eternal friendship to anyone, nor written poetry since I was eleven years old.

The score-card, you feel, will not balance up too badly. A father who constantly adjured Julia to 'be somebody' (like Shakespeare or Milton) gave her a lot to live up to, but she certainly isn't doing badly so far.

Anne Frank, writing in the throes of a first love which must have been rendered doubly sensitive by the hothouse atmosphere of the Secret Annexe, seems to be looking through the other end of the telescope, writing with a painful consciousness that things are coming at her too far, too fast:

> Am I only 14? Am I really still a silly little schoolgirl? Am I really so . inexperienced about everything? I have more experience than most; I have been through things that hardly anyone of my age has undergone. I am afraid of myself, I am afraid that in my longing I am giving myself too quickly. How, later on, can it ever go right with other boys? Oh, it is so difficult, always battling with one's heart and reason; in its own time, each will speak, but do I know for certain that I have chosen the right time?

Time Passes

It is never too early to start regretting the passage of the years. 'The last day of being sweet-and-twenty,' wrote Barbara Pym on 1 June 1934. 'And very sad it makes me to think so.' Not altogether reasonable, though most of us probably felt the same. Here is Etty Hillesum, also in her twenties:

> *22 April, Wednesday, 11.00 pm*
> I really oughtn't to be thinking stupid things like: I am already so old, I'm 28 and I haven't yet been able to express anything of all that lies buried in me and cries to be let out. One should just grow and mature and not think about the years. Perhaps it won't be until I'm 60 that I'll be able to say what I think I have to say.

Florence Nightingale was even more demanding of herself:

> *12 May 1850*
> Today I am thirty—the age Christ began his mission. Now no more childish things. No more love. No more marriage. Now Lord let me think only of Thy Will, what thou willest me to do. Oh Lord, Thy Will, Thy Will.

But Beatrice Webb, who spent the day before her twenty-ninth birthday on the assumption that 'Surely there are not many more years to live', had enjoyed a life change and changed her tune by her thirty-third one.

> *22 January 1891*
>
> Working hard and working well . . . in spite of my 33 years I feel younger than I have ever done before, except that I feel horribly 'independent', absolute mistress of myself and my circumstances—uncannily so.

Enough has been written about the fear of independence, and indeed of growing up, in women, something which Anne Truitt notes in our own age:

> *23 February 1975*
>
> Last night four women sat at my dining-room table in the candlelight: one in her forties; one in her thirties; Mary, sixteen; and I, fifty-three. We walked warily and rather sadly around the fact that no one was going to look after us but ourselves. The idea of being protected by men dies hard. We had all (except perhaps Mary) given up the feeling that such protection is our *right*. But we all, in varying degrees, decreasing with age, cherished some small hope of the idyllic warmth of male shelter. I have come, even so recently as within the last month, to the verge of preferring to look after myself . . .'

The point about Beatrice Webb's quote above is that she had for the first time found a future she could face with pleasure. As Vera Brittain puts it:

> *Tuesday, December 29th 1914*
>
> Today was my 21st birthday. There is nothing whatever to say about it. To be of age according to the law & to be one's own mistress does not impress me at all, nor does it fill me with grave & sober reflections. It is having nothing definite to do that makes another year seem a burden; when one is at least on the way towards achieving one's object, & things are happening, one's life is made up by events & not increasing years.

But then Vera Brittain makes her own comment just eight years later, preparing for publication the diaries which were to be published as *Chronicle of Youth*:

> Some of those who read these pages may have followed a recent controversy in one of our leading newspapers concerning the respective merits of age and youth. Perhaps those who agreed with some of the disputants that the young are intrinsically noble, and that age is a falling-off from the pure wisdom of youth, will exclaim in horror when they finish this chronicle: 'If this is the wisdom of youth, Heaven help the old!' They may conclude, as I upon re-reading these pages concluded, that the arrogance, the cruelty, the

sentimentality and the hopeless anguish of youth are the price that has to be paid for knowledge, the stuff out of which experience is made—but they are not wisdom. It is surely only when we can look back upon them, and feel sorry that we hurt ourselves so cruelly, and others so thoughtlessly, can even sigh a little because we suffered so much, and laugh a little because we were so foolish, that we can even begin to be wise.

Perhaps trouble comes when one is forced not to look forwards, but to start looking back. It is a position in which Toni Bentley, as a ballerina, found herself at the age of twenty-two:

November 30 1980

Damn this body of ours, it goes eventually, and even if one moves on in life and survives, that physical career will always have been one's high point. How could it be otherwise in retirement for us, at thirty or forty. One is so aware it is due to inability, physical inability. What greater reminder of one's slow decay toward death. It's like growing old far too early; instead of one's mind dwindling, one's body dwindles, with one's mind totally intact, filled with the same desire and energy as ever—probably more.

Unlike some European and Soviet companies, we are not provided for in retirement. We get no pension, no security and no retirement plan. After all, at thirty-five or forty we are still able-bodied in the eyes of society. The fact that one has given one's entire being—energy, time, body, thought, care and love—from age eight to age forty to one's art makes no difference.

Our work is taken from us through no fault of our own, except maybe the fault of choosing to dance at all. But nobody warns a ten-year-old that he will be finished at forty, and what ten-year-old would listen?

None, of course. At ten, a month is a very long time... The telescopic effect by which the years get shorter as they roll on is something we are all too aware of, and which several diarists have pointed out. Eugenia Wynne:

New Year's Day 1797

Good God how swiftly time passes and if now that I am only seventeen I complain of its rapidity, what shall I do when I am thirty?

Or forty, or... 'Do the years really get shorter and fly faster,' asked Mary Gladstone in 1871, 'or is it that in childhood all is exaggerated, and that we are only approaching gradually to reality, to be reached in mature age?' It is an *Alice in Wonderland* world where things suddenly shrink or grow more than lifesize again. Virginia Woolf knew it well:

Wednesday, January 13th [1932]

...can we count on another 20 years? I shall be fifty on 25th, Monday week that is: and sometimes feel that I have lived 250 years already, and sometimes that I am still the youngest person in the omnibus. (Nessa said that she still always thinks this, as she sits down.) And I want to write another four novels: *Waves,* I mean; and the *Tap on the Door;* and to go through English literature, like a string through cheese, or rather like some industrious insect, eating its way from book to book, from Chaucer to Lawrence. This is a programme, considering my slowness, and how I get slower, thicker, more intolerant of the fling and the rush, to last out my 20 years, if I have them.

Change of Life

Must all the news be bad as time goes on? Of course not. George Eliot, heading for forty, spends New Year's Eve, 1857, in thankfulness for her reason 'to think the long sad years of youth were worth living for the sake of middle-age'. And in her diaries (published under the title of *Everything to Lose*) of the fifteen years after the Second World War—a period which covers the last years of her husband Ralph's life—Frances Partridge takes a positive view of middle age, all the more welcome for being rather surprisingly rare:

> *December 10th 1950*
>
> Pouring with rain again, yet at breakfast our spirits were high and we talked about enjoying life. Who would have expected when young that in middle age there is such intense excitement to be had just from being alive. That is justification enough, Ralph said, for having brought a child into this wicked, frightening world—no need to seek further.

Fourteen months later, though, she is less optimistic when she thinks of Ralph: 'I am seriously worried about his thus giving up and accepting old age before he is sixty.' Six years later, 'age' is something she feels impelled to look in the face:

> *September 27th 1958*
>
> A visit to Alix and James, such as we made today, gives us a glimpse of our own futures. They are just so much older and crazier than Ralph and me; like hens they have been chivvied a little closer to the execution shed, and are cackling louder and losing more feathers though they aren't yet inside...
>
> One of the few consolations of age, I agreed with Bunny the other day, is its irresponsibility. This world is no longer any of my making, or much to do with me. Take it away and do what you like with it. I don't even greatly care if you drop it and break it. I'm interested in a detached way by your antics, that's all. No, I'm afraid that won't do. Nobody wants to end up as a selfish old person insisting on having the railway carriage window up (or down, as the case may be), besides which it's physically impossible to be so disengaged.

Under the stress of circumstance, of course, anyone can feel old before their time. As housewife Nella Last wrote in 1940, enduring a World War and the sight of her sons setting off to it:

I'm very old inside me, far older than my fifty years [she said to a son]. Perhaps if I live to be old, my shining memories of happy laughing boys and girls will come back—I feel they *must* be somewhere. Such happiness and fun could not be gone forever, and only pain and suffering endure. They were such nice boys, with ideals that were so high. They never wearied me when they used to sit and 'rave'. I felt it was a privilege that they let me see their hopes and plans.

All Passion Spent?

What Nella Last is describing surely has more to do with the pressure of the world around her than with the toll of experience, far less the physical changes that real old age must bring. And even they can be fought up to a point. 'My great lameness, etc, makes me feel how age is creeping on,' wrote Queen Victoria on her seventy-eighth birthday, in 1897. At seventy-eight, one might reasonably expect it to have crept. Her birthday, she writes, seems sadder each year—'but I pray yet to be spared a little longer for the sake of my country and dear ones. . . .' Draw your own conclusions.

The passion for living is surely there still. And Ellen Newton, imprisoned in a geriatric home ('Haddon') by reason of a heart condition, but mentally as forceful as ever, fights against the assumptions all around her:

Today, in a questing frame of mind, I ask our very professional Sister
Gareth when does one begin to be geriatric.
'Oh, at about forty-five,' she tells me.
So, old age with its diseases and alleged disabilities begins at a time when
most of the world's most gifted men and women have not yet done their
great creative work. But Sister, Paganini, long past sixty, was still playing
that Concerto of his, which they say has so many hazards that no concert
violinist cared to tackle it until Menuhin came along. And Sybil Thorndike
was still creating parts, in good company, at eighty. Discipline, and a
fantastic memory were on her side, of course.
Yet Ninon de l'Enclos, that alluring seventeenth century charmer,
towards the end confided to a friend that 'Old age is woman's hell'. Just
what would she have said of Haddon? And Ninon was by no means
neglected. At eighty she still had lovers who came to enjoy her beauty and
her wit, and more intimate favours as well, it is very reliably stated. Nearly
all the great autobiographies have come from men well past
forty-five—from Gibbon to Bertrand Russell, who was still writing, with
humanity and sweet reason, forcefully enough to excite the younger
generation when he was all of ninety.
And what about Michelangelo, Renoir, Picasso and Chagall? Or Verdi,
Toscanini and Arthur Rubinstein? Alfred Hitchcock, adventuring into his

seventies, is still cinema's master of suspense—and Churchill, leader when there was no one younger with the heart to lead. If you think about it for a moment, it's plain that at eighty or so Tito is not doing too badly either, keeping Jugoslavia out of reach of Big Brother, and out of economic strife, as well. No, Sister Gareth. No one can convince me that any age in itself is a disease, or quite ineffectual. Old age is a state of mind. And its ruthless enemy is convention, not the biological clock. Experience, maybe a long working life, and memory reaching back to a past crowded with men, women and events, are not often the stuff that apathy and disease feed on. Somewhere, environment and lack of occupation take over.

The forbidden thing should be to brand all elderly men and women as senile. Everyone who lives grows older. The majority don't grow soured, helpless, or bitter and irresponsible, simply because the passing years slow down their tempo of living ... One of my favourite visitors, well past her eightieth birthday, gets her car out and drives herself and a sister over to see me every ten days or so. And there's no special calendar to measure the time or capacity to think, or to feel. Exquisite singing, or a violin or oboe superbly played can send sensuous shivers of delight down an elderly spine. Besides, people do fall passionately in love at seventy, when 'with-my-body-I-thee-worship' still means precisely what it says.

That, to some of her younger readers, could be the unkindest cut of all. The delusion that physical love is only for the young, persists—at least where women are concerned. And some men (like Hamlet!) have not hesitated to set the age of celibacy unreasonably low. Liane de Pougy recalls one of her lovers taunting her:

'Think! Soon you'll be forty, my girl. You'll be *forty years old*'—leaning on the words. 'No one will want you any more and what tears of blood you'll weep when you remember your Henry and how much he would have loved you.' I had just turned thirty-five at the time!

It is a feeling to which teenagers are particularly prone where their parents are concerned. Here, Ellen Newton writes chidingly of her sister Helen's children.

Helen is youthful and perceptive, and in no way claims possession because she has given life. Yet already one or two of her young, who should know better, are making her feel the generation gap. It's an ugly phenomenon in this permissive age which has so many attractive ways. We're leaving our world, stuffed with outworn creeds, for them to renovate. They have the drive and the courage to do it. But courage, even like theirs, isn't enough. Neither is the belief that if you have youth nothing else matters.

Since I was a talkative five-year-old I've been drawn to older people. At first, because they could usually tell the most enthralling stories. In my reckoning there's no age-test for friendships. And I've never been aware that one age, in itself, is more repulsive than another. There are bores for all seasons. Helen, darling, you should remind your offspring that middle-age breathes exactly the same air, knows the same joys of desire and being desired, as your endearing young.

Ellen Newton stresses age's energy, not its tranquillity. Situated as she was, in the midst of daily unpleasantness at Haddon (howlingly disturbed patients, pain, discomfort and isolation), we could hardly expect her to express that sense of 'emotion recollected in tranquillity' which is supposed (by the young?) to be one of the perks of later life. Never mind. George Sand, such a stormy petrol in earlier days, really says it all:

September 1868

And now I am very old, gently traversing my sixty-fifth year. By some freak of destiny I am stronger and more active than I was in youth. I can walk farther. I can stay awake longer. My body has remained as supple as a glove. My sight is somewhat blurred, so that I have to wear spectacles, but they have increased my interest in natural history, as they enable me to see in the grass and sand tiny objects I might have overlooked. I go in bathing in icy water and find it pleasant. I never catch cold, and I have forgotten what rheumatism is. I am absolutely calm. My old age is as chaste in thought as it is in deed. I have no regret for youth, no ambition for fame, and no desire for money, except that I would like to have a little to leave to my children and grandchildren. I have no complaints to make of my friends. My one sorrow is that humanity does not go forward fast enough. Society seems indifferent to progress...

I no longer live in myself. My heart has gone into my children and my friends . . . If there were no other people in existence I should, therefore, be perfectly happy—happy, that is, as a stone, if one could imagine a stone capable of looking on at life—but other people do exist and through them I live. I rejoice with them and I grieve with them. I have no more needs for myself. Shall I live much longer? Is this astonishing old age without infirmity and without weariness a sign of long life? Or shall I drop off suddenly? No use wondering. One may be snatched away by an accident any moment. Shall I keep on being useful? Ah, that is worth wondering about. It seems to me that I shall. I feel that my service is more personal, more direct than ever. I have acquired considerable wisdom without knowing where it came from. I could bring up children much better than I once could.

It is a mistake to regard age as a downhill grade toward dissolution. The reverse is true. As one grows older one climbs with surprising strides. Mental activity increases with age, as physical activity develops in a child. Meanwhile, and nevertheless, one approaches the journey's end. But the end is a goal, not a catastrophe.

Chapter 3
~ Looks

'...and only God, my dear
Could love you for yourself alone,
And not your yellow hair.'—W. B. Yeats (For Anne Gregory)

Faces and Fortunes

Like it or loathe it, Yeats probably had a point. Or, to put it another way, how many of us are so sure he was wrong that we do not care about our own physical attractions, even now? And in the days when many of our diarists were writing, when marriage was the best if not the only career for a woman, 'making the most of yourself' must have seemed more important still.

Here is someone who did not have to worry. Or, perhaps, who had got presentation down to a fine art:

August 24th 1919

Shall I draw my physical portrait? Tall, and looking even more so: 1.66 metres, 56 kilos in my clothes. I run to length—long neck, face a full oval but elongated, pretty well perfect; long arms, long legs. Complexion pale and matt, skin very fine. I use the merest touch of rouge, it suits me. Rather small mouth, well shaped, superb teeth. My nose? They say it's the marvel of marvels. Pretty little ears like shells, almost no eyebrows—hence a little pencil-line wherever I want it. Eyes a green hazel, prettily shaped, not very large—but my look is large. Hair thick and very fine, incredibly fine, a pretty shiny chestnut brown. Hardly any grey hairs. One or two, to prove that I don't dye.

Not all self-assessments are so satisfactory as Liane de Pougy's. Most of us doing the silent assessment in front of the mirror could no more dream of that kind of complacency than we could of solo flight. And even that accredited beauty of the elegant Edwardian age, Daisy, Princess of Pless, proves that if no man is a hero for his valet, no woman is really beautiful ('not so bad', maybe) to her own reflection in the glass:

> My dear diary, I am really not vain, for honestly I cannot see where my beauty lies. This is what I am really like: I would look much plumper if I did not wear long and well-made French corsets; blue eyes with fair eye-lashes which I make black; pretty-coloured fair hair; good eyebrows; straight yet somehow turned up nose; short upper lip with the front two teeth rather longer than the others (like a rabbit or a mouse I think), thick bottom lip and a very slight double chin—which I keep in hand by dint of frequent massage. There is nothing to boast about in that, is there?

In Liane's case, of course, one has to remember that she knew what she was talking about. Not only was she as generous in her estimates of other women as she was about herself—on Mimy: 'tall, slender, white as a magnolia flower, her enchanting gestures so graceful, small, rare, precise, fiery eyes; an almost unreal fineness'—but in essence hers was a professional's estimate of the tools of her trade. Take those gestures she is so fond of talking about. Do you think they just happened? Listen to this:

> *July 27th 1918*
>
> This morning I went for a long walk with Steinilber and we talked about gestures. Each period, each fashion, gives rise to its own. That of the snuff-box, mittens and curved arms over crinolines, handkerchiefs held by the middle. What a charming gesture it was to lift the skirt to show just enough to excite desire by suggesting the rest... Now we wear low-cut dresses. Is it cold? There's a pretty, shrinking way of spreading your fingers over a fur crossed at the throat. Skirts are short, no more need to lift them. One stretches an arm, lifts the wrist to eye-level: how else read the time from one's wrist-watch? There have been the charming movements of the lips against the mesh of a veil; the lipstick gesture, so frequent that one no longer notices it, and the powder-puff, which has become so natural; the sharp little tap of the walking-stick, or the way of tucking it very high under one's arm-pit when not using it. I like taking a stick when I go out. It gives my spirit a touch of virility! I feel protected, and truth to tell, when I'm a little tired—well, I'm quite glad to lean on it a little; not much, not so that you would notice.

It sounds as exaggerated as Beatrix Potter's wonderfully bitchy comment:

> *April 17th 1883*
>
> Miss Ellen Terry's complexion is made of such an expensive enamel that she can only afford to wash her face once a fortnight, and removes smuts in

the meantime with a wet sponge. The Crompton Potters know someone who knows her well.

But then, even in her sixties, Liane de Pougy, then Princess Ghika, was a public beauty, with duties and a position to keep up:

> *July 6th 1932*
>
> Because life has become so difficult, Colette—whom I admire and like to see from time to time—has opened a shop selling beauty products in the rue Miromesnil. I went to the opening and she exclaimed: 'My fortune is made—here is Liane, beautiful Liane!' and she threw herself into my arms. I reeled—she is no mean weight—and let her sell me everything she wanted.

The legend lingers sometimes longer than the beauty. Liane knew better than most that she had had a good run. On entering a restaurant a year later, 'dressed divinely by Lanvin':

> Someone cried out: 'Oh how beautiful Princess Ghika is, she looks just like Liane de Pougy!' Laughter. An unknown lady looked me over, shrugged and said: 'She's a very good-looking woman but how can you compare her with Liane de Pougy?' – 'But it *is* Liane,' someone explained. 'Oh, go on with you!' said the lady. 'Liane de Pougy must be as old as the hills.'

Equally concerned with her physique and for an equally professional reason is the dancer. Here is Toni Bentley in *A Winter Season:*

> *November 21st 1980*
>
> I sometimes worry that when I stop dancing and start living, my incredible consciousness of physical beauty is going to be a real problem. Especially with men. I thought a giant step had been taken when I found a big round tummy not only not disagreeable but quite lovely and cuddly. I thought to myself, I can grow to love normal people. A few years ago I was convinced beyond a doubt that I could never ever love a man who had flat feet. Feet were incredibly important to me. And as for having no calves or muscle tone—well, I still have my doubts. But by mistake, I liked a man who did have flat feet. I liked him first, then noticed his feet—and then, thank God, it was too late to say no! I suppose everyone has prejudices, and ours are physical. We can't help it; the first things we notice are bodies.

In a sense she is only taking to extremes something that operates on us all. To judge by modern surveys, perceptions of acquaintances on apparently intellectual and emotional levels are significantly altered by physical appearance. Especially men's perceptions of women? It's something that sixteen-year-old Maud, a hundred years before, worked out for herself:

I'd give all I own for one good true girl-friend who would honestly love me.
There's Eva, dear Eva, she likes me well enough (when Edith [Martin] isn't
around) but she doesn't love me at all while she seems to worship
Edith—Edith so frequently cold and sharp. But Edith is pretty, when she
laughs her face lights up and her eyes sparkle, so you see it is mostly Edith's
looks.

I compare us sometimes, we two girls, and wonder how it is—Edith
doesn't seem to care for their love—I am *hungry* for it, she doesn't even try to
be even decently *polite* to them half the time while I always speak as kindly
and pleasantly as I know how, she is no smarter than I, cannot compose as
well, and is more selfish I *know* and there's only one other thing, Edith is
lovely and I'm homely.

Poor little blind fool! I used to think that my mouth was small and rosy,
my eyes bright and black, and my movements easy and free. Today I'm
actually afraid to look in the mirror. I'm so repulsive looking,—all I can see
is black hair, ugly and ill fitting in front, red eyes, swollen with crying, a
sallow, freckled face, and pug-nose. Then I think of Edith's clear pretty
pink and pearl complexion, her large brown eyes, and fringed, curling
eye-lashes, and her nut-brown hair, with the pretty graceful curls dancing
all around her forehead, and I pray even while I think it wrong, that God
will make me pretty.

Or, as the poet Sylvia Plath put it, writing in a time of depression:

Nose podgy as a leaking sausage: big pores full of pus and dirt, red blotches,
the peculiar brown mole on my under-chin which I would like to have
excised. Memory of that girl's face in the med school movie, with a little
black beauty wart: this wart is malignant: she will be dead in a week. Hair
untrained, merely brown and childishly put up: don't know what else to do
with it. No bone structure. Body needs a wash, skin the worst: it is this
climate: chapping cold, desiccating hot: I need to be tan, all-over brown,
and then my skin clears and I am all right. I need to have written a novel, a
book of poems, a *Ladies' Home Journal* or *New Yorker* story, and I will be
poreless and radiant. My wart will be non malignant.

Women's 'crowning glory' assumes special importance in some diary
entries: Margaret Fountaine, a Victorian ugly duckling who suddenly
found herself blooming into rather an unusual swan, quotes her uncle:
when a woman becomes attractive, it usually means she has found a
new way of doing her hair. Twelve-year-old Helen Morley's mind also
seems to be running on her crowning glory as she masters a new fact of
life:

When I said that I was homely, Ester exclaimed, 'You homely? Just let me
fix you up and you'll see.' I agreed, and she got the scissors and cut my

bangs and combed my hair, then she put rice-powder on my face and when I looked in the mirror I saw that I wasn't homely at all. They laughed when I told them that what we do here is to grease our hair with chicken fat to keep it plastered down. She told me that I should wash my hair and then put it in curls and then go there for her to comb it. How nice that I've become friendly with Dona Gabriela's family. They're so kind! If it weren't for them I never would have thought to have my bangs cut and my hair combed in the latest style. Ester thought it was funny when I told her that Mama Tina used to say, 'The pretty lives, the homely lives.' She said, 'It's true, but the pretty ones live better.' How happy I am today to be pretty at last!

Barbara Castle wrote at the time of her dismissal from the Cabinet:

'Breakfast over, my first concern was to go and have a comb-out.' (The Castle motto throughout the ages: 'When the sirens sound, make sure you look your best!')

Almost everyone seems to care about their appearance and some unexpected people make no bones about admitting it—like the middle-aged, confirmed invalid Alice James:

January 12th 1890

You would be amused if you saw the paces thro' which I put poor little Nurse; in the winter she has to applaud me Mind in summer me beauty! In my moments of modesty, don't scoff, I have 'em, I consult her about my letters and you may be sure she knows too well which side her bread is buttered to do aught but admire. In the summer when we pass an old frump more sour than the last I throw myself upon her mercy and ask her if I am as dreadful to look upon as that. When she comes up to time with a reassuring negative, and I sink back on my cushions, in my black-goggled, greenery-yallery loveliness, pacified—for the moment!

The Language of Clothes

If people are assessed on the colour of their hair and the shape of their body, they are also judged on the wrappings in which they choose to present themselves. Clothes talk—they tell us about the wearer and her social standing. If fashion sends out messages, so does our approach to the subject. Queen Victoria: 'fashionable dressing—anything but that!'

It was Barbara Castle who wrote: 'Another conference is launched! My best hat, the one I've had for two years, rose to the occasion triumphantly....' She wasn't necessarily giving proof of a frivolous or, in a derogatory sense, feminine mind. Nor should the journalists who commented on the hat ('I was amused to read in the press that I had been out specially to buy it') necessarily be reproved as chauvinists. Admittedly, it is unlikely that any of the male Ministers' suits came in for much comment on the same occasion. Men have traditionally liked to laugh at women for an excessive interest in dress. But given the importance of clothes as a communication tool—who is it who laughs last?

'Betsey and me we held a council of war about the gown cap sash shoes we want to wear if we are asked to the Ball,' wrote Eugenia Wynne. 'Womanish, childish will a rigid censor say but very natural I think.' Hear hear. You needn't expect to find the impressive, intellectual and distinctly un-'childish' woman disdaining the importance of dress either. Witness Vera Brittain's protective concern over the way her newly successful friend Phyllis Bentley presented herself to the world:

> *Monday, May 9th 1932*
>
> Mother & Aunt Lillie turned up to help with the food just after dinner & Phyllis to my delight appeared looking really nice in a very pretty black & silver dress that revealed to me the fact that she had a quite beautiful figure. After the oranges and greens of the previous days, & Winifred's remarks about her clothes being terribly provincial & all hung about with beads & things, it was a pleasant surprise; also her face seemed better looking as on Saturday I hinted gently how becoming her horn-rimmed spectacles were, & she thereafter abandoned the pince-nez & stopped looking like a school-mistress. She looked animated too and happily expectant, like a pleased child.

The social reformer and historian Beatrice Webb is fascinated, if shamefaced, when she describes the purchase of a new wardrobe:

> *11th January 1898*
>
> The old Eve in me is delighted with buying a trousseau for our nine months' journey. It is a long time since I have really had a good 'go' at clothes and I am revelling in buying silks and satins, gloves, underclothing, furs and everything that a sober-minded woman of forty can want to inspire Americans and Colonials with a due respect for the refinements of attractiveness! It is a pleasure to clothe myself charmingly! For the last ten years I have not had either the time or the will to think of it. For this tour, I harmonize some extravagance with my conscience by making myself believe that I must have everything new and that I must look nice! I believe that it is a deliberate expenditure because six months ago I determined that I would do myself handsomely as part of a policy, but I daresay one or two of the specially becoming blouses are the expression of concrete vanity. My childish delight in watching these bright clothes being made is a sort of rebound from the hard drudgery of the last two years.

It is the dancer Toni Bentley who spells out the message, though:

November 27th 1980

There are some basic rules for rehearsal clothes. Everything must be soft, old, borrowed, pinned, cut up and oversized. And worn only once—variety is essential. Only new company members wear anything that actually fits, a sure giveaway of their youth. We go through fads: big sweat shirts, Capezio's latest leg warmers, or triple layers of leg warmers. New articles are very suspicious; they contain no personal identity, so the scissors are instantly applied to the neckline (as low as possible, please!). The basic premise is to cover up and keep warm. Layer upon layer is essential so that we can peel off at appropriate intervals when sufficient warmth and confidence for self-exposure is reached. When we are on stage in tutus and leotards, it is the most naked we've been all day. Layers also give a wonderful feeling of possibility; after all, one can always take them off. Adding layers also happens but less frequently; it's a sign that things aren't going so well in the security area.

Clothes are also about belonging and keeping up with, or ahead of, the Joneses. Witness the teenage Maud Rittenhouse in 1881:

April 30th

Auntie brought Edith 2 new dresses, a silk parasol, silk mitts and new hat from Chicago. Friday at recess Edith took me over to show them to me. On the way I asked, 'Is the bonnet a poke?' 'No.' 'Cottage?' '*No*—and has no strings to it—the people of Chicago just hoot at strings under the chin, they won't think of them.'

I know how much good it did her to say that and so I didn't dispute it (you know my bonnet ties under the chin) and any-way she knows as well as I, that they are worn all over the U.S. and as much at Chicago as any place. Besides in one of Auntie's letters (guess Edith forgot that she showed it to me) she said, 'The most of the bonnets worn are like Maud's.'

I think it is the best joke of the season.

Maud's diary is full of descriptions of clothes, the details showing a real relish. Just a fortnight later it is a 'light regular ladies' evening dress':

Mrs James just 'laid herself out on it' and home it came, light and fluffy, trimmed in the loveliest satin and silk cords, with square neck and puffed sleeves. Wore my little bonnet (that I made of satin and lace and flowers)....

But she also has the strongest sense of matching the appearance to the occasion: 'Mabel had her sweet girlish white dress being made suitable and pretty (while half the ninnies are getting white satins—think how inappropriate—graduates in satins!)'

Dress can convey a whole host of different messages. It has traditionally been used to signal the different stages of life—Maud on her 'regular ladies' evening dress, Frances Partridge recording a child's delight in her hideous new school tie, just as she records the speculation on an elderly lady who still employs what could be considered the young woman's arts to attract. Lady Anne Clifford, in the seventeenth century, records the first time her toddler puts on 'a pair of whalebone bodice', 'her first coat that was laced with lace', 'the first velvet coat she ever had'. Mary Brabazon, in 1882, writes:

Sunday 18th June was a very sad one for me, as Normy for the first time put on manly attire, and it made me realize how time had passed, and that I must very soon bid him farewell. It is sad to feel his childhood is passing away.

Dress also has to conform to contemporary standards of propriety with all that *that* implies: Witness Fanny Burney:

Brussels, 23rd May 1815

At Madame de la Tour du Pin's I kept the Fête of Madame de Maurville, with a large and pleasant party; and I just missed meeting the famous Lady C[aroline] L[amb], who had been there at dinner, and whom I saw, however, crossing the Place Royale, from Madame de la Tour du Pin's to the Grand Hotel; dressed, or rather *not* dressed, so as to excite universal attention, and authorise every boldness of staring, from the General to the lowest soldier, among the military groups then constantly parading La Place,—for she had one shoulder, half her back, and all her throat and neck, displayed as if at the call of some statuary for modelling a heathen goddess. A slight scarf hung over the other shoulder, and the rest of the attire was of accordant lightness. As her Ladyship had not then written, and was not, therefore, considered as one apart, from being known as an eccentric authoress, this conduct and demeanour excited something beyond surprise, and in an English lady provoked censure, if not derision, upon the whole English nation. . . .

Fanny Burney was writing at a time when the hooped skirt had been discarded for (to quote the *Connoisseur)* 'flowing "Classical" robes' worn over 'a minimum of underclothing which revealed the outlines of the body to the astonished spectator. . . .' The same source quotes an 1806 viewpoint: 'What delicate man can view with unconcern the *nudes* we meet everywhere. . . the bosom shamefully exposed, and far more, the ankle.'

Dressing to reflect one's place in society can become a tiresome duty, as it appeared to Mrs Carlyle, the wife of a Victorian public man:

December 11th 1855

—Oh dear! I wish this Grange business were well over. It occupies me (the mere preparation for it) to the exclusion of all quiet thought and placid occupation. To have to care for my dress at this time of day more than I ever did when young and pretty and happy (God bless me, to think that I was once all that!) on penalty of being regarded as a blot on the Grange gold and azure, is really too bad. *Ach Gott!* if we had been left in the sphere of life we belong to, how much better it would have been for us in many ways!

It can also signify, rather than keeping up with the Joneses, the necessity (to self-respect) of keeping up certain standards under adversity. You can see it in the American and Canadian pioneer women. Here is one of them, Anne Langton, writing from Upper Canada, in 1839:

We ladies have been exeedingly busy getting up our muslins, a very difficult operation with arrowroot as a substitute for starch.

Tuesday April 9

I have been cutting open a pair of my new shoes, lacing them up, and concealing the lacing with a row of little bows down the front. If the novel appearance attracts attention, and I am asked if such is the fashion, I shall say I have just got them from England.

Though not to the exclusion of a certain practicality.... 'The bride wears hoops...Would not recommend them for this mode of travelling—the wearer has less personal privacy than the Pawnee in his blanket,' writes Helen Carpenter, making the wagon-crossing to California in 1857. But you can see the same 'brave face' in housewife Nella Last, writing towards the end of the Second World War on the 'queer hybrid creatures' in pants and pixie hoods pushing prams and 'making the streets so untidy':

I could not help but think that many women are seizing the excuse of there being a war on to give full reign to the sloppy lazy streak in their make-up. When the raids were on, *anything* could be understood or forgiven—but WHY NOW?

A few pages later Nella is trying 'not to purr with delight' as a 'pet of a hat' (not the 'doll-eyed Hollywood sort') is wrapped up for her: '*just* the kind of coarsely-woven straw, the *exact* shade of wine colour, the perfect *dream* of a hat—and only 16s 11d.' She has that love of clothes, all right. But a diary entry earlier in the war, in 1940, touches on another aspect of the language of dress:

Monday, July 1st 1940

It's getting easy to recognize the haves and have-nots now—womenfolk I mean—by the wearing of silk stockings and the frequent trips to the hairdresser's. I think silk stockings and lovely soft leather gloves are the only two things I envy women for. I can dodge and contrive dresses and, as I'm light on my feet, my shoes last a long time with care, but there is such an *uplift* about seeing one's feet and legs so sleek and silky, or in peeling off a pair of lovely leather-smelling gloves.

The haves and the have-nots—yes, dress has always been a vital way to tell them apart. And if it is so in our own age, how much more so in the Victorian, when a lady and her kitchen maid might have been taken for denizens of different planets. In her relationship with, and final marriage to, the upper-class Munby, maidservant Hannah Cullwick was called upon to play both roles in turn.

In the extraordinary dual life she lived [see page 98], Hannah's belief in the validity of her own work and identity was an essential constant. When her life was exclusively a servant's, there are strong indications that honest dirt and a plainness in her dress had for Hannah a significance beyond necessity:

Tuesday, 10th March 1873

Mrs Wood the charwoman was to dinner—she's cleaning upstairs for Mary this week. She laughs at me for having my frocks so short & she's very particular not to get dirty over cleaning. I'm sure she despises me for being so black & even *she* wears gloves & all her children too when they goes out. And the poor woman's sorry they won't let her little boy wear gloves at the Orphan School where some lady got him into. She's very particular how herself & children look, still she doesn't mind going to ladies a-begging. Her husband was a coach-man only, so it's extremely disgusting of her to be so proud & particular.

Walking through Hyde Park on her day off she observes:

... there was such a lot of proudly dress'd people—some on horses & some ladies with their beautiful silk trailing quite half a yard on the ground, which I thought was disgracefully extravagent and ridiculous.

Occasionally she comments that a silk is 'beautiful' or a kerchief 'remarkably pretty'—but vanity cannot really have been one of Hannah's sins when you think that she often wore a print dress sixty years old. Hannah is obviously determined never to confuse fine feathers and fine birds. Witness the wedding trip on which she is uncomfortably arrayed in fashionable attire:

Saturday, 30th August 1873

Massa says I behaved nicely & look'd like a lady too. He bought me a felt hat & plume of cock's feathers to wear, & a veil, & a new brooch to pin my shawl with, & a new waterproof cloak. But I generally wore my blue skirt & jacket over my grey frock, with frill round my neck, & white cuffs, & grey kid gloves, & carrying my striped sun shade. All so different to anything I had got used to, but one day in the train I got almost ill-temper'd at being so muffled up, & I felt I'd much liefer feel my hands free as they used to be. But M. made me put the gloves on again, & I thought it was hard to be forced to wear gloves—even harder than it was to leave 'em off altogether before I was married, as I did for over 16 year I think. When I started I wore my old black bonnet to Folkstone, & changed it there, & the same back again, & put my plaid shawl over my skirt so I wasn't noticed coming into the Temple nor going out.

She is 'very glad to get back home again' (to resume her servant's life): 'I've doff'd all my best clothes & put my own on again—my dirty cotton frock & apron & my cap....' You can't get a better picture of the degree to which dress, like the proverbial manners, maketh man. But for a more flippant approach you might try Katherine Mansfield's mother:

'Oh dear,' she said, 'I do wish I hadn't married. I wish I'd been an explorer.' And then she said dreamily, 'The rivers of China, for instance.'

'But what do you know about the rivers of China, darling,' I said. For mother knew no geography whatever, she knew less than a child of ten. 'Nothing,' she agreed. 'But I can *feel* the kind of hat I should wear.'

Part II
Men and Women

- Parents and Children
- Love
- Marriage
- Sex

Chapter 4
~ Parents and Children

*'All women become like their mothers. That is their tragedy. No man does.
That is his.'*—Oscar Wilde, *The Importance of Being Earnest*

*'Children begin by loving their parents; after a time they judge them; rarely, if
ever, do they forgive them.'*—Oscar Wilde, *A Woman of No Importance*

I: AS A MOTHER

Motherhood, as reflected in diarists' entries on the subject, is not all
joy—far from it—but here is a passage expressing the pleasure of
childbearing. The writer is the sculptress Anne Truitt:

Sam was born in November 1960, six months after we returned from San
Francisco to Washington, early in the coldest, snowiest winter I can ever
remember. The freezing weather made us cozy together, Sam and me. I
used the guest room, two steps and one room away from ours but within
hearing distance, for Sam's nursery. There he lay peacefully in the
well-used crib. Against one of the two large windows was a spacious white
table, the one I now use for drawing. This was his bathing and changing
place. Against the other window, placed so I could look out easily, was my
nursery rocker.

When I heard his first tentative cry in the middle of the night, I used to
get up instantly, turn my electric blanket on high so my bed would be warm
on my return, slip into a bathrobe, and tiptoe quickly to his crib. I never
turned on a light. Part of the magic closeness was the semi-darkness of the
high-ceilinged room lit only by a street light. I would immediately turn him
on his back so he would be happy knowing that he would soon be
comfortable, fill and plug in the bottle warmer, put in the bottle brought up
in the ice bucket the previous evening, change him (lovely warm water, nice
dry double diaper), and wrap him in a soft knitted blanket. By this time, the

bottle was just right. Then we would sit by the window, rocking gently, both warm and happy in a little world isolated by snow and sleeping people, rich with the homey smell of baby and milk.

'I had forgotten how sensuous babies are—all skin and touch and need,' adds Anne Truitt later, with delight, when her daughter Alexandra's first baby is born.

This note of pleasure is one that needs to be borne in mind when reading the entries that follow. Anne Truitt herself describes motherhood as composed of 'prides and disappointments, of angers and joys, of calls on endurance that had to be invented as events demanded it. And of pain, the inevitable pain that marks the mother, peaking into a watershed that cuts off forever the playing fields of childhood.' Yes, there is a good deal of pain in the entries ahead. There are plenty of mothers who shift a little uneasily under the burden of parenthood, desirable though it may be, or who even reject their role.

Bearing

For those who decide to have children, the process often takes its physical toll.

'I do think a woman *em beraso* has a hard time of it,' writes Susan Magoffin, pregnant, in America in 1846, 'some sickness all the time, heart-burn, head-ache, cramp, etcetera. After all, this thing of marrying is not what it is cracked up to be.' Many others, it seems, would agree. Like the pioneer woman Mary Walker, also in America, a few years earlier:

> Began to feel discouraged, felt as if I almost wished I had never been married. But there was no retreating: meet it I must... Soon I forgot my misery in the joy of possessing a proper child.

The anticipation of delivery must have been terrifying in an era without the benefits of pain relief, when puerperal fever was common and the infant mortality rate was as high as 20 per cent. Mary Timms, writing in the nineteenth century:

1833

> Sometimes I think I shall never again enter this house, death may have marked me for his prey... The hour of trial is approaching. Nature shrinks. O for grace—for patience—for resignation to the will of my heavenly Father, that I may be enabled to bear all that my God sees fit to lay upon me. Thousands have been supported; may the strength of the Lord be perfected in my weakness; and if my life be spared, I trust it will be to glorify him.

(And, indeed, giving birth can still look like an ordeal in the twentieth with stories... 'of pain, bleeding, tearing and stitches'.)

Sometimes the anticipation seems to have been worse than the actual event. Witness Charlotte Guest in 1883:

> I have to thank God that my hour of trial is over, and that I am now fast recovering, for which mercy also I ought to be very grateful after having suffered about as little as was possible... I had written home, and had got half way through a long letter at twelve o'clock, when I was taken ill. At two my dear child was born. I was soon pretty well. Merthyr had gone to the House soon after eleven, and did not return till past three. No one had told him of the little one till he reached the top of the stairs, when Mamma met him and told him that he had a little girl. He was quite overcome when he entered my room immediately after and he kissed me and our dear infant.

and Betsey Wynne in 1789:

> I woke in great pain this morning, continued poorly all day, but minded it as little as possible. To my no small happiness and everybody's surprise I was brought to bed by seven o'clock in the evening of a boy, before Dr. Savage had time to come, the nurse delivered me. A small child but a sweet boy.

On her second labour:

> I was surprised and frightened at being taken ill in the middle of the night as I did not expect to be brought to bed till the end of the month and my nurse was not to come till the twentieth—I called up the women at four o'clock in the morning and sent immediately for Dr Tooky—it was all over a little after six. The *cook* was *headnurse* and dressed the child. It is a nice little girl but owing to her being born three weeks before her time is very delicate and small.

By way of contrast, Elizabeth Drinker's record of her daughter Sally's labour and (breech?) birth in America in 1795 continues well over twenty-four hours: '...she has been all this evening in afflictive pain though unprofitable...she sufffered much to little purpose....'

It is small wonder that, even for an Elizabeth Fry, the expected pleasures of happy motherhood proved elusive immediately after the event:

12th September 1801

> I have hardly had time or strength as yet to describe the events I have lately passed through. I did not experience that joy some women describe when my husband first brought me my little babe, little darling! I hardly knew what I felt for it, but my body and spirits were so extremely weak, I could only just bear to look at those I loved, and I felt dear baby at first a quiet

source of pleasure, but she early became a subject for my weakness and low
spirits to dwell upon, so that I almost wept when she cried; but I hope, as
strength of body recovered, strength of mind will come with it.

On the birth of her sixth child less than nine years later, she wrote:

23rd September 1809

On Fourth day, my lovely boy was born, a willing mind to suffer was hard to
get at; I longed to have the cup removed from me. I had to acknowledge
present help in trouble, so that I could only give thanks; indeed I have
renewed cause for thankfulness and praise, which my poor unworthy mind
has felt little able to render since, being weak at times, tempted and tried;
but I desire to abide near, and cling to that power, that can pardon and
deliver.

Four years after that first entry above, Mary Walker, already the
mother of three, is writing:

I find my children occupy much of the time; that if their maker could see fit
to withold from me any more till they require less of my time and attention,
I think I should be reconciled to such allotment.

A Grave Responsibility

It seems to be their duties towards their children that most preoccupies
women. Linda Pollock's fascinating *Parents and Children*—to which I am
indebted for much of the early American material in this
chapter—bears out this point. Her anthology selection is not taken
primarily from diaries, nor exclusively from female sources. (A
surprising amount—given that the period covered runs from
1600–1900—is written by men.) But it certainly suggests that the moral
responsibilities of parenthood demand as many pages as the practical
pleasures or problems.

Fanny Longfellow's journal entry, coyly announcing the impending
arrival of her first child, has a period charm about it...and a fairly
dramatic indication of the note struck by many new mothers as well:

February 21, 1844

Stopped with Henry for dressmaker...I have outgrown my wedding dress,
and it will no longer cover one beating heart only! O Father, let the child but
be as happy, and far better, than the mother and I pray for no other boon.
Feel sometimes an awe and fear of myself, a fear that my heart is not pure
and holy enough to give its life-blood, perhaps its nature, to another. What
an awful responsibility already is upon me! God alone knows how much my
thoughts and temper may mould the future spirit. Let me strive to be all
truth and gentleness and heavenly mindedness, to be already the
guardian-angel of my child....

Fanny Longfellow kept a second journal to record the progress of her children. And in 1848 it tells a sad story which exposes that painfully close tie between mother and child:

> *August 29 1848*
>
> Poor baby drooping today, and at night very feverish with symptoms of dysentery.

> *August 30 1848*
>
> Very hot. Darling baby very feeble, though without fever.

> *September 1*
>
> Baby confined to her bed and lying there so sadly patient, with her poor pale face and hollow eyes....

and so on, until:

> *September 11*
>
> Sinking, sinking away from us. Felt a terrible desire to seize her in my arms and warm her to life again at my breast. Oh for one look of love, one word or smile! Mary was with us all day. Painlessly, in a deep trance, she breathed. Held her hand and heard the breathing shorten, then cease, without a flutter. A most holy and beautiful thing she lay and at night of look angelic and so happy.

A month later, on October 14, the entry reads:

> Very weary and wretched. I seem to have lost interest in the future and can enjoy my children only from hour to hour. I feel as if my lost darling were drawing me to her—as I controlled her before birth so does she me now.

It is a variant on the experience of American sculptress Anne Truitt in our own time. Her *Daybook,* a journal kept over a period of seven years during which her children completed the long process of growing up and leaving the nest, represents a coming to terms with the artist—and also, inextricably, the mother—within herself. Her sense of her children's (and in turn, *their* children's) independent identity is both spoken and self-evident, in operation from the moment of their birth. But when Sam, the 18-year-old youngest, is seriously hurt in a car crash:

> An inner lock slipped smoothly into place and my bond with my son Sam became abruptly whole, as it had been before he was born. Through this placental connection I began to feel, and into it I began to pour energy.

Just a month earlier, she had written:

> *September 1978*
>
> The pangs of labor are a metaphor for the startlingly painful and difficult process by which a child is delivered into adulthood. The curve of physical

41

motherhood peaks over the watershed of labor into a shining Shenandoah, a broad alley that seems to new parents to stretch forever. For me it had the same smiling lavishness as the first days of delicately greening marriage: a lovely open space with brown-furrowed fields snugly bounded by ramparts of love on either side. It never forcefully occurred to me that the children would scramble up these very mountains out of the valley to see what lay beyond. Paradoxically, the more hospitable the valley, the more energetically they climb. The end of parenthood is implicit in its beginning: separation.

The first birth is documented. A doctor stands by; physical facts are readily available: literature bounds in accounts of birth. Folk knowledge hammocks the pregnant woman: she sways in a gentle wind of attention.

Not so with the second birth into adulthood. That is a solitary business for the parent. The course of events is not documented—cannot be, as each child tears the connective tissue differently. The process cannot be examined in advance and prepared for with specificity. . . . Another child appeared to become more and more indifferent to me. Instead of chatting—and we are a chatting family—the child turned laconic. I was lucky to be told, 'Good morning'. Until I recognized this cutting off for what it was, I thought the child surly. Another simply ran in and out of my heart as if it were a drafty old barn with doors creaking in a desultory wind; only straw and shelter were needed.

'Since I am the parent,' she continued, 'the burden of foresight and consideration lies squarely on my heart and intelligence.'

With such an awesome burden to bear, small wonder that most mothers, far over and above the practical day-to-day chores, seem to be concerned with Getting It Right so far as the moral instruction, disciplining and education of their children is concerned.

Getting It Right

Not many mothers can have had things quite as cut and dried as Nancy Shippen, writing for herself in America in 1883, a list of 35 'Directions Concerning a Daughter's Education'. They range from the severely practical:

Let her eat deliberately, chew well, and drink in moderate proportions.

To the dauntingly moral:

Discreetly check her desires after things pleasant, and use her to frequent disappointments.

As Elizabeth Fry put it:

I feel at times, deeply pressed down, on account of my beloved children. Their volatile minds try me, but amidst my trials, I have a secret hope concerning them, that all will end well; and a blessing attend them, if they bow to the blessed yoke (for so I feel it) in their youth.

And in her turn, some thirty years later, Elizabeth Fry's niece Priscilla Johnston, is writing:

How little does this book convey any idea of the almost ceaseless engrossment of my heart, mind, and time about them! Every day seems marked by care about the body, conduct, or circumstances of one or other these precious, anxious treasures!

She, of course, is thinking of the practicalities as well as the moral points. But concern about the latter seems to be remarkably widespread. Here is Susan Huntingdon writing in America in 1813:

There is scarcely any subject concerning which I feel more anxiety, than the proper education of my children. It is a difficult and delicate subject; and the more I reflect on my duty to them, the more I feel is to be learnt by myself!

The song goes on and on—hovering anxiously, very often, around the rightness or otherwise of the old saying 'Spare the rod and spoil the child'. For Honoria Lawrence, writing in 1842, that was literally the dilemma: On one particular occasion, an instance of trivial disobedience from her son Alick mushrooms into an issue which, apart from anything else, casts grave doubts on the long-term effectiveness of corporal punishment:

Saturday, May 28th 1842

I whipped him with a little slip of whalebone, but with no effect. While smarting he called out 'Yes, yes Mamma, I will be good, I will reckon,' but the next moment returned the same resolute look, and 'No, I will not reckon.'

After about half an hour spent thus, I did not know what to do, feeling I had got into a contest which I must win. As he stood resolutely before me he saw me rest my head on my hand. 'Mamma are you praying to God?' 'Yes, my boy, I am asking Him to make you good.' He immediately knelt at my knee and said earnestly, 'Oh God make me good, take away this naughty and make me good.' I was in hopes the evil was subdued, but the next moment the case seemed as hopeless as ever. I tied his hands behind him and left him for a little while, from five to ten minutes, in the bathing room. But I returned too soon. I had no patience. Half an hour might have done the work. I found Alick as firm as ever, whipped him again and tied him to the bed post. I was glad to see such resolution in his character and afraid to break his spirit. Yet I could not give up. I lifted up my heart in prayer and was composed and calm through all, but I hardly felt such pain when I thought him dying. I think if I had had more patience all would have been well, but the moments seemed as long to me as to him. Several times I left the room for a few minutes and returned finding him the same. 'Will you now reckon one, two, three, etc?' 'No, I will not.' 'Then I must whip you again.' 'Yes, do,' and with a sore heart I again whipped him. Once or twice he said 'Mamma, I'm afraid of the rod.'

Then I feared I had gone too far. I immediately laid it down saying, 'My boy, I don't wish to touch the rod again, only count as I bid you.' 'I will not.' Then at other times he would yield. 'I will Mamma, I will count,' and then he would begin 'One, two,' the evil seeming to rise up again. 'No, I can't Mamma.' 'Then say it after me.' 'No, I won't.' Sometimes he took the stripes like a Spartan, sometimes cried out 'Dear, dear mamma, you hurt me, kiss and make better?' Several times too he said, 'Just pray to God once more,' but I thought it dangerous to let him make religion a pretext for disobedience and replied, 'No, my boy, God will not listen to you while you are obstinate. You must try now to be good, or He will not help you.' Then he would say, 'Just give me one more whipping and then I will say it.' This went on for three hours, from four, till seven and I was deeply grieved. He seemed to have made up his mind to pass the night tied to the bed post and I could do no more.

At last, when the servant announced tea was ready and I was going away, he yielded, and in a different tone said, 'Yes, Mamma, I will be good, I will make you glad.'

'Then my boy reckon as I bid you.' He did so, reckoned to eight several times without hesitation. With a glad heart I released him, but then felt puzzled what to do. I longed to take him in my lap, and make up with caresses for all the punishment I had inflicted. But this would have been only self-indulgence. I merely told him I was glad he was good.

I was rather disappointed at seeing him in one moment as merry as ever, seeming not to remember what had passed, but I avoided saying anything that might lead him to affect feeling. When we went to bed I spoke seriously to him, told him of God's displeasure and prayed with him. Through the night he was restless, starting from his sleep. 'Yes, yes, mamma, I will be good, I will reckon,' and frequently wakening saying he was thirsty. Darling child, with what costs to myself I punished him! I think he was subdued, not merely exhausted, but I am by no means sure I took the right method. Perhaps, had I left him for a longer time in the first instance, I might have avoided the conflict. Perhaps had I prayed more fervently God would have made him yield. For one thing I am most thankful, that he was not the slightest estranged from me, but on the contrary clings more than ever to his 'own, dear mamma'. I hope the remembrance will be enough now and that we shall never again have such a conflict.

Vera Brittain's account of her son John comes as welcome relief in the circumstances:

Sunday, August 21st 1932

John rather trying all day; when I mentioned the possibility of a smack he merely replied: 'Smack! Smack! If you want to smack anybody, smack yourself!'

Doubly welcome, in fact. Both in the contrast between John's clearly unbroken spirit, by contrast with Alick's—who, you can't but feel, was clearly headed towards a future psychiatrist's couch—and for the casual amusement with which Brittain relates the little incident. Most mothers seem to be more preoccupied with the rule-book—or books. Mrs Gaskell, in 1835, writes of her baby daughter Marianne:

> Once or twice we have had grand crying, which have been very distressing to me; but when I have convinced myself she is not in pain, is perfectly well and that she is only wanting to be taken up, I have been quite firm; though I have sometimes cried almost as much as she has . . . Crying has been a great difficulty with me. Books do so differ. One says 'Do not let them have anything they cry for', another (Mme Necker de Saussure, 'Sur L'Education Progressivé', the nicest book I have read on the subject), says 'les larmes des enfants sont si amères, la calme parfaite de l'ame leur est si necessaire qu'il faut surtout épargner des larmes' ('Children's tears are so bitter, and complete calm of spirit so necessary, that one must at all costs spare them crying'). So I had to make a rule for myself, and though I am afraid I have not kept to it quite as I ought, I still think it a good one. We must consider that a cry is a child's only language for expressing its wants. It is its little way of saying 'I am hungry, I am very cold,' and *so*, I don't think we should carry out the maxim of never letting a child have anything for crying. If it is to have the object for which it is crying I would give it *directly*, giving up any little occupation or purpose of my own, rather than try its patience *unnecessarily*. But if it is improper for it to obtain the object, I think it right to withhold it steadily, however much the little creature may cry. I think, after one or two attempts to conquer by crying, the child would become aware that *one* cry or indication of a want was sufficient, and I think the habit of crying would be broken. I am almost sure even my partial adherence to this plan has prevented many crying fits with Marianne.

We would tend to agree, based as the rule is on the premise that 'a cry is a child's only language for expressing its wants'. The rule George Sand made for herself, at once more high-flown and less specific, stressing the need to balance education of the head and of the heart, is sometimes a little harder to relate to:

> More than anything else it is important to understand the child and help the child to understand his own character, so that he may be in harmony with himself. Point out where he has failed and where he is on the right track, keep encouraging him as he makes progress. If the child is avid for knowledge, make it clear to him that intelligence counts for nothing without goodness and love. If the child be lazy and slow but gentle and sweet, make him understand that he should make an effort to apply himself for the sake of those he loves.

But her comments about the need to protect children from an education at school (where 'equality is won by fist fights, discipline is brutalizing, and authority is cruel and puerile') would have found an echo in the heart of one mother across the Channel. Charlotte Guest, in 1845, faced with the socially inevitable prospect of sending her ten-year-old son to public school:

> When I thought of all the sorrow and temptation my poor boys would have to go through in that place I quite shuddered and prayed that assistance might be granted them from above. It seems a sad prospect, but everybody says it is the only way to bring up boys; and what is to be done? How can I, a poor weak woman, judge against all the world?

Poor women, 'weak' or otherwise. George Sand's diatribe had been triggered by the sufferings of her sensitive nine-year-old Maurice, placed in a military school by his father, who used his legal authority to deny the boy's pleas to stay with his mother instead.

Sometimes seemingly under attack from every angle at once, it is poignant to find, at the beginning of the journal Mrs Gaskell kept to record the progress of her Marianne, the following 'dedication'. And a pre-Freud one, at that:

> ...And you too, my dearest little girl, if when you read this, you trace back any evil or unhappy feeling to my mismanagement in your childhood, forgive me, love!

The Most Difficult Relationship

In keeping a diary for and about their children, Mrs Gaskell and Mrs Longfellow have a rather unexpected companion. Lady Cynthia Asquith, wife to the son of Prime Minister Asquith, was a society beauty, prominent in the most elevated political and literary circles. And against that glittering background the personal tragedy of her eldest son John, suffering from a condition then undiagnosed, but which would now have been described as autism, stands out in even more striking relief.

Lady Cynthia's general diaries (as distinct from the notebooks on each child) began in 1915 and one of the first entries on John, at four already recognizably a 'problem' child, comes in the context of a seaside visit with D. H. Lawrence and his wife:

Tuesday, 11th May, 1915
> The Lawrences were riveted by the freakishness of John, about whom they showed extraordinary interest and sympathy. The ozone had intoxicated him and he was in a wild, monkey mood—very challenging, just doing

things for the sake of being told not to—impishly, defiant and still in his peculiar, indescribable detachment.

If Lawrence's diagnosis of John as a 'static challenge, ... symbolic of real Descartism, the negation of all accepted authority' is open to question, the medical profession (who spoke hopefully of the effects of time and training to take him out of himself) cannot be said to have done much better. By 13 May 1916:

> I feel cold terror about John now more and more often. It is just because the word 'stupid' is so inapplicable and because of a strange completeness about him as he is, that makes one despair of any reason why he should ever change. Oh God, surely nothing so cruel can really have happened to me myself? I must just hope and wait and hope.

Limited hope came in the form of a new governess who opined 'that there is nothing *mentally* wrong with John, though of course he is undeniably eccentric.' She considers him 'superhumanly obstinate and self-conscious'. She did indeed produce some effect—though to see John doing his counting and his drill was, Lady Cynthia noted acutely, rather like watching a performing animal at work. On the governess' insistence, she and John lived separate from the family. In July 1917, Lady Cynthia writes:

> He is no better and alas, alas, it is a nightmare to me to be in the room with him now. I must struggle against this.

If it is a reaction which can produce the instant, knee-jerk response of 'How could any mother...etc', it is at a more profound level an intensely understandable one. The intricate relationship between mother and child—the mother's idea of herself and of her child, and the child's idea of itself and of the mother—has some strange byways. Perhaps Lady Cynthia is just being more honest than most when she writes:

> *Wednesday, 24th October 1917*
> Woke up to terrible morning misery. The dreary detail of the John tragedy blackens life. One can never dismiss it from one. It is a past, present, and future nightmare. I loved my idea of that baby more than I have ever loved anything—and it was just something that never existed!

The public criticism of her apparent detachment was there, all right, but she had the answer:

> *Tuesday, 18th December 1917*
> ... I gathered someone had been critical of me, and had said she couldn't imagine not concentrating on him if he were her child. I said if I believed him to be really curable, I would never leave him, but I had long really

inwardly realized the hopelessness of the case and determined to keep the cruel sorrow within certain limits—not to *allow* it to blacken the whole of life for me, but to keep myself sane for Michael and the best way to do that was to fix one's thoughts as much as possible on the latter.

It was to Michael, Lady Cynthia's beloved second son, and to Simon, born in 1919, that her diaries passed after her death. (John had died in 1937.) Those entries dealing with the years 1915-1918 were edited for publication. And though what is left is undoubtedly striking enough, references to John, says a note in the index, have been cut 'as too personal and too painful'.

II: AS A CHILD

Difficult Relations

What Oscar Wilde had to say about parents in general goes for mothers in particular. Of all the popular explorations of women's psychology published in recent years, the prize for the most telling title must go to Nancy Friday, author of *My Mother, My Self*. Only some daughters are moved to write about their family relationships but when they do, they tend to have a lot to say and, yes, the most vehement writing —positive or otherwise, but more often otherwise—is aimed at their mothers. In view of the entries that lie ahead, it is probably a good idea to start off with an appreciative assessment. Fifteen-year-old Helena Morley is concerned to right a very common wrong—that of women being taken for granted:

Wednesday, July 10th 1895
Papa is much beloved in my family. Everybody likes him and says he's a very good man and a very good husband. I like hearing it but I'm always surprised at their just saying that papa's a good husband and never saying that mama's a good wife. Nevertheless, from the bottom of my heart I believe that only Our Lady could be better than mama.

   I don't think anyone could be a better wife to papa or a better mother to us than she is. With papa leading a miner's life, most of the money he gets goes back into mining; there's not much left over for the house. We complain about things sometimes, but never a peep from mama. She never says a word that might upset my father; she just keeps telling him: 'Don't be discouraged; to live is to suffer. God will help us.' But I, being less patient, build castles in the air before I go to sleep, about being invisible and taking money from the rich and bringing it home. I've discovered it's a good way to get to sleep.

When I see mama getting up at five in the morning, going out in the yard in all this cold, struggling with wet, green wood to start the kitchen fire to have our coffee and porridge ready by six, I feel so sorry I could die. She begins then and goes without stopping until evening, when we sit on the sofa in the parlor. I sit holding mama's arm on one side and Luizinha's on the other, to keep warm. Renato and Nhonho sit on the floor beside the stove, and mama tells stories of bygone days ... But this pleasant time never lasts very long. At half-past eight mama goes back to the kitchen to struggle with green firewood and get our porridge.

And yet nobody ever says mama's a good wife.

But even though—hard work apart—the Morley home sounds like a happy one, Helena's words remind us of some important issues: How fathers tend to get the good bits of 'parenting' and how mothers' image suffers in consequence. How, by parental example, daughters acquire the image of male and female roles. And how many daughters—even outside the 'broken home' situation— seem to feel a need to compare their parents, and almost to choose between them. None of the extracts quoted in this chapter conveys one message alone—of love without responsibility, or tyranny without dependency. That is what made the chapter so very hard to write.

'How beautiful they were, those old people,' wrote Virginia Woolf of her parents. And yet:

Wednesday, November 28th, 1928

Father's birthday. He would have been 96, 96 yes, today; and could have been 96, like other people one has known: but mercifully was not. His life would have entirely ended mine. What would have happened? No writing, no books;—inconceivable.

Woolf is in her forties, saying that she used to think of her parents daily until writing *To The Lighthouse* 'laid' them in her mind. Etty Hillesum is twenty-seven, not too old to be violently irritated by her parents (who is?) but old enough to reproach herself for it:

'Stop whining, for goodness' sake, you shrew, you nag, carrying on like that.' Such are my inner reactions when my mother sits down to have a chat with me. My mother is someone who would try the patience of a saint. I do my best to look at her objectively and I try to be fond of her, but then surely I'll find myself saying emphatically, 'What a ridiculous and silly person you are.' It's so wrong of me, I don't live here, after all, I just allow myself to vegetate, and I put off my life until I have gone again. I have no impetus here to do any real work, it is as if every bit of energy were being sucked out of me. It is now eleven o'clock and all I have done is to hang about on this chilly windowseat, looking at the uncleared breakfast table and listening to my mother's pathetic complaints about butter coupons and her poor health, etc. And yet she is not really a shallow woman. That's the real tragedy of it. She wears you out with all her unsolved problems and her quickly changing moods; she is in a chaotic and pitiful state, which is reflected all about her in the utterly disorganized household. And yet she is convinced that she is an excellent housewife, driving everyone crazy with her perpetual fussing over the housekeeping. As the days go by here, my head feels more and more leaden. Well, all one can do is just get on with it. Life in this house is bogged down in petty details. They smother you and nothing important ever happens. I would denegrate into a real melancholic if I were to stay here for any length of time. There is nothing one can do either to help or to change things. The two of them are so capricious.

Perhaps her reaction is not only more comprehensible—more believable—than that 'how beautiful...', but more natural as well. Certainly, the sound of the American teenager Alice praising her parents, and lashing herself by comparison, has a worrying sound: 'I really have a great family,' she enthuses—after she has run away from home, become seriously involved in hard drugs, and returned to a 'prodigal son' welcome. Months earlier, before the drugs, there had been no doubt about the ambivalence of her feelings toward her parents' all too shining virtues:

> Imagine my long-suffering, sweet-mouthed mother being tempted to utter a slimy phrase about my drab-looking nobody friend. I wonder why she doesn't take a second look at her drab-looking nobody daughter, or would that be too much for the well-groomed, thin, charming wife of the great Professor, who might be the President of the school within a few years?

But as the clouds gather and Alice's problems become more acute, the two strands in her writing about her parents become more disparate. Idolization on the one hand, alienation on the other—certainly no real communication:

> This is the funniest thing I have ever heard: Mom is worried and hinting that something might have happened to her little baby in those words she can't bring herself to use... do you know, she finally wound up actually feeling guilty for ever even suspecting such a thing.

Needless to say, 'something' has happened to Alice: sex, drugs, a drop-out life. Soon Alice runs away again, and then seeks help:

> I finally talked to an old priest who really understands young people. We had an endlessly long talk about why young people leave home, then he called my Mom and Dad. While I waited for him to get the call through I looked at myself in the mirror. I can't believe that I have changed so little. I expected to look old and hollow and gray, but I guess it's only me on the inside that has shrivelled and deteriorated. Mom answered the phone in the family room, and Dad ran upstairs to get the extension, and the three of us

almost drowned out the connection. I can't understand how they can possibly still love me and still want me but they do! They do! They do! They were glad to hear from me and to know I am all right. And there were no recriminations or scoldings or lectures or anything. It's strange that when something happens to me, Dad always leaves everything in the whole world and comes. I think if he were a peace mission involving all humanity in all the galaxies he would leave to come to me. He loves me! He loves me! He loves me! He truly does! I just wish I could love myself. I don't know how I can treat my family like I have. But I'm going to make it all up to them, I'm through with all the shit. I'm not even going to talk about it or write about it or even think about it anymore. I am going to spend the rest of my entire life trying to please them.

Her boyfriend gets on so well with her parents (according to Alice) that he makes her promise to 'enjoy and appreciate them enough for both of us'. With friends like that..? One way and another, Alice's relations with her parents, who clearly make her feel inadequate, read like a primary psychology lesson almost too textbook to be true. And it is quite impossible not to connect the relationship with her desperation, her drug addiction, and her death.

Almost impossible, too, not to feel that when Frances Partridge's diary quotes her friend Gerald Brenan as saying: 'Parents have to learn that they are to their children what a lamp-post is to a dog' he may have got hold of more than a cynical and half-true *bon mot*.

He may just conceivably be reflecting what is by comparison with the other possibilities a desirable state of affairs in this most difficult of all relationships.

Mommies Dearest

As mentioned earlier, the mother-daughter relationship is one often explored by diarists. Queen Victoria's difficult relationship with her domineering mother is too well known to need much documenting. Here is an entry from her journal:

> *16 November, 1839*
>
> Talked of Mama and the necessity of speaking to her about . . . leaving the house; Lord M. said he feared I should have great difficulty in getting her out of the house. 'There must be no harshness,' said Lord M, 'yet firm.'

Other entries on the subject of mothers by daughters are at once less pragmatic and more revealing. Here is Beatrice Webb:

24 March 1874

What is this feeling between Mother and me? It is a kind of feeling of dislike and distrust which I believe is mutual. And yet it ought not to be! She has always been the kindest and best of mothers, though in her manners she is not over-affectionate. She is such a curious character I can't make her out. She is sometimes such a kind, good affectionate mother, full of wise judgement and affectionate advice, and at other times the spoilt child comes out so strong in her. But whatever she is, that ought not to make the slightest difference to my feeling and behaviour towards her. Honour thy Father and Mother was one of the greatest of Christ's commandments...'

The same dissatisfaction, the plea for more affection and attention, comes from Anne Frank:

Wednesday, 12th January, 1944

I believe Mummy thinks there could be no better relationship between parents and their children, and that no one could take a greater interest in their children's lives than she. But quite definitely she only looks at Margot [Anne's sister], who I don't think ever had such problems and thoughts as I do. Still, I wouldn't dream of pointing out to Mummy that, in the case of her daughters, it isn't at all as she imagines, because she would be utterly amazed and wouldn't know how to change anyway; I want to save her the unhappiness it would cause her, especially as I know that for me everything would remain the same, anyway.

As the 'difficult' Alice grumbles: 'If only parents would listen! If only they would let us talk instead of forever and eternally and continuously harping and preaching and nagging and correcting and yacking, yacking, yacking!' Anne Frank, like Alice and Beatrice Webb and countless others, blames herself for her hostility towards her mother:

2nd January, 1944

This morning when I had nothing to do, I turned over some of the pages of my diary and several times I came across letters dealing with the subject 'Mummy' in such a hot-headed way that I was quite shocked, and asked myself: 'Anne, is it really you who mentioned hate? Oh Anne, how could you?'

'I can't really love Mummy in a dependant child-like way,' she says, 'I just don't have that feeling.' But perhaps she wishes she could:

Wednesday, 5th January, 1944

You know that I've grumbled a lot about Mummy, yet still tried to be nice to her again. Now it is suddenly clear to me what she lacks. Mummy herself has told us that she looked upon us more as her friends than her daughters. Now that is all very fine, but still, a friend can't take a mother's place. I need my mother as an example that I can follow, I want to be able to respect her.

I have the feeling that Margot thinks differently about these things and would never be able to understand what I've just told you. And Daddy avoids all the arguments about Mummy.

The figure of an imaginary ideal mother is one that occurs in other diaries. It is almost what Beatrice Webb is expressing when she looks back a few months after her mother's death with very different eyes.

27th August, 1882

A woman gives much when she consents to become mother and wife. I put the mother first because it is the relationship which absorbs her life, for which she suffers and should be loved. Poor little Mother. Looking back I see how bitterly she must have felt our want of affection and sympathy and for that I feel remorse.

Poor little Mother! Her death was so sad—so inexpressively sad in its isolation. Is all death like that? Can we not in that supreme moment bind the past with the future and through our influence force one link in the chain of human development, and our last mortal act be one of prayer and blessing? And who knows that Mother did not bless us with her last breath and that we, that I, am not now feeling the working of that blessing within me. It is strange, how I now feel the presence of her influence and think of her as an absent friend who does sympathise with my new life, but cannot tell it me. I never asked for her sympathy when she lived, but now she, through the medium of my memory, gives it me.

When I work, with many odds against me, for a far distant and perhaps unattainable end, I think of her and her intellectual strivings, which we were too ready to call useless, and yet will be the originating impulse of all my ambition, urging me onward towards something better in action or thought. When I feel discouraged and hopeless, when I feel that my feeble efforts to acquire are like a blind grasping in space for the stars, the vision of her will arise persistent always in action and in desire. Persevere.

Six years later, the sense of blessing and protection has not disappeared. Rather, it has grown stronger. In the case of Henriette Dessaulles, the idealized figure is, again, the dead mother: the 'Mama' mentioned is her stepmother:

July 7th, 1875

Yes, a mother—a real mother— that must be 'the someone' I dreamt about last night. Well, as far as *that's* concerned it's all over. I may as well lock up my heart with everything in it because the mother I have finds me a bother, she hardly speaks to me, I feel I'm in her way like a little nuisance. Could it be that I am the cause of her coldness? I know I have a lot of faults. Even though I feel things deeply, I'm shy and reserved and undemonstrative. Perhaps she doesn't know how I long for a sign of love from her. Oh! this summer I would like to be friendly and affectionate to her—but I'm afraid, and when I reach out to her and she rejects me, I always feel bruised—as if someone has stepped on my heart, and a heart that is stepped on is

53

crushed—it shrinks back, cowers and recoils, ready to flee and hide for fear of being crushed again. I had been so happy these last few days!

The same theme is repeated again and again:

February 21, 1877

Oh, how I wish I were at the convent and how far off tomorrow evening seems! Papa is away and I am frozen, chilled to the bone, in this arctic atmosphere. Chatting is impossible, faces are glum, gestures and tone abrupt, and when I'm downstairs all I want to do is run away to some dark spot and retreat into the peaceful world of my dreams. It would be so easy to be happy if we all tried, but oh! how utterly miserable I am now. I pray to my little mother in heaven to come and console me tonight and hold me and love me. God, oh God, why did You create orphans—You, who knew what mother love was?

Stepmothers, it would appear, do deserve some of their bad press, and Henriette doesn't always feel inclined to shoulder even a share of the blame:

August 25, 1877

There isn't a colder, pricklier, harder-to-please person in the whole wide world; I am utterly weary of it.

One is aware of hearing only one side of the story; even so, 'Mama's moods' do seem excessive. But three years later, when Henriette has turned from teenager to a twenty-year-old on the verge of engagement, she herself recants up to a point:

December 8, 1880

It's truly amazing how friendly I'm becoming with Mama. Was I bewitched before, I wonder? Did her attitude towards Maurice divide us as much as all that? I keep asking myself how it's possible that there was so little mutual understanding, so little harmony between us. Even her temper outbursts don't affect me any more; I know they are short-lived and I know she is genuinely fond of me; therefore nothing she says hurts me.

She must be as pleased as I am about this improvement in our relationship. Without wishing to boast, I suspect she is quite bowled over by my cheerfulness, my good humour, and that whole side of my nature she knew nothing about; she is discovering that we have a great deal in common. I'm a revelation to her—I see it in her eyes, in her whole attitude. And she is beginning to like Maurice; she enjoys chatting with him, thinks he is such a serious, well-informed young man, and so witty too!

In short, it's heaven!

Daddy's Girls

Ellen Peel was another nineteenth-century stepdaughter to whom 'Mama' proved unsympathetic—if less menacing than maddening:

'... she is abominably cheeky.' She was another who seems by the most objective standards to have suffered from a distinct lack of demonstrative affection. But Ellen, suffering under Mama, found no refuge, actual or emotional, in Papa ('the only man I can NOT get on with') and in that she is unusual.

Look at Henriette. Mama's coldness has hurt her:

Thursday

Her tone made it clear that her indifference was genuine, and I am stupid enough to feel terribly, terribly hurt and upset. After sobbing in my room for a while (where I could die without anyone noticing) I had to dress to go out. Papa, meeting me on the stairs, saw that my eyes were red from crying. 'Is my little girl unhappy about going back to the convent?'

'Oh no, I'm ever so glad to go!' and I leaned my head on his shoulder to hide the tears that threatened to reappear.

'It's not nice of you to dislike us so much,' he teased.

'Be quiet, don't say such hideous things. I love you.' I kissed him and ran away, but not before he had seen the tears that had started to run down my face again.

He watched me go and I don't know what he thought. He wasn't there at lunch, so he doesn't know about that ugly scene... fortunately.

Her father is 'dear sweet papa, his hugs and kisses—I always felt so happy when I was with him'. He is 'that wonderful father of mine' who can be relied upon to react with the most flattering and urgent concern to a hint (a faked one) of ill-health.

Anne Frank, without any question of real and step-parents being at stake, is almost equally sure where her allegiance lies:

Saturday, 7th November, 1942

It's obvious that Mummy would stick up for Margot; she and Margot always do back each other up. I'm so used to that that I'm utterly indifferent to both Mummy's jawing and Margot's moods.

I love them; but only because they are Mummy and Margot. With Daddy it's different. If he holds Margot up as an example, approves of what she does, praises and caresses her, then something gnaws at me inside, because I adore Daddy. He is the one I look up to. I don't love anyone in the world but him. He doesn't notice that he treats Margot differently from me. Now Margot is just the prettiest, sweetest, most beautiful girl in the world. But all the same I feel I have some right to be taken seriously too. I have always been the dunce, the ne'er-do-well of the family, I've always had to pay double for my deeds, first with the scolding and then again because of the way my feelings are hurt. Now I'm not satisfied with this apparent favouritism any more. I want something from Daddy that he is not able to give me.

I'm not jealous of Margot, never have been, I don't envy her good looks or her beauty. It is only that I long for Daddy's real love: not only as his child, but for me—Anne, myself.

Later she reacts against her family *en masse:* 'When I was in difficulties you all closed your eyes and stopped up your ears and didn't help me.' But afterwards, it is not her family *en masse* that she is so concerned and ashamed at having hurt: 'I will take Daddy as my example, and I *will* improve.'

Fanny Burney's approbation of her father may be expressed in less familiar language: 'never was parent so *properly,* so *well*-judgedly affectionate!' But it goes deep. Oddly enough she is yet another with a reputedly unsympathetic stepmother. The decorum of smooth-faced family life, though, is preserved even in the diary entries: the tone doesn't heat into hostility for 'my mother' though it warms into ardent affection for 'my father'. For his sake she took an unpleasant post at court; to him she returned afterwards:

> *Chelsea College London, October 1791*
>
> I have never been so pleasantly situated at home since I lost the sister of my heart and my most affectionate Charlotte. My father is almost constantly within. Indeed, I now live with him wholly; he has himself appropriated me a place, a seat, a desk, a table, and every convenience and comfort, and he never seemed yet so earnest to keep me about him. We read together, write together, chat, compare notes, communicate projects, and diversify each other's employments. He is all goodness, gaiety, and affection; and his society and kindness are more precious to me than ever.

Her talent and career he accepted and appropriated (at least, that is the unsympathetic interpretation). Her marriage he refused to attend. How reminiscent of another famous father, Dr Barrett, father of Elizabeth Barrett Browning.

When Elizabeth Barrett kept her diary for the space of ten months, the family's last months at their old home of Hope End, Robert Browning had not yet appeared on the horizon. Not only that—Elizabeth's invalidism, so famously established in *The Barretts of Wimpole Street*, was also a thing of the future. Elizabeth was twenty-four (though often she sounds younger), active and ardent, the clever girl whose intellectual tastes and talents were fostered by her father—whatever other restrictions, unreasonable even in those days, he may have imposed. You have to read between the lines a little to get much hint of the martinet Mr Barrett has been painted elsewhere. But there's little doubt the domestic tyrant is there:

> *June 17th, 1831*
>
> After dinner, papa unfortunately walked after me out of the room...The

consequence of this was a critique on my down-at-heel shoes; and the end of that, was my being sent out of the drawing-room to put on another pair. So while Anne is mending the only pair I have in the world, I am doing my best to write nonsense and catch cold without any.

The Victorian Father didn't believe in taking his family into his confidence: with financial difficulties and the possible sale of Hope End looming menacingly in the air, Dr Barrett's children were left to glean what information they could from watching his mood and his countenance. But when the move comes closer, Elizabeth is far from blaming Papa:

> *26 August*
>
> I may have to leave this place where I have walked and talked and dreamt in much joy: and where I have heard most beloved voices which I can no more hear, and clasped beloved hands which I can no more clasp: where I have smiled with the living and wept above the dead and where I have read immortal books, and written pleasant thoughts, and known at least one very dear friend—I may have to do this; and it will be sorrow to me.—But let me think of it calmly. I can take with me the dear members of my own family,—and my recollections which, in some cases, were all that was left to me here: I can take my books and my studious tastes, and above all, the knowledge that 'all things', whether sorrowful or joyous, 'work together for good to those who love God'. And my dear Papa's mind,—(should he not be dearest to me?) will be more tranquil when he is away from a place so productive of anxieties.

It's only too easy to know what to make of the final entry in the Hope End saga (as it remains after Elizabeth's brother edited it much later in life):

> *April 23, 1832*
>
> Mr. Boyd pressed me earnestly to go to see him for two or three days— 'There is no harm in asking!—Do ask your Papa.' I was obliged to say 'I will think of it': tho' thinking is vain. Went away in pouring rain. Left.

Wimpole Street, here we come.

How different from Joan Wyndham's 'Daddy Dick'—

> *Tuesday, 22nd August, 1939*
>
> ... I don't know why everybody calls him that, as if I had a choice of other, more suitable daddies. Unfortunately all I have is DD, maddening, self-centred and never there. I suppose he'll be late as usual, although it's nearly a year since he last saw me.
>
> *Later*
>
> DD finally arrived in a very expensive looking car called an Alvis, and we drove out for a cream tea in Marlborough. His face is tanned and he wears a

blue shirt with a red tie. He looks much better now he has stopped drinking. The tea was supposed to be a kind of treat, to make up for neglecting me for so long. He seemed unusually friendly and interested, and asked me about Mummy and whether she was OK. I said yes, but we could do with a bit more money if he could spare it, which he jolly well ought to, considering what his paintings fetch nowadays.

'And how is the exotic Sidonie?' he went on, very sarcastic because he can't stand her. 'Still painting her face white and going to Mass every morning?' I don't know why he should be so down on her, Mummy's jolly lucky to have someone to look after her and love her—it can't be much fun being divorced at twenty-three.

The clotted cream and scones arrived and we laid into them. 'We're both rather greedy aren't we?' Daddy observed. 'It's strange how like me you are, in spite of our hardly ever seeing each other. I wonder how you'd have turned out if you'd been brought up by me instead of by two religious ladies.'

Us in Them

...A recurrent theme, from both the parents' and the child's point of view, is what you could call 'us in them'—the echo of characteristics, experiences, standpoints down the generations (as we saw in the extract above). To anyone who has seen politician Shirley Williams' face on television there is a particular relish in reading the diary entry her mother, Vera Brittain, made for 28 July 1932:

> Shirley, after being put to bed, climbed right over the rails of her hired cot, which is an inch or two lower than the one at home, and fell with a terrific bump on the floor; I heard it in my room and dashed in to find her already at the door, roaring but apparently unhurt. She will now have to be strapped; where she gets all this adventurous rashness from I cannot imagine. As Gordon's mother is the only unknown element I suppose she must be responsible for S.'s terrifying traits.

And, six months later:

> Shirley turned her back on the party and played in a corner with one jig-saw puzzle all afternoon. Mrs Davies says that she has got through all the Montessori apparatus in the school (i.e. up to six years old) and ought by right to be moved up to an older group but is still too tiny—the youngest but one. Feministically I am glad that in orthodox ways she seems likely to be cleverer than John, but I have an instinctive fellow feeling for John and do hope the poor child hasn't inherited *only* my failings!

Teenagers may be more concerned with establishing their independence, but a number of grown-up daughters, reached (or past) the age of having children themselves, are concerned suddenly to look back, to trace the path of 'My Mother' and 'My Father'—'My Self.'

It's striking how often a voyage of self-exploration seems to start with exploring that mysterious, ever-present other. Anne Truitt, in her fifties, started a journal in which she hoped to come to terms with the artist within herself. What theme recurs through the first months' pages?

13 July 1974

I cannot remember ever not knowing that my father loved me more than anyone in the world. I abided in that love, loved and honored it as he loved and honored me. But I never truly understood this central stove of warmth and light in my life until long after my father was dead, until I reached the age he had been in my childhood. Because I was born when he was forty-two, it is only in the last few years that I have wholly loved him. When I was younger, his love seemed excessive, embarrassing because of a proportion I could meet only decorously, never realistically.

It was my mother's cooler hand that guided, apparently effortlessly and rather unemotionally, my efforts to learn how to live.

15 July

My mother's moral force radiated from her like a gentle pulsation. Sensitive people picked it up and found her presence delicately satisfying. Tall, slender, light-boned, fair-skinned, everything about her was fined down almost to transparency. She moved over the ground lightly, and her golden brown hair (never cut until her head was shaved for an operation to excise the brain tumour that was already killing her) was piled up softly and allowed to fall over her high forehead, above which it seemed to float. Fine, like the rest of her, it would have radiated like an aureole around her head had she not decisively worn a net, invisible, made of real hair.

She was herself only when alone. I used to watch her brace herself for people; even, occasionally, for me. And then watch her straight, narrow back relax, her shoulders drop a little, as she set out for a walk. A few steps away from the house and her feet would begin to skim.

This satisfaction with being solitary was a tremendous source of freedom for me. It implied a delight in self and affirmed my own obsessive sieving of experience. By taking her mind totally off me, she gave me my own autonomy. I knew from experience that she was careful and responsible. I realized that she would have watched me had she not been sure that I was all right. And, if she were sure, I could be sure. Very early in my life, I set out stoutly to look around at everything.

Nothing is perfect: Mother's restraint added up to excessive demands on her energy. Only fortune, Truitt writes, prevented her in middle life from 'stiffening into my mother's pattern'. Father, though loving, was weak, an assessment that turns up again in the journals of Anaïs Nin. *Her* father left the family when she was a child (her journal began as an extended letter to him). Now she is an adult he turns up again:

> I find my father again when I am a woman. When he comes to me, he who marked my childhood so deeply, I am a full-blown woman. I understand my father as a human being. He is again the man who is also a child . . . The father I imagined cruel, strong, hero, famous musician, lover of women, triumphant, is soft, feminine, vulnerable, imperfect. I lose my terror and my pain. I meet him again when I know that there is no possibility of fusion between father and daughter, only between man and woman.
>
> Henry says this will reconcile me to God. My father comes when I no longer need a father.
>
> My father comes when I have gone beyond him; he is given to me when I no longer need him, when I am free of him. In every fulfilment there is a mockery which runs ahead of me like a gust of wind, always ahead. My father comes when I have an artist writer to write with, a guide I wept for in Allendy [her analyst] a protector, brother, symbolic children, friends, a world, books written. Yet the child in me could not die as it should have died, because according to legends it must find its father again. The old legends knew, perhaps, that in absence the father becomes glorified, deified, eroticized, and this outrage against God the Father has to be atoned for. The human father has to be confronted and recognized as human, as a man who created a child and then, by his absence, left the child fatherless and then Godless.

The analysis goes on for pages as letter follows letter and meeting meeting, sometimes in pleasure, sometimes in pain. More than once Anaïs speaks of her father as her other half, her double. He, she writes, is 'amazed and at first delighted, for every narcissist dreams of a twin'. But is he her double, or her *doppelganger*?

> I had always lived not to be my father. Through the years I had made a portrait of him which I had sought to destroy in myself. On the basis of a few resemblances, one fears total resemblance. I did not want to be him. That may be why I sought a more sincere life, real values, disregarded the outer forms, took flight from society, wealthy or aristocratic people.
> We love music.
> We love the sea.
> We dread squalor. (But I never pursued money to avoid it.) I was unflinchingly poor many times. I can make real sacrifices. I never calculated. I am capable of immense devotions. I set about scrupulously to destroy in myself any over-attachment to luxury, beauty. Frivolity. Grand hotels. Cars. Salons.
>
> My father is a dandy. When we were children, his cologne and his luxurious shirts, were more important than a toy for us, or clothes for my mother.
>
> When he left, I felt as if I had seen the Anaïs I never wanted to be.

Roles that have been played before are all too easy to play again:

March 1934

'Go on,' he said, 'now tell me I have no talent, tell me I do not know how to love, tell me I am an egoist, tell me all that your mother used to tell me.'

'I have never believed any of those things.'

But suddenly I stopped. I knew my father was not seeing me any more, but always the judge, that past which made him so uneasy. I felt as if I were not myself any more, but my mother, with a body tired with giving and serving, rebelling at his selfishness and irresponsibility. I felt my mother's anger and despair. For the first time, my own image of my father fell on the floor. I saw my mother's image. I saw the child in him who demanded all love and did not know how to love in return. I saw the child incapable of an act of protectiveness, or self-denial. I saw the child hiding behind her courage, the same child now hiding behind her courage, the same child now hiding behind Maruca's protection. I was my mother telling him that, as a human being and as a father, as a husband, he was a failure. And perhaps she had told him, too, that as a musician he had not given enough to justify his limitations as a human being. All his life he had played with people, with love, played at love, played at being a concert pianist, playing at composing playing; because to no one or to nothing could he give his entire soul.

Certain gestures made in childhood seem to have eternal repercussions. Such as the gesture I had made to keep my father from leaving, grasping his coat and holding on to it so fiercely that I had to be torn away. This gesture of despair seemed to prolong itself all through life. I repeated it blindly, fearing always that everything I loved would be lost. It was hard for me to believe that this father I was still trying to hold on to was no longer real or important, that the coat I was touching was not warm, that the body of him was not warm, not human, that my tragic desire and quest had come to an end, and that my love had died.

Fifteen years later, another long separation having followed the failed reconciliation, her father dies and Nin weeps for what she lost—or never had:

20th October 1949

San Francisco

So many memories. Why did he build a wall around himself? Why did he always seek the flaws in others, why were his blue eyes so critical? No memory of tenderness or care, and yet my mother tells me that he took thousands of photographs of us, naked. He was full of aesthetic admiration for his children. It was the only moment in which he showed interest. Or was it interest in a new hobby, photography? I do not know. But the moment of photography was the only moment we received attention. I wonder if my dislike of photography came from that.

Did he bring out the woman's coquettishness in the little girl? Eyes of the

61

father behind a camera. But always a critical eye. That eye had to be exorcised, or else like that of a demanding god, pleased. I had to labor at presenting a pleasing image. Of course, that is where it came from. Not to displease the Photographer God and Critic.

Joaquin wrote me about our father: 'I tried to be friendly but he had already locked himself away from everybody. He was lost in the pit of his own loneliness and frightened at the sound of his own voice.'

He had discarded all photographs but those of himself which were hung around the walls.

A little later it is her mother who dies. 'I rebelled against death. I wept quietly. The guilt came from my rebellion against her. The anguishing compassion for her life.'

'How we love people after their death,' Nin wrote then:

> Conceding with love and admiration to my mother meant an acceptance of traits inherent in me which I considered a threat to my existence, as, for example, my maternal qualities, and I had to fight them in her. She sought to make of me the woman I did not want to be, who capitulated to wifehood and motherhood, and while she lived she threatened all my aspirations to escape the servitude of woman. When she died I was forced to take into myself this conflict, and I realized I had long ago lost the battle. I am a woman who takes care of others on the same level my mother did. As soon as she died this rebellion collapsed.

Sylvia Plath's journals show her in the process of exploring the ambivalence of her feelings towards her mother (her father had died when she was a child). Probably she didn't live long enough to emerge from this ambivalence—if indeed one ever does. Once again, on this subject as on so many others, the journals show a very different Plath from the buoyant *Letters Home*. It is a difference Plath herself explores. 'In the safety of letters', she wrote, 'we could both verbalize our desired image of ourselves in relation to each other: interest and sincere love, and never feel the emotional currents at war with these verbally expressed feelings.' It was in analysis, in Boston at the end of 1958, that these other currents begin to emerge, to be reflected in long, questioning, repetitive pages.

It was her therapist, Dr. Ruth Beuscher, who, 'like a shot of brandy, a whiff of cocaine', gave her, as she phrased it, permission to hate her mother:

> *Friday, December 12 [1958]*
> But although it makes me feel good as hell to express my hostility for my mother, frees me from the Panic Bird in my heart and my typewriter (why?), I can't go through life calling Dr. Beuscher up from Paris, London, the wilds of Maine long distance. [Omission] Life was hell. She [Sylvia's

mother] had to work. Work, and be a mother, too, a man and a woman in one sweet ulcerous ball. She pinched. Scraped. Wore the same old coat. But the children had new school clothes and shoes that fit. Piano lessons, viola lessons, French horn lessons. They went to Scouts. They went to summer camp and learned to sail. One of them went to private school on scholarship and got good marks. In all honesty and with her whole unhappy heart she worked to give those two innocent little children the world of joy she'd never had. She'd had a lousy world. But they went to college, the best in the nation, on scholarship and work and part of her money, and didn't have to study nasty business subjects. One day they would marry for love, love, love and have plenty of money and everything would be honey sweet. They wouldn't even have to support her in her old age... Me, I never knew the love of a father, the love of a steady blood-related man after the age of eight... the only man who'd love me steady through life: she came in one morning with tears... in her eyes and told me he was gone for good. I hate her for that.

'What to do with your hate for... all mother figures?' she asks. 'What to do when you feel guilty for not doing what they say, because, after all, they have gone out of their way to help you?'

Friday morning, December 26, 1958
A good Christmas. Because, Ted [Plath's husband] says, I was merry. I played, teased, welcomed Mother. I may hate her, but that's not all. I... love her too. After all, as the story goes, she's my mother.

In Plath's dreams, she's also Ted... who is also her father. Nothing is simple. There are no answers, but the questions are all consuming:

What do I expect or want from Mother? Hugging, mother's milk? But that is impossible to all of us now. Why should I want it still? What can I do with this want? How can I transfer it to something I can have?

Chapter 5
~ Love

'It's love that makes the world go round!'—Gilbert and Sullivan (and others)

'The love that moves the sun and the other stars.'—Dante

Monday, October 1st, 1979

Walk with Rosie, who has a new boyfriend.
'Half of me's in love with him,' she says.
'Which half?' I ask. 'Bottom or top?'
(Rosie says she hasn't been to bed with him yet, so probably top half.)—Jilly Cooper, from *The Common Years*.

Love is... the teenage diaries sent in to Valerie Grove. Love is 'living in a perpetual state of hypothesis', being 'overwhelmed by him and his very existence'. Love is 'not knowing what I'd do without him'. Its object is—from the same teenage writer and in remarkably quick succession—Hamlet, John Lennon, Peter O'Toole, John Wood and James Booth. 'Older than me', the writer stipulates. 'In his 20's', 'skilled', 'reasonably vicious'.

The teenage diaries are a good place to start because, inevitably, they chart the first painful, delicious plunge into romantic waters—the inviting glitter on the water, the sudden shocking chill... A month of courtship rates more words than a year of connubial bliss. But that doesn't make it only for the young. Love is also Beatrice Webb making her slow pact with Sidney, Dora Carrington remembering 'the special perfectness of Lytton', Queen Victoria praising Albert's 'pretty mouth', and Virginia Woolf on Vita Sackville-West: 'her maturity and full-breastedness: her being so much in full sail on high tides'. When it comes to learning to swim, all types and ages of women are much the same. Love is the great leveller.

Love at First Sight

'Love is blind' says the proverb and it is borne out by a collection of extracts describing first encounters between men and women who were destined to mean a great deal to one another, but who were probably unaware of it at the time.

The first prize has to go to Lady Caroline Lamb on Lord Byron—'mad, bad and dangerous to know'. But Beatrice Webb—then Beatrice Potter— is deservedly famous for her description of an early meeting with her future husband:

> *February 14th 1890. Devonshire House Hotel*
> Sidney Webb, the socialist, dined here to meet the Booths. A remarkable little man with a huge head on a very tiny body, a breadth of forehead quite sufficient to account for the encyclopaedic character of his knowledge, a Jewish nose, prominent eyes and mouth, black coat shiny with wear; regarded as a whole, somewhat between a London card and a German professor. To keep to essentials: his pronunciation is Cockney, his H's are shaky, his attitudes by no means eloquent, with his thumbs fixed pugnaciously in a far from immaculate waistcoat, with his bulky head thrown back and his little body forward he struts even when he stands, delivering himself with extraordinary rapidity of thought and utterance and with an expression of inexhaustible self-complacency. But I like the man. There is a directness of speech, an open-mindedness, an imaginative warm-heartedness which should carry him far. He has the self-complacency of one who is always thinking faster than his neighbours, who is untroubled by doubts, and to whom the acquisition of facts is as easy as the grasping of matter; but he has no vanity and is totally unselfconscious.

A classic of its kind, despite the promise of mild warmth in the 'I like the man'. But hardly more unpropitious than Fanny Longfellow (née Appleton), hearing of *her* future husband's approach:

> *July 20th 1836*
> Professor Longfellow sends up his card to Father. Hope the venerable gentleman won't pop in on us, though I did like his *Outre-Mer*.

The venerable gentleman, did she but know it, had not yet reached thirty at that point. Queen Victoria, by contrast, was in ecstasies from the start of her acquaintance with Prince Albert:

> *October 11th 1839*
> Albert really is quite charming, and so excessively handsome, such beautiful blue eyes, an exquisite nose, and such a pretty mouth with

delicate moustachios and slight but very slight whiskers; a beautiful figure, broad in the shoulders and a fine waist; my heart is quite going . . . it is quite a pleasure to look at Albert when he gallops and and valses, he does it so beautifully, holds himself so well with that beautiful figure of his.

Victoria knew perfectly well that a possible marriage was in the air: Albert had been invited to England for no other reason and she must have been glad to find him quite charming—any other decision might have been a little awkward. But Betsey Wynne's opinion of her Captain Fremantle is equally positive:

> *June 24th 1796*
>
> How kind and amiable Captain Fremantle is. He pleases me more than any man I have yet seen. Not handsome, but there is something pleasing in his countenance and his fiery black eyes are quite captivating. He is good-natured, kind and amiable, gay and lively; in short he seems to possess all the good and amiable qualities that are required to win everybodies heart the first moment one sees him.

It is almost enough to make one believe that, as the saying goes, 'There is always the thought of marriage between a single man and a personable female: if not in his mind, then certainly in hers.'

It wasn't marriage Joan Wyndham was thinking of when she set eyes on her first fancy, but the same principle applies. She was ready to fall in love:

> *Saturday, October 14th 1939*
>
> . . . I turned round and saw—well how can I describe him? If I was feeling romantic I should say I saw Pan; if realistic, then the most depraved long-haired Bohemian, in a blue shirt and corduroy pants, that ever drank cheap red wine in the Artists' Cafe.

One woman's meat . . . A 'depraved Bohemian' would not have suited Betsey Wynne, and certainly not Queen Victoria, but for Joan Wyndham, it was a case of love—or, at least, attraction—at first sight.

Testing The Water!

Is 'the readiness all'? Thirteen-year-old Anne Frank knew just what she was and was not ready for:

> *Saturday, June 20th, 1942*
>
> I expect you will be rather surprised at the fact that I should talk of boy friends at my age. Alas, one simply can't seem to avoid it at our school. As soon as a boy asks if he may cycle home with me and we get into conversation, nine out of ten times I can be sure that he will fall head over heels in love immediately and simply won't allow me out of his sight. After a

while it cools down of course, especially as I take little notice of ardent looks and pedal blithely on.

When she met Peter who was to be the love of her Secret Annexe life, her first reaction was indifferent. 'He's not 16, a rather soft, shy, gawky youth; can't expect much from his company.' A week later she has certainly seen no reason to change her mind: 'What a fool!' His parents pushing her towards him may have hindered or may—improbably— have helped ('Imagine it!). Either way, it was a surprising eighteen months before propinquity began to do its work. But work it did:

Thursday, 6th January, 1944

Dear Kitty,
My longing to talk to someone became so intense that somehow or other I took it in my head to choose Peter ... I tried to think of an excuse to stay in his room and get him talking, without it being too noticeable, and my chance came yesterday. Peter has a mania for crossword puzzles at the moment and hardly does anything else. I helped him with them and we soon sat opposite each other at his little table, he on the chair and me on the divan.

It gave me a queer feeling each time I looked into his deep blue eyes, and he sat there with that mysterious laugh playing round the lips. I was able to read his inward thoughts. I could see on his face that look of helplessness and uncertainty as to how to behave, and, at the same time, a trace of his sense of manhood. I noticed his shy manner and it made me feel very gentle; I couldn't refrain from meeting those dark eyes again and again, and with my whole heart I almost beseeched him: oh, tell me, what is going on inside you, oh, can't you, look beyond this ridiculous chatter? ...

When I lay in bed and thought over the whole situation, I found it far from encouraging, and the idea that I should beg for Peter's patronage was simply repellent. One can do a lot to satisfy one's longings, which certainly sticks out in my case, for I have made up my mind to go and sit with Peter more often and to get him talking somehow or other.

Whatever you do, don't think I'm in love with Peter—not a bit of it! If the Van Daans had had a daughter instead of a son, I should have tried to make friends with her too.

The 'affair' took its natural course: 18 February: 'Whenever I go upstairs now I keep on hoping that I shall see "him". Because my life now has an object, and I have something to look forward to, everything has become more pleasant.' Plenty of clues to motivation there—not that young love is always 'pleasant'. 19 February: 'Oh, if I could nestle my head against his shoulder and not feel so hopelessly alone and deserted!' By 22 March she is sure that he loves her, 'but just how, I myself don't know yet ... As a girl, or as a sister?'

After the first kiss and the first experiments in 'necking—a word I can't bear'—comes the parental pep-talk about trust, plus a warning from Anne's father that in the artificially enclosed world in which they are all living things are bound to look different from how they would outside. Good advice... but is it advice of which Anne stands in need? There are hints (poignantly enough, in one of the penultimate entries) that she may know it herself:

Saturday, 15th July, 1944

...I know very well that I conquered him instead of he conquering me. I created an image of him in my mind, pictured him as a quiet, sensitive, lovable boy, who needed affection and friendship. I needed a living person to whom I could pour out my heart; I wanted a friend who'd help to put me on the right road. I achieved what I wanted, and, slowly but surely, I drew him towards me. Finally, when I had made him feel friendly, it automatically developed into an intimacy, which, on second thoughts, I don't think I ought to have allowed.

Youth does seem to keep an unexpectedly cool eye on its own ardours at times. Take the student Barbara Pym. On 25 January 1933 she wrote: 'This diary seems to be going to turn into the Saga of Lorenzo.' She wasn't far wrong—but there is, about all the early references, a tone of schoolgirl relish. 29 April: 'Oh ever to be remembered day. Lorenzo spoke to me!' 30 April: 'I was very happy thinking about Lorenzo and the funny way he talked and everything. I had that funny kind of gnawing at the vitals sick feeling if that describes it at all'—Romeo at Stratford is 'awfully like Lorenzo'. On 31 July she feels the need of an original cure: 'After lunch I took some Yeastvite tablets and continued to take them after tea and supper. A slightly unromantic way of curing lovesickness I admit, but certainly I feel a lot better now.' In November: 'his smile of self-conscious fatuity is sweet—but one day it may seem silly'. And on 28 May the following year:

I suppose the truth is that I belong to a cruel sweet Englishman called Henry Stanley Harvey [Lorenzo's real name], but at the age of not quite 21, it is not possible to be certain.

'Mississippi' Maud Rittenhouse in the 1880s is inclined to use her youth, perhaps not altogether ingenuously, as a kind of handle against fate:

I think how moral and kind Elmer is and then go to bed and dream of Robert calling me 'Sweet little woman' and then wake up mad and wish I'd never seen a male creature in my life.

I could hardly sleep for thinking. This state of indecision seems really wicked, but I don't know how to help it.

The idea of an infant of 16 having to bother her head about lovers and sich [sic]. I'll declare it's horrid.

Sixteen isn't too young for her to have learnt teasing tactics: 'If it takes him 15 days to answer my letter it takes me 30 to answer his.' The hapless Robert soon gets his cards: ('Mama, upon Friday and Saturday last so vividly pictured the wasted, unsatisfactory heartbroken life of the woman who married a man without a good moral foundation, that I cannot but think it best.') He wasn't long mourned (the very next day she wrote: 'I'm beginning to despise him now as earnestly as I once loved him. Everything is done between us.') and there was always Elmer …and Will, and Jim. 'Oh! dear. I wish I'd never seen a boy—so I do.'

On the one hand, it is hard to disagree with her bosom friend's assessment of Maud's character:

> 'Maud, you haven't any heart at all, you're the worst specimen I ever
> saw—you're a—a—'
> *'Flirt*, and done with it, why don't you say,' I exclaimed impatiently. 'Well,
> what shall I do about it?'

On the other hand, isn't she rather ahead of her time in questioning the assumption that she must always be the emotional watchdog?

Maud wanted her experiences—she only objected to being faced with the consequences. What a pity she couldn't experiment without reproach, as Joan Wyndham seems to have done. In fact Joan's freedom—of thought, speech and even deed—seems extraordinary for the 1930s, though a lot must be put down, presumably, to the unusual world in which she lived.

At the beginning of her teenage diary, so appropriately published under the title *Love Lessons*, Joan is nearly seventeen and still concerned to show she knows love's alphabet. 'I am in love with Harold the butler, and Macrae who looks after the horses,' she writes in the first entry on 22 August 1939. A week later she is becoming 'more and more infatuated' with an older (female) drama teacher.

From there, she was ready to fall in love properly. After the wonderful description of her first encounter with the 'depraved' Gerhardt, it is no surprise that Joan's ready and roving fancy should light on him. And she is clearly getting past the stage of testing the waters. Even if the waters are scalding, she could find herself taking the plunge:

> Watching him ladling cooked dog biscuit out of a saucepan, I saw all my
> future feelings mapped out before me like a chart. Days of sour boredom,
> melancholia and touchiness, followed by days of bliss and delirium (usually
> quite uncalled for), living from one milestone to another. No more
> aquarium life.

Taking The Plunge

NATURAL PROGRESSION

Joan Wyndham's 'plunge,' in one sense, is chronicled in a later chapter. To her, and those around her (friends and boyfriends), it took the form of a conventional question: sex, to have or not to have. In another sense, an emotional one, she seems to have taken her plunge much earlier on—as she stood outside Gerhardt's window, watching through a chink in the curtains another woman's long bare legs moving bedwards as the lights went out.

> They say in novels 'something died in me,' but that's not true. It's all you ask for to have the love die. The worst thing is that it goes on living and redoubling its love, and is wounded to the quick and cries aloud. I only wish a lot of things would die in me.

But then again, despite the pain of this first love, one can detect a note of detachment in the references to, and even the relationships with, subsequent lovers. Joan Wyndham does grow up in the course of *Love Lessons*, but she does it imperceptibly. And it is only the final diary entry that signals the progression:

> *Tuesday, 13th May 1942*
>
> I'm in the train going to Leighton Buzzard, with my belt and buttons newly shined, ready to start training for Special Duties. At least it will keep my mind occupied.
>
> I suppose I could meet someone new, a pilot or something, who won't be queer or paranoid or schizophrenic, who won't be self-centred and cynical or have had VD, or take drugs or play the guitar, and who certainly won't be a painter! And what's more he won't be a hypochondriac or a hedonist, or hate children or laugh at religion or think the lower classes ought to be shot at sight; he'll have a heart and a soul, and all the right feelings at the right time.
>
> And he won't beat women up and have rushes of adrenalin and smash things or keep two mistresses at the same time; he'll do the washing-up and buy me flowers and take me dancing, he'll see me home in air-raids, think I'm beautiful and write me love-letters and ask me to marry him!
>
> But I'm sure I'll never like him half as much as Rupert.

Note the name: Rupert, *not* Gerhardt, her first love.

The Southern Belle, Maud Rittenhouse, despite her more restricted circumstances, continues to move through men with even more alacrity. 'Life is a knotty problem,' she writes in 1885, 'and my days of love-winning are over and gone. I candidly believe I shall never marry. I can never marry a man not mentally equal to me or above me, and, without egotism, I do not find that man.' But just a few days later she notes in her diary: 'After all my self-congratulation I find I am still a creature of extremes—every new scholar for instance fills me with animation and sets me castle building.'

In the same extract, Elmer appears to be going to some trouble to lead the field of suitors:

> Do you notice how careful he is that I shall not outgrow him? Do I go wild over art, Elmer immediately studies catalogues and circulars, reads up artworks, orders art periodicals, affects galleries, makes me presents of sketch-boxes and art-folios. Do I go horse-mad, Elmer sends me a copy of the *American Horse-woman*, gives (or tries to give me) a pony, orders himself the handsomest of saddles, whips and horsey etceteras. Do I rave over Browning, Elmer immediately orders Browning complete and begins to study. Do I praise Norfolk jackets and heliotrope-perfume, Elmer suddenly appears in the most stylish Norfolk possible, and wafts about him a delicate odor of heliotrope. And so on ad infinitum. Where thou art, there am I also—*right there* as Wint puts it.

Elmer, in fact, makes it as far as an engagement, only to be forced into 'releasing' Maud from that engagement when he loses his money through a real-estate collapse in the West and is (falsely) accused of fraudulent discrepancies in his book-keeping. Enter Earl and Ned—more vacillation—an engagement to Earl who (the boot being on the other foot for once) blows hot and cold to the point where Maud is forced to take what was then considered the lady's prerogative and press the release button:

> *Wed, Aug. 19 [1891]*
>
> Of course I wrote to Earl at once releasing him from the engagement, and saying in what way I preferred him to return my letters, and I, his, etc.
>
> Nobody speaks of it in the family, though I see Harry watching me a good deal—wondering, I suppose, how a girl acts anyhow, when her sweetheart decides he doesn't love her well enough. It is the strangest thing how my mind teems with all the pros and cons of the case.. while I do everything as if handsome Dr. Mayne had never existed. I am exercising a good deal at tennis, and walking. George Corliss was here all Sunday afternoon and evening and took me walking. I was with George the first time I ever saw Earl. And Earl once thought me engaged to George. Earl says he feels 'strange and unnatural', that it made him 'half wild' to write what he did. Well, but I don't mean to enter into any of this. I think, think, think, a thousand things about it. But it will do me no good to write them down. I believe, if it killed me, I could keep from showing him or anyone the hurt. What a blessed thing a little decent womanly pride is... And people talk about 'deathless love'! And some folks actually believe in it.

Two years later: 'Old Journal, it is a ghastly confession to make here in my room with the curtains down, the door tight shut and our two selves alone. I believe I am an *old maid*. I found a white hair this morning; and I haven't had either a love-letter or a gentleman caller in *two weeks*—I mean one with any paraded "intentions".'

Her fears are unfounded—eighteen months later Earl reappears on the scene, re-proposes, and is re-accepted. With the wedding-gown in the making and her new cards ordered, Maud's fourteen-year journal ends for good. The curious thing is that in all those fourteen years the tone is so little changed. After a love life (in thought if not in action) that would make the much-married Wife of Bath blink, Maud at thirty still sounds much as she did at sixteen. At first, her amours are enchanting: Scarlett O'Hara lives, in an Anne of Green Gables (and Louisa M. Alcott, and *Katy*) setting of Temperance Picnics and sunny summer afternoons. But towards the end of the journal, in its very sameness, doesn't a slightly sinister note creep in? Faint echoes of Dickens' jilted Miss Haversham, sitting in the sixty-year-old tatters of her bridal finery; even of *Baby Jane*? It is as if Maud never braced herself to take that emotional plunge. Until, presumably, her eventual marriage— and there the journal doesn't follow her.

What of the other girls or women whose love stories began earlier in the chapter? Anne Frank's went no further. But novelist Barbara Pym continued in 'that divine madness for which she [Sandra—a pet name for herself] can only be thankful'. Over the next two years, in 'Lorenzo'/Henry's frequent absences, she never forgot him. In May 1936, while acting as his secretary (!) 'I've fallen in love, and with Henry... Feel just as bad as I did three years ago—almost worse because he has been extremely nice to me and we have got on much better together than ever before.' In a rather telling entry a little later, she writes: 'I often think that Henry is never so nice as when he's standing at the door of the flat saying goodbye.'

Six months later Henry was married – to someone else. Barbara writes in her diary of envying his wife ('after all, I love him, too!') but her letters continue, in a friendly spirit, now addressed to both of them.

A Man's World

Queen Victoria, by the fact of her public position, had been forced to take the plunge almost before she met Albert. She protested, when Lord Melbourne broached the matter of marriage to her. 'I said I dreaded the thought of marrying: that I was so accustomed to have my own way, that I thought it was 10 to 1 that I shouldn't agree with any body.' But once she had been pushed into meeting Albert, and admired him, her way was clear:

14th October 1839

After a little pause I said to Lord M., that I had made up my mind (about marrying dearest Albert).—'You have?' he said; 'well then, about the time?' Not for a year, I thought; which he said was too long; that Parliament must be assembled in order to make a provision for him, and that if it was settled 'it shouldn't be talked about,' said Lord M.; 'it prevents any objection, though I don't think there'll be much; on the contrary,' he continued with tears in his eyes, 'I think it'll be very well received; for I hear there is an anxiety now that it should be; and I'm very glad of it; I think it is a very good thing, and you'll be much more comfortable; for a woman cannot stand alone for long, in whatever situation she is.'.. Then I asked, if I hadn't better tell Albert of my decision soon, in which Lord M. agreed. How? I asked, for that in general such things were done the other way,—which made Lord M. laugh. When we got up, I took Lord M.'s hand, and said he was always so kind to me,—which he has always been; he was so kind, so fatherly about all this. I felt very happy ... Talked to Lord Melbourne after dinner of my hearing Albert couldn't sleep these last few days; nor I either, I added; that he asked a good deal about England, about which I tried to give him the most agreeable idea.

October 1839

At about 1/2 p.12 I sent for Albert; he came to the Closet where I was alone, and after a few minutes I said to him, that I thought he must be aware why I wished [him] to come here, and that it would make me too happy if he would consent to what I wished (to marry me); we embraced each other over and over again, and he was so kind, so affectionate; Oh! to feel I was, and am, loved by such an Angel as Albert was too great a delight to describe! he is perfection; perfection in every way—in beauty—in everything! I told him I was quite unworthy of him and kissed his dear hand—he said he would be very happy [to share his life with her] and was so kind and seemed so happy, that I really felt it was the happiest, brightest moment in my life, which made up for all I had suffered and endured. Oh! how I adore and love him, I cannot say!! how I will strive to make him feel as little as possible the great sacrifice he has made; I told him it was a great sacrifice,—which he wouldn't allow ... I feel the happiest of human beings.

When she spoke to Lord Melbourne about her fears of not having her own way he had told her 'Oh! but you would have it still'. Elsewhere, however, it was a man's world. Victoria might pity herself for having, by her position as Queen Regnant, to make the proposal: other young women, in theory at least, might envy her the power.

Here is Betsey Wynne poised uncomfortably on the brink ('For all I only think of Fremantle I can hardly live without him I scarcely believe

I am in love.') Increasingly certain of her own feelings, hoping she is sure of his but, without the protection of an official engagement, finding that the presence and attentions of the wrong man are almost as bad as the absence of the right one:

Friday and Saturday 9th & 10th September 1796

We had these two days the most delectable weather. A fine Mediterranean skye, the sea like a mill pond and only a little pleasant breeze enough for it not to be too hot. Captain Sutton and Sir Charles Knowles came both days to see us. The old Baronet is a real bore. Captain Sutton is a pleasant good sort of man. We danced Saturday evening with them but I was forced to do it, I heard something which quite broke my heart. Papa complained very much of me to Mamma. He says I am quite changed, that I grow a downright Coquette, that he sees I shall be a second Montalban and with Fr. I was a great fool if ever I thought he would let me marry him, that I might do it if I chose but that he would never see me again if I did etc. and a thousand other such things. Good God, how mistaken he is if he thinks that I am flattered by the partiality shown to me and that I endeavour to please, far from it, Captain Foley's attachment is a torment to me, and it makes me wish still more for Fremantle's return. But then if Papa persists in his present resolution how miserable shall I be. All that I suffered till now is nothing to what is to come. Hope still keeps up my spirits a little. Papa changes so often perhaps he will yield to our prayers.

By January 1797, with nothing yet fixed and no formal proposal from Captain Fremantle, Betsey's sister Eugenia (both girls' diaries have been preserved), feels impelled to take a hand:

Tuesday, January 3rd [1797]

No wind, or if there is a little it is foul. Fremantle is a riddle to me. I cannot doubt but he is in love, all shows it, the most trifling incident a new proof of it, and yet he does not talk of marriage and if he does he contradicts himself again the next moment.

Wednesday, January 4th

I had again a great deal of talk with Fremantle, he gives his word that his intentions, his sentiments are the same as they were when he went to Smyrna, and then he adds what would do if you was in my position? as far as delicacy will permit it, I try to hint to him what I would do, if I were in his place.

Eugenia's words met with more success than such efforts usually do. The entry for 31 December 1796 in Fremantle's own diary reads:

Am amazingly attached to Betsey, but cannot make up my mind to marry. I can't say I have on the whole behaved very well.

And for 10th January:

> Sent a proposal to Mr Wynne about marrying his daughter. Everything concluded as I could wish.

Margaret Fountaine, born a country clergyman's daughter in 1862, arrogated to herself the privilege then usually reserved to men, of making the first move. In youth she reproached herself for it:

> *April 15th 1883*
> A few months ago I heard that Mr Muriel, our doctor, had said that both Evelyn and I had got a monomania and that was the love of men! It seems a dreadful thing for him to have said, and still more so as I am certain he was not mistaken, though I think Evelyn's monomania is restricted to curates *only!* Sometimes I feel afraid when I think how desperately, how awfully, wicked I am…

It's not pleasant to watch her thrashing around at this time, choosing a man by her own judgement 'beneath' her, repelled in turn by married life ('a hencoop existence') and spinsterhood ('it made me shiver at the thought').

Later in her 'wild and fearless life,' amid a series of amours from an aristocratic Hungarian to the married Syrian dragoman with whom she spent twenty-eight years, the 'monomania' seems to have remained and the sense of sin diminished:

> I often reproached myself for Neimy's attachment to me, but how could I help it? The man swore he had no wish on earth except to make me his wife. I didn't care a damn about him. But I began to find his untiring devotion and constant adoration decidedly pleasant…

Jump or Be Pushed?

Beatrice Potter's initial working acquaintanceship with Sidney Webb soon ripened into something warmer on his part—but she was reluctant… (She was thinking of her earlier tortured affection for Richard Chamberlain—she had, after all, just written in her diary: 'that terrible time of agonizing suffering seems to have turned my whole nature into steel'.) By the end of May, Webb was pressing to declare his feelings, but the chances against anything stronger than friendship, Beatrice told him, were a hundred to one. 'Think of me as a married woman, as the wife of your friend.'

She was attempting a course he condemned as 'emotional suicide': 'I regard everything from the point of view of making my own and another's life serve the community more effectively.'

'I gave you leave to think of me,' she quotes herself in the diary as saying, 'when you would be thinking of yourself, but not when you have sufficient power to work. I am willing to replace self in your consciousness, but never, never would I oust work or others.'

So they continued. As he grasped, she still eluded, but the 'marriage of true minds' at least grew closer through their intellectual companionship and 'Dear, Sidney, I will try to love you', she promised in a letter, 'but do not be impatient'.

On December 1, to her diary:

December 1st 1890

That is exactly it: marriage is to me another word for suicide. I cannot bring myself to face an act of *felo de se* for a speculation in personal happiness. I am not prepared to make the minutest sacrifice of efficiency for the simple reason that though I am susceptible to the charm of being loved I am not capable of loving.

And summing up the year, on 31st December: 'The tie that was tightening between me and another I have snapped asunder and I am alone again, facing work and the world.'

Her withdrawal was for a time decisive but correspondence between the two, though its tone was chilled, continued. By April they were friends again; in May, Beatrice finally ceased to reject Sidney's proffered attention. On 22nd May, with due reference to the probable feelings of her father, she was still writing in her diary 'If I marry...' While her ailing father lived, the engagement was to be hidden but rapidly, it became something from which Beatrice could draw a secret strength:

August 11th 1891

It is very sweet this warm and close companionship in work. The danger is that I shall lean on him too much and get into a chronic state of watching him at work and thinking that I am working too. But our happiness in each other takes naught from the world... and it should exalt our effort, strengthen our capacity to make this happiness possible to other men and women.

'I need him once a week,' she wrote later, 'to rest me in the sublime restfulness of love.'

'Dear Father passed away' on New Year's Day 1892: the engagement was announced. On 21 January she wrote:

And now the old life is over—or rather the old shell is cast off and a new one adopted. Past are the surroundings of wealth, past the association with the upper middle class, past also the silent reserve and the hidden secret. Now I take my place as a worker and a help-mate of a worker, one of a very modest couple living in a small way.

'In essentials I remain the same,' she added hastily. But on the day of her marriage, 23 July:

Exit Beatrice Potter. Enter Beatrice Webb, or rather (Mrs) Sidney Webb.

In the social, as well as the emotional sense, it was a rite of passage.

Rites of Passage

A formal betrothal, with the engagement ring as a token of commitment, marks the half-way house between courtship and marriage.

When Vera Brittain became engaged to her Roland on 21 August 1915, the event, as she tells her diary, was more redolent of embarrassment and misunderstanding than of rapture:

Then I said vaguely 'What we were talking about last night... I didn't
know what to do, but I do want to do the right thing, but if you still want me
to...'
'Well?' he said.
'Alright,' I answered.

Her reservations, however, were not to do with the strength of her feelings: those had been made clear eight months earlier, in what was her own rite of passage:

Thursday, December 31st [1914]
It was just dawning upon me that I was a different person from the one who
had received his books on my 21st birthday. It seemed an age since then.
Everything these two days had been dreamlike & incomplete; almost
everything we could have said to each other had been left unsaid, but I
knew the one thing that made all the difference in the world— that the
feelings which, ever since I had known him I had thought might quite
possibly arise between us, were no longer a dream but a reality....
    At last the train moved. He took my hand once again in a long warm grip,
& once again I said *au revoir,* for I would not say the Goodbye that I thought
it might be. I leaned out of the carriage window & waved to him once &
then could not look any more, but sat silent & motionless, capable of neither

words nor tears or anything else, & yet extraordinarily conscious of that very feeling of incapability.... I felt then that I would give all I had lived or hoped for during the brief years of my existence, not to astonish the world by some brilliant & glittering achievement, but some day to be the mother of Roland Leighton's child...

Fanny Longfellow is another who prefers to decide for herself the moment of supreme importance, with feeling not fact as the guiding star. 10 May 1843 had been the day of her engagement; on 10 May 1844:

What can I say of thee, thou birthday of my new life of love and blessedness? Scaredly and silently must thou be honored in my heart as is the day of its freedom...

This was indeed my marriage-day, although another bears the title. He who can alone create the mystery of two hearts fused into one was the only witness and priest of the holiest, happiest union.

May this day ever bring Him nearer then to our hearts than any other.

Walked through the little lane and sat under a tree, sending joy into the blithe air like the birds, the insects and every living thing. Alone alas! for though Henry stole this day from college last year, he dutifully returns the theft this.

But it is the formal state of betrothal in which Honoria Lawrence, sailing to India to join her fiancé, takes refuge:

Thursday, April 6th

Captain Warner came a little before noon to ask me to walk, so I went out for half an hour and found myself much the better for the exercise. I was determined to tell him how I am situated, for as Annette sagely remarked to me, 'His being the Captain gives him no dispensation against falling in love'. So I took my opportunity when he told me he has a brother in the Bengal Artillery. I quietly replied 'Very likely I may see him for I am going out engaged to marry a gentleman in that service.' My voice was quiet enough I fancy, and the crimson I felt mounting to my temples was concealed by my bonnet and veil. Having made known my engagement also to Mrs Stewart and Miss Mackey, I suppose it will be no secret to anyone on board, and it is my desire to be looked on as a married woman. This saves all troubles.

And while on the one hand she was just taking a sensible and timeless precaution, equivalent to dropping the worlds 'my boyfriend' into a conversation with a new male acquaintance today, there are one or two pointers which act as a reminder of how total a rite of passage, or life change, marriage for a woman once was. (And, incidentally, of how completely a formal betrothal was accepted as a half-way house.)

Even a reigning Queen Victoria, it seems, may have had difficulty establishing her independence without the bit of gold which officially made a woman of a girl:

> *April 17th 1839*
>
> Said to [Lord Melbourne] how dreadful it was to have the prospect of torment for many years by Mama's living here, and he said it was dreadful, but what could be done? She had declared (some time ago) I said she would never leave me as long as I was unmarried. 'Well then, there's *that* way of settling it,' he said. That was a schocking [sic] alternative, I said.

Even after the arrival and acceptance of the all-conquering Albert, the alternative went on being a little 'schocking'.

> *February 7th 1840*
>
> We were seated as usual, Lord Melbourne sitting near me. Talked...of the Marriage Ceremony; my being a little agitated and nervous; 'Most natural,' Lord M. replied warmly; 'how could it be otherwise?' Lord M. was so warm, so kind, and so affectionate, the whole evening, and so much touched in speaking of me and my affairs. Talked of my former resolution of never marrying. 'Depend upon it, it's right to marry,' he said earnestly; 'if ever there was a situation that formed an exception, it was yours; it's in human nature, it's natural to marry; the other is a very unnatural state of things; it's a great change—it has its inconveniences: everybody does their best, and depend upon it you've done well; difficulties may arise from it,' as they do of course from everything.

A good pragmatic way of going into the ceremony.

At almost the other end of the social scale, Nella Last also cites her mother's domination as one reason for her determination to get married.

> *Sunday 17th May 1942*
>
> My wedding anniversary—thirty-one years. Time flies quickly. I cannot believe it's so long since. My mother never let me choose a dress—and I was always weak-minded and preferred peace to battle and discord—so I wore what she liked, and looked forward to the day when I should do everything I'd wanted to, when I was married! I was married in a quite lovely shade of 'Alice blue', but as no make-up was worn then by a respectable girl, it robbed me of what colour I had. I can remember my huge dark eyes blazing in my poor little white face—and my attempts to rub and pinch a bit of colour into my cheeks. Mother thought I looked lovely. My husband thought I looked white and afraid. My friends told me I looked 'transparent'. And I knew I looked *awful*—all from my blue outfit! Dad said, 'Such tommy-rot, wanting to get married when you are such a child, in spite of your twenty-one years—but you can always come back home again,

you know.' Me, I thought it would have to be a very hot fire indeed to make me climb back into the frying-pan that was home. I never went.

A few weeks after Betsey Wynne's marriage, her mother is still cropping up in her diary entries:

Sunday, January 29th 1797

It was with inexpressible satisfaction I received letters from Naples, but nothing can equal the mortification and pain I felt in reading the one Mamma wrote to me. It made an impression on me which I shall never forget. She expresses how unhappy it has made her to see her daughter leave her without shedding a tear, which proves so much indifference and ingratitude on my part and will ever be a sorrow and chagrin to her. But how ill she knows me. How bad she has interpreted my feelings! If she can suppose taking leave I did not cry, I certainly did not feel less for that, I know how much I am indebted to so indulgent, so good a parent. I shall ever have regard and love for the best of Mothers and ever be thoughtful for all she has done for me.

The following account in Eugenia Wynne's diary, a few days before her sister's marriage, gives a slightly more sympathetic sidelight on the feelings of the family left behind:

Monday, 10th January 1797

I was very low spirited all day. I cannot help thinking that in all probabilities my sister will soon be torn away from me, and notwithstanding the thought bathes my cheeks with tears of grief I cannot help wishing that the affair may soon be brought to a conclusion because I shall always be ready to sacrifice my own private interest to her happiness. Fremantle was here in the morning, he charged Mr French with a letter for Papa in which he made him his proposals but had as yet received no answer. We waited for his return in the evening with the greatest anxiety. Papa was serious and silent. He came in the evening and told us that Papa's answer to Mr. French was that he had no objections but that he would consider upon the subject with Mamma. That answer is decisive enough, I have no doubts that my sister will be very soon Mrs. Fremantle. I smile at her happiness whilst my own distress exacts my tears.

Often, of course, Mamma was only too glad to get her daughters off her hands. Probably she felt she had failed in her duty otherwise. These extracts from the 1887 diary of Miss Ellen Peel illustrate contemporary assumptions:

Wednesday, 30th March 1887

In the afternoon we walked to Cefn and Uncle Roger and General Mostyn as usual. We had tea in the cottage. Mary and he flirted as usual. They ought to leave off, he is behaving shamefully as he always does. Willy came down with a grave face to smoke. He had been talking to Mama. She does not intend taking Mary and me out this year, she says she is tired of it. In fact we are evidently *de trop* in this establishment. I suppose one ought to marry. It would be horrid even if one could, to marry someone one don't care a bit about, but I suppose one must come to that. It is sad, when one thinks of all one's dreams, working together for some noble aim in perfect concord, but one soon gets *disillusionee*, especially when one is *de trop* everywhere, and it doesn't mend matters to write sentiment in middling French and English mixed. Willy was much taken with the idea of Cecil Slade (for Mary). He says he is a thorough gentleman and really 'straight' and it would be a very good thing. He says the General is not, he has heard things about him, though he would not say what, and if he meant to propose he would have done so. I am afraid that is so, and she certainly ought to break it off.

On 30 August, Ellen writes, 'Mary's birthday and mine, 25 and 24. I feel very old, very idle, very useless, and rather *de trop* altogether.' The place of an unmarried daughter at home cannot have been an easy one, especially if she were past the age at which parental authority is natural. The following month the entry in Ellen's diary reads:

Monday, 24th September
Had a real row with Papa. He began. I don't know when I have been so angry. I felt I could marry anyone who came handy, no matter who, but no-one turns up when one is angry or I could have proposed myself.

Eighteen months later, salvation of a sort appeared. Ellen's erratic brother Willy, suffering from mental aberrations of an unspecified but apparently sexual nature, was ordered to Australia, and Ellen, suddenly useful to her family, was seconded to take care of him. But in the summer of 1889, Ellen is home again, tipped from a position of often daunting responsibility back into dependence:

Saturday, 29th June
I am still here which is the last thing I expected, but Willy does not seem to want me now. I can't understand his being allowed to stay in London, and nobody tells me anything or only scraps. It seems hard. I have tried so hard to do for the best, and now everything we had planned seems to be being undone, and I can only look on while things are blurted out to him he need never have known, and he is practically on the loose in London. I suppose I fancied myself too necessary, people were too kind to me while I was away ... I don't know what or how much they have told him, or how he bore it or anything; I might as well be almost buried, and after living for that for the last 9 months, it does seem a little hard. I was so tired when I got down here and so low that it got on my nerves but now I am almost apathetic, one

can't do more than one can and though one can never say one has done absolutely one's best, still I have tried, and that must and shall content me.

My own position is somewhat unpleasant. I had my own money 6 months ago, so I have no right here and they are not on good terms with me. Papa was very fond of me just before he went [he, Mama and Fanny had gone to London] but since then Mama read a letter of mine to Fanny and I am supposed to be corrupting her. And I can't get on here. So that outlook isn't rosy, especially as it seems practically for good, you are so walled in here. I might marry. A good many people have liked me since I have been away, and there are two who would marry me now, both like me a thousand times better than I deserve...

Insofar as marriage was a woman's goal, it was naturally something at which she was expected to excel—not just in the performance of her married duties, but in the selecting and attaining of the man for and with whom she was supposed to perform them. If marriage was a passage into a new life, then it was important to make as good a match as possible, so that the new life was, to coin a hackneyed phrase, one to which you would like to become accustomed. Here is the Duchess of Northumberland in the eighteenth century recording two imprudent matches:

25th October 1764

Lady Harriet Wentworth, youngest sister to the Marquess of Rockingham, a Girl of admirable good sense and an unblemish'd Character, eloped with John Sturgeon, a Lad of about 19 who was her own footman, so illiterate when he came into her Service that he could not even write (his) name, but she had taught him Mathematicks, Writing, Music &c. She parted with all her fine Cloths, she should for the future wear only Washing Gowns as was fit for his Wife. They hired a Room in Conduit street & she lay that Night with the Landlady & the next day they were married.

2nd November

At the latter End of the Year (1764) the News of Paris was that the Prince of Conti was certainly to marry Mme de Boufflers who I had before seen in England. People thought it very extraordinary in every way, as the Princes of the Blood seldom marry women so much their Inferiours [sic] & still more extraordinary that any Man would marry a Woman who was once his mistress and who he had quitted as such, for the last seven Years. It is true his friendship has always appear'd to continue in the strongest manner, but it is seldom people marry for friendship. Her character was very high at Paris in all other respects & that was a blemish easily excused there.

Her husband was so complaisant as to dye about six weeks before this report prevail'd. & gave her a chance to be rais'd to a very high station, for the Princesses of the Blood are upon a great footing in France & have Ladies of the Bedchamber, &c &c. However at last Prudence prevail'd. &. as the P of Conti as Grand Pieur de Malta would have lost 15,000# Sterling a year of his Income & the Palace in which he resided (Le Temple) by the Marriage, He & the Lady agreed it would be better to live on upon the terms of Friendship as they have continued to do ever since.

And recording one eminently suitable (indeed, entirely 'arranged') match, she still put a precise cash value on things:

3rd August 1767

Lord Thanet was married to Miss Sackville. beauty without Art had in this case its reward; he had never spoken to her when he wrote to her Mother the following proposals: 8001 a year Pin Money, 3000 Joynture & 50,0001 for younger Children. He follow'd his Letter so soon that he got to her Ladyship before her Answer had reach'd his Lordship, & as may be supposed was favourably received by Mother and Daughter. Nelly O'Brien (whom he had kept some Years) thought it hard that Ld Thanet should turn her out of his House before she was brought to Bed, &, as she says, he had so good a Precedent to follow, the Duke of Grafton permitting the Duchess to bed before he sent her away.

A more shocking instance—shocking because it is told from what we cannot but think of as the 'victim's' point of view—comes in the *Diary of My Honeymoon*. There have been too many fakes for any anonymous diary of sensational content to be taken entirely on trust but, when this one was published in 1910, the publishers (John Long) in a note assured readers they believed it to be genuine:

CALAIS, 2nd March

I was married yesterday: I'm eighteen today; and I wish I was dead!

I've had two horrible months, all like a fever, being driven about and played with, and seeing things I didn't want to see, and hearing music I didn't want to hear, so to wake up now and then to feel horribly, horribly frightened and shocked.

And at last I began to think I should be glad when it was all over and I could be quiet and rest.

Rest! Shall I ever rest? Shall I ever be quiet? Or shall I go on and on till I go mad?

Oh, Mama, Mama, how could you let me do it? Why didn't you let me know?

And Papa, how meanly you left your daughter in the lurch! It wasn't like you, it wasn't fair!

It's twelve o'clock and I am alone at last, thank God! I can see Sir Lionel [her husband] walking down the street with that heavy, waddling walk, swinging first to one side and then to the other, as if he were crushing things as he goes along. Oh, I wish he would never come back!

I'm so tired that I can scarcely keep my eyes open; but I can't rest, I must just write, write, and so I've opened my poor old book and I'm going on just where I left off two months ago, when I first knew I had been sold.

Sold! Sold! Papa and Mama wouldn't like to be told that by anyone but me! Mama didn't mind me when I told her so yesterday, before I came away. She just laughed, and told me I was a silly child, and said that some day I should be thankful I had had such a good mother, who went on steadily doing her duty in spite of difficulties put in her way by the very people who ought to help her! And then she began to cry, and I know people must have said, when they saw her red eyes, how sad it was for Lady Rushbury to part from her daughter.

But I knew better. She was just angry that I'd found her out.

Does Mama repent when the event turns out even more disastrously than might have been predicted? Apparently not:

She turned upon me in that vivacious way of hers, like bright bird. 'No, I couldn't tell you anything,' she said quickly. 'If I had it wouldn't have come off. One can never tell a girl, or she would never make a good marriage.'

I shuddered. How could she use such a word to me now?

'A *good* marriage!' I echoed in a disgusted tone.

But Mama was quite herself again. She frowned imperiously at me.

'Yes, a good marriage,' she repeated. 'There is only one sort of marriage that is good, even tolerable, and that is marriage with money. It is a horrible thing to have to acknowledge, but there is no use blinking the fact. Marriage, life itself, is impossible without money.'

Implausible? Not considering that, when American heiress Consuelo Vanderbilt sued for an end to her turn-of-the-century marriage, her mother told a Vatican court that 'when I issued an order nobody discussed it. I therefore did not beg her but ordered her to marry the Duke.'

To a certain extent, the social status of a prospective partner is bound to be a factor in the mind of the girl (or woman) as well as in that of her parents. Can it ever cease to be? Nowadays, it probably wouldn't be expressed, but in the 1880s, women, however 'nice' or romantic or independent, were moderately open about it. Witness Margaret Fountaine:

His desire to do all he could for me had flattered my vanity, yet do all I could the thought would force itself into my mind that he had only gone to wait on me as became his station and I had ordered as a servant the man who in my secret heart I had sought to think of as a husband. A sense of shame crept over me for having stooped to love a man who was inferior to me in rank and position...

Witness, even, Beatrice Webb, though thinking on another's behalf: 'owing to [Sidney Webb's] social status I could not marry him during father's lifetime without grieving the poor old man past endurance'. This 'poor old man' had presumably already been acclimatized to some fairly extraordinary public campaigning activities on his daughter's part.

Nor were worldly concerns confined to the upper-classes. Here is maidservant Hannah Cullwick writing in the 1860s:

> Mrs Davis came—a friend of Mary's. She's been nurse to some children of Lord Garbros in her time & is pension'd off. They had tea in the room downstairs and she was here & I wash'd myself & put a clean apron on & went in to have my tea. Mrs Davis is a grand sort of woman in her way, & wears lots of rings. She ask'd me how I did & said I look'd rosy & well enough. At tea time she began about marriages, & how Lord R Montagu had married his nursemaid & that what a fine thing it was to marry well, as she call'd it. When I said love & honour & this & one's word was more than riches she laugh'd at me. 'Cause she said what odds if the girl had another sweetheart anyway, she had seen more of the world than I had & she would always give one thing up for a better, & she told us how she gave up her young man when he'd got a house ready & all, for another. But poor woman she's had all her work, for her husband only lived about ten years & left her with six children, & then she went to service & put 'em out to nurse. But she said they're all well of what lived, for the youngest & another died, & *they're* married well too. Mrs Davis, poor woman, seems as worldly minded as possible & rather vulgar I think. I call'd her Ma'am of course & said good-bye to her & came out with the tea things.

It is almost a relief to turn to the Quaker reformer Elizabeth Fry, newly come to her full strength of religious faith, receiving the proposals of a man she knew comparatively little. Her qualms are different ones:

> *Twelfth Month 12th (1799)*
> I believe the true state of my mind is as follows. I have almost ever since I have been a little under the influence of religion, rather thought marriage at this time was not a good thing for me; as it might lead my interests and affections from that source in which they should be centred, and also, follow as far as I am able the voice of Truth in my heart; are they not rather incompatible with the duties of a wife and mother?

'Marriage is too much treated like a business concern,' she was to write more than thirty years later, 'and love, that essential ingredient, too little respected in it.'

As the actual marriage day dawned, though, her feelings were what any inexperienced bride's must have been:

I awoke in a sort of terror at the prospect before me, but soon gained
quietness and something of cheerfulness; after dressing we set off for
Meeting; I was altogether comfortable. The Meeting was crowded; I felt
serious, and looking in measure to the only sure place for support. It was to
me a truly solemn time; I felt every word, and not only felt, but in my
manner of speaking expressed how I felt; Joseph also spoke well. Most
solemn it truly was. After we sat silent some little time, Sarah Chandler
knelt down in prayer, my heart prayed with her. I believe words are
inadequate to describe the feelings on such an occasion; I wept in good part
of the time, and my beloved father seemed as much overcome as I was. The
day passed off well, and I think I was very comfortably supported under it,
although cold hands and a beating heart were often my lot.

From the comparatively sublime to the completely ridiculous. Here
is the ubiquitous Mississippi Maud (aged sixteen) on a neighbourhood
wedding. And if Elizabeth Fry's doubts about what was in effect the
possibility of self-development within the confines of marriage have an
oddly modern ring, you cannot say the same of this:

Thursday, May 5 - 1881

While we were practising at the church Tuesday night, two couples went to
the parsonage—one to be married. We were invited in. Such a prosaic
wedding. Heavens! The groom didn't even kiss his pale and trembling
bride, or call her 'Little Wifey'. I'll be switched if I'd get married if I
couldn't be called 'Little Wifey' and have somebody's smiling eyes dancing
whole acres of love upon me . . .

Nerves apart, pre-wedding expectations are sometimes wonderfully
high. Witness Henriette Dessaulles in springtime, 1881:

I don't think I've mentioned yet that the wedding, *my wedding*, has been set
for the 19th of July. Eight weeks from now.

It is almost unbelievable . . . I can't really say that I'm impatient; no, it's
lovely, it's perfect the way it is, but I'm happy to be slowly moving towards
this wedding which will make me his. Yes, I'll be his! That's what is so
wonderful!

My beloved, to think that I wasn't even allowed to talk freely to you, yet
now they're actually giving me to you so you may take me away and have
me all to yourself—no! It's too extraordinary!

I was out driving the small blacks earlier on, and as I got home and
stepped down into the courtyard, old François said to me, 'You're going to
miss the horses, you love them so!'

'That's true, I won't be driving them any more, but I'll have children.'

'That seems almost impossible, Mamzelle Henriette. You, being a mother. What a tiny slip of a mother that's going to be!'

And so François can only see me as a little girl—the little girl he has known almost since she was a baby.

But dear François, that little girl belongs to the past, along with Kate's Irish fairies and elves. The young woman she has become is setting out on a marvellous adventure, swept along by love. She hopes and believes that her idyllic happiness will last. Even more than this—she wants to make Maurice so utterly, so completely happy that he will think he is back in the garden of Eden—this time, though, without any forbidden fruit, without a treacherous Satan, and without a curious and disobedient Eve!

Chapter 6
- Marriage

'Marriage is like life in this—that it is a field of battle, and not a bed of roses.'—Robert Louis Stevenson

'The married state, with and without the affection suitable to it, is the compleatest image of heaven and hell we are capable of receiving in this life.'—Richard Steele

'The real theatre of the sex war is in the domestic hearth.'—Germaine Greer

The Good News

EARLY DISCOVERIES AND MARRIED BLISS

Sometimes the very highest hopes of marriage are fulfilled.

13th February 1840

> My dearest Albert put on my stockings for me. I went in and saw him shave; a great delight for me...

wrote Queen Victoria, three days after her marriage. As an adults-only description of Wendy House happiness, it could hardly be bettered.

Here is the American sculptress Anne Truitt looking back across three decades, her memories not soured by the divorce which came just three years earlier:

> The first feelings of marriage are so heavenly. I remember I used to wake up on purpose just to feel how happy I was. The heady potpourri of marriage delighted me: the lavish closeness, the just balance between delight and responsibility, household decisions, the open-endedness (the whole rest of our lives!), and the incredible beauty of being allowed to love someone as much as I wanted to.

And Beatrice Webb's response to married life (after a first day spent 'reading at intervals Amiel's *Journals* by way of relieving the preoccupation') is equally happy. A few months after the wedding 'our life', she writes, is 'an even tenor of happiness'. Almost too even, too happy:

> There is nothing to tell nowadays! No interesting extract of gloom and light, no piquant relationship, all warm flat midday sunlight—little excitement and no discomfiture. I tell Sidney laughingly that I miss the exciting relationships with marriageable or marrying men, that I feel 'hemmed in' by matrimony. Truly, I am too happy to seek excitement, too satisfied to look for friendship.

She continued so:

> *21st June 1893*
>
> Meanwhile my husband and I grow nearer to each other each hour of the day. A beautiful pact, marriage. Personal love and tenderness, community of faith, fellowship in work, a divine relationship. The one and only drawback—a doubt whether happiness does not stupefy life with its inevitable self-complacency. As days and months fly by, and little is done, one wonders whether one is unduly apathetic or simply lazy. . . .

That nagging doubt resolved (see the final section of this chapter), Webb was to prove that the honeymoon can last a lifetime. Volume 2 of her published diary ends with the words of Sidney: 'He is a blessed mate for me.'

Not everyone is so explicit. Sometimes the strongest and most supportive marriages go unsung. Husbands like Leonard Woolf, credited with a vital role in Virginia Woolf's fragile stability, tend to feature in the diaries *en passant* (L. does such and such) rather than as the subject for direct discussion. To discuss one's husband in a memoir, one biographer of the Edwardian age suggests, would have been considered bad form. At other times the light cast upon a marriage is oblique, sideways, but none-the-less illuminating for that.

Here is Dora Carrington commenting on her long life with Lytton Strachey. The trigger is a tragic one; she is writing just after his death. But in mourning her loss, the strength of what they shared together is clear:

> *11th February 1932*
>
> No one will ever know the special perfectness of Lytton. The jokes when he was gay. 'The queen of the East has vanished.' I believe you ate my nail scissors, and then at lunch pretending to play a grand fugue before we got up. And the jokes about the coffee never coming because I stayed so long eating cheese. Sometimes I thought how wasteful to let these jokes fly like

swallows across the sky. But one couldn't write them down. We couldn't have been happier together. For every mood of his instantly made me feel in the same mood. All gone. And I never told him or showed him how utterly I loved him. And now there is nobody, darling Lytton, to make jokes with about Tiber and the horse of the ocean, no one to read me Pope in the evenings, no one to walk on the terrace. No one to write letters to, oh my very darling Lytton.

The girls and women of an earlier age—witness Betsey Wynne —often seem to accept the married state as a fact of life (*the* important fact of life) without feeling the need to comment upon it. Similarly, the majority of children and even adolescents (at least in pre-divorce days when they had the right to expect a united front) seem not to feel any compulsion to comment on the marriage nearest to them—their parents'. Helena Morley is the happy exception:

> *Sunday, 26th November 1893*
> When I get married I wonder if I'll love my husband as much as mama loves my father? God willing. Mama lives only for him and thinks of nothing else. When he's at home the two spend the whole day in endless conversation. When papa's in Boa Vista during the week, mama gets up singing wistful love songs and we can see she misses him, and she passes the time going over his clothes, collecting the eggs, and fattening the chickens for dinner on Saturday and Sunday. We eat best on those days.

Who knows whether Mama ever kept a diary? Or whether it would in any case have been left to Helena's outsider's eye to record her happiness?

The eyes of their world were upon the Ladies of Llangollen: Eleanor Butler and Sarah Ponsonby, two aristocratic females who eloped together in 1778 to the scandalized fury of their families, fled to Wales, and lived there for almost fifty years in a state of what one can only call connubial bliss. But the nearest you get to comment, in the ladies' journal, more a matter of factual record than of reflection, is incessant references to the activities of 'my beloved and I'.

Sometimes, even after long years of marriage, though, happiness will out and we realize just how fortunate we are. Does the realization come particularly under threat or pressure from another source? The published diaries of Frances Partridge both have titles that may be relevant in this context—*A Pacifist's War* and *Everything to Lose*. Here is an extract from the first, at the outbreak of war:

> *12th January 1940*
> In writing a diary all the most important things get left out. Only the decorations get mentioned and the shape of the building is taken for

granted. Far the greatest pleasure I have almost every day of my life is simply being with R., or, when I'm not with him, from remembering everything to tell him afterwards. In some ways the outer bleakness created by the war has intensified this very great happiness.

In the second, she is if anything more explicit. Who says the flames of love die down as time passes?

> *5th May 1948*
>
> Ralph to London to the dentist. I have sprained my ankle so cannot go with him, but as the years pass I *hate* being parted from him even for an hour or so; I feel only half a person by myself, with one arm, one leg, and half a face.

As a declaration of love, it is at least as terrifying as it is wonderful, reassuring only if one could take out a guarantee against disagreement, death or disaster. (*Everything to Lose* ends twelve years later with Ralph's death, and with Frances' brief, underlined and heartbroken entry: 'Now I am *absolutely alone and for ever.*') But she had already nailed her colours to the mast, in describing her response to a younger friend, Janetta's, plea for advice.

> *22nd October 1945*
>
> With someone so young and vulnerable we are naturally afraid of being too interfering or dominant. (I more so than Ralph, I think.) Or should I for once say what I really believe, that love is far the most important thing in life, a stronger, potentially more permanent and all-pervading force than the wildest of girlhood dreams suggests. People talk, out of a sort of prudery, as if it vanished entirely after five or six years of marriage, and only an affable, humdrum relation was left, enabling couples to jog along pretty well if they allowed each other plenty of freedom. But it needn't be like that at all. It's a hopeless failure if it is. After twenty years together one can be in a sense just as deeply in love as ever one was. Love doesn't simply fade away like 'old soldiers'; it changes its character, naturally, and matures, but its depth and richness can be as great as ever.

The Bad News

MARITAL DISCORD

How different is Frances Partridge's position from that of Mary Boykin Chesnut, the nineteenth-century American plantation owner's wife, who elsewhere (see page 175) compares wifehood with slavery:

> *1st January 1864*
>
> It is only in books that people fall in love with their wives. Is it not as with any other co-partnership, say travelling companions? Their future opinion of each other and the happiness of association depends intensely on what

they really are, not on what they felt or thought about each other before they had any possible way of acquiring accurate information as to character, habits, etc. Love makes it worse. The pendulum swings back further, the harder it was pulled the other way. Mrs Malaprop to the rescue: 'Better begin with a little aversion.' What we think of people before we know them is of no weight either way; but did two people ever live together so stupid as to be long deceived?

There are some dramatic testimonials to just how badly a marriage can go astray. One is *Journal of a Governess* from the self-styled 'Miss Weeton' in 1818:

> Is it Thy Will that I submit to the tyranny of him who so cruelly uses me, and abuses the power which he has over me? Oh, that I could say that it were any other than my own husband. He that should nourish, cherish, and protect me; he that should protect me, so that even the winds should not blow too roughly on me—he is the man who makes it his sport to afflict me, to expose me to every hardship, to every insult. Or am I right in struggling to free myself from his griping hand?
>
> Bitter have been the years of my marriage, and sorrowful my days. Surely the measure of them is full! My life, my strength, cannot sustain many more such.

If Miss Weeton's journal reads like a Victorian melodrama, the diaries of Lady Anne Clifford two centuries earlier have an unexpectedly familiar ring. The incomplete form in which they have survived still gives us plenty of sidelights on a long-running quarrel about 'the land'—an inheritance she felt she should have received from her father, the Earl of Cumberland. It was a quarrel her husband, and others more highly placed, put pressure on her to renounce:

> The King asked us all if we would submit to his judgement in this case, my uncle Cumberland my Coz: Clifford and my Lord answered they would but I would never agree to it without Westmoreland at which the King grew in a great chaff.
>
> My Lord went up to my closet and said how little money I had left contrary to all they had told him, sometimes I had fair words from him and sometimes foul, but I took all patiently and did strive to give him as much content and assurance of my love as I could possibly yet *I told him I would never part with Westmoreland*. After supper because my Lord was sullen and not willing to go into the nursery, I had Mary bring the child to him in my chamber which was the first time she stirred abroad since she was sick.

Quarrels beginning elsewhere inevitably spill over into matters affecting 'the child'. Lady Anne's husband leaves home, he sends for the child to follow:

When I considered that it would both make my Lord more angry with me and be worse for the child I resolved to let her go; after I had sent for Mr. Legg and talked with him about that and other matters I wept bitterly.

All this time my Lord was in London where he had all and infinite great resort coming to him. He went much abroad to Cocking and Bowling Alleys, to plays and horse races and commended by all the world. I stayed in the country, having many times a sorrowful and heavy heart, and being condemned by most folks because I would not consent to the agreement so as I may truly say like an owl in the desert.

It is not that matters were always bad. ('My Lord and I were never greater friends than at this time.') It may just be that even a basically—or an apparently—strong relationship has its hiatuses. To jump to the moderns, here is Katherine Mansfield on her marriage:

June 1919

Often I reproach myself for my 'private' life—which, after all, were I to die, *would* astonish even those nearest to me. Then (as yesterday) I realise how little Jack shares with me. Last week I had no idea what was going in the paper [*The Athenaeum* which he was editing at the time], no copy of the paper, and J. had not the smallest curiosity as to whether I had seen or had not seen it. He never even asked. It might have been a report from the Home Office. I found from Milne that he still goes to Somerset House. I found from him today that he is paid £250 a year for it.

Knowing my agony if anyone is *late*—having shared it with me a dozen times, saying he knows the difficulties of our domestic arrangements, he was 25 minutes late yesterday; and when he realised how he had hurt me, he sulked because he could not do as he liked—was always driven, *all* his pleasure spoilt, even at St Alban's, by worrying about my 'complex' about the time.

He went to St Alban's yesterday and stayed until four, and never told me a thing of the journey—had nothing to tell.

Today he is with his brother. We met for lunch and he discovered for me afterwards (when I asked) a number of new books which he has brought into the house and never shown me—just put away. He knows I can seldom go out—he knows I can *never* get to a bookshop; he knows how I *love* books—love dipping into them—love just a moment's chat about them, but all the same, he has never thought to share these finds with me—never for a moment.

All this hurts me horribly, but I like to face it and see all round it.

He ought not to have married. There never was a creature less fitted by nature for life with a *woman*.

And the strange truth is I don't WANT him to change; I want to see him, and then adjust my ways and go on alone and WORK.

Life without *work*—I would commit suicide. Therefore work is more important than life.

Suffering—in this case, Mansfield's tuberculosis—doesn't always draw people together. Sometimes it makes them feel farther apart:

> After a few days J.'s letters in response to *my* depressed letters began to arrive. There were a series of them. As I grew depressed, *he* grew depressed, but not for me. He began to write (1) about the suffering I caused him: *his* suffering, *his* nerves, *he* wasn't made of whipcord or steel, the fruit was bitter for *him*. (2) a constant cry about money. He had none; he saw no chance of getting any—'heavy debts'—'as you know I am a bankrupt.' 'I know it sounds callous.' 'I can't face it.' These letters, especially the letters about money, cut like a knife through something that had grown up between us. They changed the situation for me, at least, for ever. We had been for two years drifting into a relationship, different to anything I had ever known. We'd been *children* to each other, openly confessed children, telling each other everything, each depending equally upon the other. Before that I had been the man and he had been the woman and he had been called upon to make no real efforts. He'd never really 'supported' me. When we first met, in fact, it was I who kept him, and afterwards we'd always acted (more or less) like men-friends. Then this illness—getting worse and worse, and turning me into a woman and asking him to put himself away and to *bear* things for me.

Not every marriage voyage is fully chronicled, that goes without saying. But some of the gaps are surprising. The successive volumes of Anaïs Nin's journal appear to discuss past and present with exhaustive frankness, except for one rather curious exception. In 1981 it was still possible for a reference book, *Women in History*, to state with conviction that 'Anaïs Nin never married'. That was before *Journal of a Wife* came out... That book, with its portrait of Nin's early marriage, takes us from the honeymoon Nin in 1923 ('it is a joy to be consumed by flaming adoration') who writes:

> *13th July 1923*
>
> I read of women who give as a reason for their continued interest in work after their marriage the fact that they become restless and bored and lonesome in their houses. I could scarcely believe my eyes. I find an ever deepening joy in solitude and have too much with which to fill my time—to read, to study, to write, to sculpture, to sing and dance—so much, I wish my days and life were longer, and I envy those who have too much time on their hands.

to the one who states eighteen months later:

> *23rd March 1925*
>
> I understand now the spirit that pushes some married women to embrace an inane social life, to spend their afternoons in a club playing bridge, to 'go around' with other men. They are accused of selfishness because

meanwhile the poor husbands are killing themselves with work. They have no right to kill themselves with work. By doing that they kill all the living beauty of marriage—the companionship, the united enjoyment, the united growth.

And, more fundamentally, to the one who writes, at the end of the four-year journal, without any visible loss of affection for her husband: 'My very real self is not wifely, not good. It is wayward, moody, desperately active, hungry.'

The journal may represent a voyage of self-discovery, but it is not the chronicle of a break-up. Such chronicles, not surprisingly, are thin on the ground if you are thinking of women's diary writing as a whole, over the centuries. The linen would have been too dirty for public washing—public in the sense of the deliberate preservation and possibly publication of the diary. And even before the outside world has a chance to make its presence felt, there is one's own self-censorship to contend with. Women (like men) can be very reticent about troubles of one sort, however forthcoming they may be about another: for example, Ellen Peel. Finally married at twenty-seven, she discovered that her husband was an alcoholic. Her diary records her agony over the death of their first child, but as her husband becomes more impossible and they separate—though on the most amicable terms—does she confide all to the journal where, all her life, she has written with the greatest frankness? Not a word. Instead, she stops writing a diary for thirteen years, to resume within weeks of her husband's death.

One of the not-too-recent diaries in which we do see disharmony chronicled is the *Blue Notebooks* of Liane de Pougy. Her life and her legend being what they were, all questions of dirty linen must have seemed irrelevant... 'Tiny One' is Liane's nickname for the young friend who has taken up a petted residence under the roof of Liane and her husband Georges ('her happy looks are our thanks'...)

July 4, 1926

Georges loves Tiny One! Tiny One loves Georges! Crack, it has happened! Is it worse than cancer?

Georges admitted it this morning, then Tiny One was summoned and came in very white.

I have been saying to myself for a long time that something was bound to happen. Georges is so much younger than I am, he has given me eighteen years of happiness... I must think! It's a very banal situation, after all. I don't want to make a grand tragedy of it, and anyway love carries the day. If it is a true love it will bend us to its laws. If it's a passing fancy it will pass. Yes, but... my nature is a difficult one. I don't yet know how I'm going to react and how I'll behave to them or to myself. Tiny One is adorable, well-bred, very intelligent, has lovely eyes, a young body. She has neither health nor money! Perhaps she is a bit of a schemer? Georges is hooked, but he insists that he adores me and can't do without me. My great, splendid, complete, pure happiness is over.

Georges is all for a *menage à trois*: 'You'll have two people to adore you instead of just one. We'll cherish you, we'll take care of you, we'll make you so happy'—a suggestion Liane angrily rejects.

She weathers the storm (not, as is explained a few days later, without consolation from another source) to emerge the stronger, needing only the freedom which formal divorce would bring:

> How much more freely I would breathe! How much less heavy my burden would become! I am constantly afraid of what my assassin may do; even, and especially, that he may come back.

Georges does, after refusing a divorce. It provoked Liane's fury at the time: 'Oh! please, dear God, forgive him as I do and grant me the favour of never seeing him again! I want him dead, not savagely, but simply to end his suffering and his wrong-doing.'

That was in November; in January and February the diary is blank. On 1 March Georges is back and Liane, perhaps by way of explaining matters to herself, has bestowed upon him a new identity.

> Georges Ghika has gone away. He has gone away for ever. But I have a certain little Gilles at my side, grave and sweet, affectionate and very pale, thin, sad at having hurt me so much.

He did not stay so. In 1931 the diary opens:

> *August 14*
> I have now spent five years with this unhappy Georges Ghika, irresponsible and debauched, suppressing actions but overflowing with evil words. He has been drinking, smoking endlessly, reading atrocious books, blaspheming against everything which contributes to a sweet and serious life: against love, against marriage, the blessed union of two people who love each other; against order; against punctuality, regularity, good manners; against religion, beliefs of whatever kind; against divine as well as against human laws; against everything. Poor discontented, bestial being, with his great ability to illuminate directed towards the most hellish landscapes. I have suffered in my mind and in my body... He had lost his virility—he was lashed by the desire to rediscover it. So at night he would direct all his evil ardour on to me, would try and fail and begin again, all to no avail. To him that, and nothing else, is what is meant by love... He would fall asleep and snore while I, in despair, would pray...

The religion to which Liane turned provided a clear answer: it was her duty to stay by her husband's side lest worse befall him. The entries for the rest of their years together provide less black and white a picture. 'I breathe more easily when we are apart,' she writes once when he is away, 'but still...' In 1933 she is writing of 'the existence we are condemned to lead at each other's sides'. But in 1937 the entry in her diary reads:

> *February 8*
> My husband has just gone out: a little shopping, a letter to post. I often stand by the window to watch him leaving. He always looks up, we smile and throw kisses. The people going by and the taxi-drivers on the rank watch us and must say to themselves: 'How those two do love each other.' At bottom they are right. I would detest him so much if I were not fond of him!

In marriage, nothing is ever as simple as it looks. If it seems inevitable that the rather feeble Georges should have gone back to the forceful Liane, it also seems inevitable that they should have broken up. The young man of title who braves his family's displeasure to marry the older woman of tarnished (or more properly, non-existent) reputation, is a stock scene which signals trouble ahead.

With hindsight, it is easy to say the same about the young married couple Lady Shelley was dragged to visit in 1815, one Lord and Lady Byron—especially if you know that Mrs Leigh is the half-sister Augusta with whom the poet was later accused of incest:

> At Mrs Leigh's request I yesterday accompanied her to Piccadilly Terrace, to call on Lady Byron. On the way, Mrs Leigh spoke a good deal about Byron, to whom she is much attached. She is by no means insensible to her brother's faults, and hopes that a good wife will be his salvation. Very few young men have been so run after, and spoilt by women, as Lord Byron has been, and marriage will, she hopes, have a sobering effect upon him. I fancy, however, from the little I saw of him, that he will not be at all easy to manage.
>
> We mounted the stairs, and were about to be ushered into the drawing-room, when the door suddenly opened, and Lord Byron stood before us. I was, for the moment, taken aback at his sudden appearance; but I contrived to utter a few words, by way of congratulation. Lord Byron did not seem to think that the matter was adapted to good wishes; and looked as though he resented my intrusion into the house. At least I thought so, as he received my congratulations so coldly, and the expression on his face was almost demoniacal.
>
> Lady Byron received us courteously, but I felt, at once, that she is not the sort of woman with whom I could ever be intimate. I felt like a young person who has inadvertently dipped her finger into boiling water.

But evil, like beauty, seems often to be in the eye of the beholder. The diaries of Hannah Cullwick, Victorian maidservant, tell a story as appalling, to the modern eye, as it is extraordinary. They were kept at the instigation of Arthur Munby, an upper-class author, with what one can only call an extremely worrying obsession for working-class women—a kind of *nostalgie de la boue* run wild. From 1854 to 1873 they conducted a secret courtship, during which Munby seems to have sucked a vicarious pleasure from every pair of boots Hannah blacked and she patiently relayed through the diaries every detail of her daily round for which 'Massa' waited so greedily.

In 1873 they were secretly married and Hannah came to share Massa's lodgings in the Temple... or the 'downstairs' part of them, at least. The story goes from bad to worse: married, Hannah masqueraded as her husband's servant, only showing herself in her dual role to the few intimates to whom he had confessed their story. The situation outrages every cannon now, contains every discrimination in one. At times, it even outrages Hannah—though not for long enough:

Tuesday, 26th November 1872

M. came to the entry corner & spoke quite unexpected, for I'd forgotten about him coming & it was nearly dark—'Is that you, Hannah?' 'Yes, Massa, it is,' I said, but quite low. It seems he didn't hear me say it, & then he said, 'What time did you come?' I felt confused & said, 'This afternoon,' still low, & I crept in at the window. Then M. came down to the kitchen & spoke again. I didn't say 'sir' of course, 'cause I'd no idea any one was above likely to be listening. Then M. went upstairs & rang the bell, & I thought, well that is showing off certainly, & I went upstairs with my temper up to its highest, & M. began to question me about not saying '*sir*' to him, as the lad was on the stairs. I felt so *angry* 'cause I thought if M. knew the boy was on the stairs he oughtn't to o'come down, not only for the humiliation the first day, but because I didn't even know Mr Rees kept a lad as clerk. So I was really in a passion & I said a great deal I didn't *mean*, & I declar'd that if M. tantalized me in that way again I would leave him whether we was married or not, for I didn't care a straw for that. Of course I meant that for the moment, for I felt I couldn't stand to be treated as such a 'nothing' & with no consideration after having [unreadable] so much all these years, & coming at last to be only as a servant to everyone's eyes except his. And being really & truly a servant to him & willing to endure all things for his sake, whether it was life or death, so long as I was near him. So that my passion was only the effect of love, & I thought M. knew me so well that he'd soon forget and forgive that.

A week later he is at it again. 'When M. came out of his room he said good morning and kiss'd me, but instantly after spoke angry as I'd not open'd the windows and doors wide. "Any servant ought to know that"…' The peace is made up that evening, in a way too many wives know only too well. She told him '*how* much I'd suffer'd; M. seem'd almost *surprised*, & yet I thought he knew everything, & he seem'd *sorry* at last, & told me there was no one in the world he cared so much for as me.' The worst of it is, the surprise could possibly have been genuine. Stripped of its horrific context, the emotional situation existing between Hannah and Munby is not without elements the wives in *The Women's Room* would recognize. And if *his* emotional ineptitude is one, *her* readiness to shoulder the blame when blameless is another. You can see it also in the young Anaïs Nin:

> *9th December 1925*
> Lately Hugh and I have had three differences between us. Oh, they are little enough in themselves, but I don't understand why there should be *any*. I am struggling to discover if it is my fault… If we are to be happy, or at least if he is to be happy, I must never *go against* Hugh, I must not *contradict* him, I must never *argue* with him.

You can see traces of it, too, in Honoria Lawrence, making a list of her moral inadequacies while being dragged, a new bride, from pillar to post around Victorian India:

> *12th November 1837*
> My chief deficiency is, I think, in making the most of circumstances. When I am settled down in a routine I can adhere to it steadily, and fill up every hour, but if I get off my track I am all adrift, my time slips by and I am altogether unhinged. This is a disposition peculiarly unfitted to the life I now lead. Let it then be my endeavour to be always prepared with some occupation, and to be satisfied with the employment that is most convenient, without considering whether it be the one I at the moment might fancy. Since our marriage I discover in myself an impatience and irritability which I did not formerly give way to.

One is happy to see that in the journal 'to' Henry she does list his faults as well as her own—even if her artless account seems to let him off rather lightly:

> *19th June 1838*
> One word more, darling, I do think you are not aware of the way in which you habitually speak to those around you. Their provokingness I fully feel, but dearest, do you recollect that you scarcely ever address a man without an abusive epithet? This you do, too, when you are not angry. Oh my husband, let not our child hear such words from its parent's lips.

And one is happy to hear that the maidservant Hannah Cullwick did, in the course of her thirty-six-year marriage, gain a considerable degree of independence from and even ascendancy over her appalling Massa, even if the first use she made of her freedom was to stop writing those diaries....

Coming Through

21st November 1855—O me miseram! *Not one wink of sleep the whole night through! So great the 'rale mental agony in my own inside' at the thought of that horrid appealing [to the Tax Commissioners, on her husband's behalf]. It was with feeling like the ghost of a dead dog, that I rose and dressed and drank my coffee, and then started for Kensington. Mr. C. said 'the voice of honour seemed to call on him to go himself.' But either it did not call loud enough, or he would not listen to that charmer.*
—Jane Welsh Carlyle

At what point do you call a marriage a success? At what point a failure? At what point does a wry comment like Mrs Carlyle's cease to be just par for the course? The goalposts have obviously been moved in the last couple of decades, to the point where the game has changed almost beyond recognition. Or has it? If you took a 'happy mean' of marriages, would you find that they are not about the dramatic break-up, if and when there is one, any more than they are about that flaunting honeymoon happiness, but are, less spectacularly, about coming through?

There were no notable dramas taking place in Barrow-in-Furness—or, if there were, Nella Last did not record them in the diary she kept for the duration of the Second World War and long beyond it. But it is in its way a fascinating 'read', and among the many reasons for that has to be the voyage of self-discovery upon which Nella Last found herself embarking within the confines of her long marriage. A lower middle-class housewife, the mother of grown-up sons (the published version of her wartime diaries, *Nella Last's War*, is sub-titled 'A Mother's Diary'), is saying to herself the things the women's movement would be shouting aloud thirty years later.

The war, compelling women who would not normally do so to take work outside the house (in Nella Last's case at a WVS Centre, where she was invaluable) helped to free them from the chains of domesticity...

Thursday, 14th March 1940
I reflected tonight on the changes the war had brought. I always used to worry and flutter round when I saw my husband working up for a mood; but now I just say calmly, 'Really dear, you *should* try and act as if you were a grown man and not a child of ten, and if you want to be awkward, I shall go out–ALONE! I told him he had better take his lunch on Thursday, and several times I've not had tea quite ready when he has come in, on a Tuesday or Thursday, and I've felt quite unconcerned. He told me rather

wistfully I was 'not so sweet' since I'd been down at the Centre, and I said, 'Well! Who wants a woman of fifty to be sweet, anyway? And besides, I suit *me* a *lot* better!'

'We wondered if this dreadful mess of war,' she speculated later, 'would release people from taboos and inhibition, as the last war undoubtedly had done'. But the war wasn't the start of the things or Nella Last: 'Dr Millar started me off when I was so ill three years ago, and I find his words truer every day—that "repression is deadly".' This in answer to her husband, who had protested once again that in this new, argumentative woman he found himself living with a stranger. (Tellingly, the illness of which she speaks was nervous.)

Inevitably, Nella Last's new discontent is focused upon her husband. Not that the man is a monster, far from it. She quotes him speaking with a degree of kindness and perception about the boys who had gone to war:

December 1941

I felt the warm tears on my cheeks and, as I turned for a handkerchief to wipe them away, I was surprised to see my husband's eyes wet. He said, 'What a slice went out of our lives at one stroke. I've only realized lately, my dear, how you must have missed them all—you seemed to mother them all, didn't you?' I just nodded. It's a wild wet night and the moon's light is veiled. Another full moon passed without big raids. It seems too good to be true somehow.

And it is just one instance of several. But when your perceptions suddenly change, the familiar figure blocking out the light can look just that—monstrous in its very normality.

10th May 1945

I looked at his placid, blank face and marvelled at the way he had managed so to dominate me for all our married life. . . . His petulant moods only receive indifference now.

It's not that she's no longer the sweet woman she used to be, she writes. It's just that she never was. 'Rather was I a frayed, battered thing, with nerves kept in control by effort that at times became too much, and "nervous breakdowns" were the result. No one would ever give me one again, *no* one.'

You could try putting some of her vehemence down to the strain of five and a half years of war. But two months later, her feelings are none-the-less strong. Indeed, she's broadening her thoughts out:

Wednesday, 25th July 1945

I felt tired, but ironed my washing, as I'm going out to the Centre in the morning. My husband is very sulky about it. He said, 'When the war got over, I thought you would always be in at lunch-time.' I said, 'Well, you always have a good lunch left—much better than many men whose wives are always at home.' He said, 'Well, I like you there always.' No thought as to either my feelings or to any service I could be doing. I thought of the false sentiment my generation had been reared with, the possessiveness which stood as the hallmark of love, with no regard to differences in temperament, inclination or ideals—when the 'head of the house' *was* a head, a little dictator in his own right; when a person of limited vision, or just plain fear of life, could crib and confine more restless spirits. I looked at my husband's petulant face and thought that, if I'd never done anything else for my lads, at least I'd left them alone and had never given advice at pistol-point, shrinking from imposing my will in any way. A little chill fell on me—not from the dusk which was creeping on the garden, either. Rather did it blow from the past, when to go anywhere without my husband was a heinous crime—and he went practically nowhere! I had a pang as I wondered what I would do when all my little war activities stopped, when he *could* say plaintively, '*Must* you go?' or 'I don't feel like...'—and I wondered if my weak streak would crop up as strong as ever, and I'd give in for peace and to that unspoken, but *very* plain, Victorian-Edwardian accusation, 'I feed and clothe you, don't I? I've a right to say what you do.' It's not love, as the sloppy Vic-Eds. sang, it's sheer poverty of mind and fear of life. If you love a person in the real sense, you want them to be happy, not take them like butter and spread them thinly over your own bread, to make it more palatable for yourself.

Better To Marry Than To Burn

'Better to marry than to burn...' said Chaucer's Wife of Bath, defending marriage, or the sexually active life, against the insistence of the mediaeval Church on the superior virtues of out-and-out celibacy. In our own day, marriage, in its capacity as a restrictive institution, has come under attack from almost the opposite angle, and particularly from the woman's point of view. Not only in our own day, come to think of it... you can go back to tenth-century Japan to find the court lady Sei Shonagon writing in the 'Pillow Book', where she noted her observations, pleasures and displeasures in daily life:

> When I make myself imagine what it is like to be one of those women who live at home, faithfully serving their husbands—women who have not a single exciting prospect in life yet who believe that they are perfectly happy—I am filled with scorn. Often they are of quite good birth, yet have had no opportunity to find out what the world is like. I wish they could live for a while in our society, even if it should mean taking service as Attendants, so that they might come to know the delights it has to offer...

Women who have served in the Palace, but who later get married and live at home, are called madam and receive the most respectful treatment. To be sure, people often consider that these women, who have displayed their faces to all and sundry during their years at Court, are lacking in feminine grace. How proud they must be, nevertheless, when they are styled Assistant Attendants, or summoned to the Palace for occasional duty, or ordered to serve as Imperial envoys during the Kamo Festival! Even those who stay at home lose nothing by having served at Court. In fact they make very good wives. For example, if they are married to a provincial governor and their daughter is chosen to take part in the Gosechi dances, they do not have to disgrace themselves by acting like provincials and asking other people about procedure. They themselves are well versed in the formalities, which is just as it should be.

A rare witness, a solitary voice speaking from her culture to our own, she stands alone. There is a huge jump to be made, from tenth-century Japan to nineteenth- and twentieth-century England before we pick up the threads of that particular argument, but having made it, we find a time when it became almost universal. No, not in the 1970s—it pre-dates that latest and greatest wave of the woman's movement. When that wave broke, indeed, the edgily self-conscious qualms of a minority of intellectual and upper-middle-class women forty years earlier must have seemed almost irrelevant.

The fight of the suffragettes, the conscious dawn of feminism, is dealt with elsewhere (see Chapter 10, Politics and Public Affairs). But in the 1920s and 1930s those who had taken advantage of it suffered peculiar qualms. Don't they still? Of course—but the emphasis of the argument has shifted slightly. Then, as anyone who has read Dorothy L. Sayers' *Gaudy Night* will know, it was often seen as a straight dichotomy between the woman (unmarried) who had chosen to step out of her sex and live in the life of the mind, and the 'womanly woman' who lived the life of the emotions and the flesh. The implication, quite clearly, was that no one can do both.

To anyone who has read *Gaudy Night*, it is uncannily evocative to hear a young Vera Brittain in 1915 reassuring the possible prospective mother-in-law who thought she might be 'very academic and learned': 'I refuted this accusation with vehemence, telling her how much isolated I am at college, and how little affinity I have with the typical college woman.' But if Vera was not entirely on the collegiate and presumably cerebral side of the fence, she certainly couldn't be placed entirely on the other... On the occasion of her engagement eight months later:

Saturday, August 21st 1915

Again there was silence & then I began to talk again, seriously this time &

on a difficult subject—which however I had to touch upon in order to explain my somewhat strange attitude. I spoke of the lack of faith I had in men & their love—& expressed my doubts whether the intellectual & spiritual in love could rise & live untarnished in spite of its constant association with the physical that is in us all. I told him how I had hated the idea of marriage & how I had determined before meeting him that I never would marry anyone . . . I told him all about B.S. [an earlier pretendant]. 'He didn't want a *companion*,' I said, rather fiercely. 'He just wanted a wife.' 'I'm not like that,' said Roland in the gentle, considerate voice I have learnt to associate with the rousing of his emotion. 'In fact, rather the opposite.' 'I know,' I said. 'I wouldn't stop in this carriage another minute if I thought you were.' He laughed—a little bitterly, and his eyes looked rather distressed.

Almost twenty years later, from the stronghold of a 'semi-detached' marriage to Gordon Catlin (Roland having died in the First World War), Vera Brittain hasn't forgotten the contemporary view that you can't have your cake and eat it too, and what's more that either way it is likely to turn to ashes in your mouth. She doesn't have much chance to forget. On 17 June 1932 she spent the morning listening to the problems ('inhibitions') of her novelist friend Phyllis ('She ended by crying again and asking how she could possibly be expected to make gestures of seeking towards anyone at all after a girlhood like this'). She spent the afternoon at a Conference on 'The Family in a Changing Society':

> Talked on the usual topic of changing position of married women, denunciation of present wasteful domesticity; need for most women both to marry & to make their special contribution of whatever kind to politics, art, literature, social service, etc. For some reason I kept the audience laughing all the time though I *meant* it to be a serious speech. Ellen Wilkinson spoke with her usual animation on the position of the ordinary married woman made uncomfortable like Naomi (Mitchison) & me, or unmarried like herself, insisted on stirring things up.

And she spent the tag end of the evening consoling a maid, Dorothy, who had just quarrelled with her young man. After which exhausting day, she reflected:

> How strange it was that within the same day I should have under my roof the successful & extremely intelligent woman novelist of 37 crying bitterly because (it amounts to that) she hadn't had a man, & at the other end of the intellectual scale the little housemaid of 20 crying just as bitterly because she had. I decided that on the whole it was probably far more bearable to be Dorothy . . .

With two children, a successful marriage and career which rarely come into collision, she herself has found fulfilment, but she is aware of being in a tiny minority.

2nd October 1932

I seem to be lucky over Gordon; most women writers seem either to have husbands who put upon them, like Delafield, or whom they have divorced, like Lady R., or else to be like Phyllis tormented with a sense of frustration because they haven't had sex experience at all. Companionate marriage is a partial solution but it doesn't meet the desire for children which physiologically-normal women like Phyllis do feel. Probably the only solution—and a slow one—is the education of men to the point where they really do give and take, really can be companions to women & feel as strong a sense of obligation to be unselfish and responsible as most women feel.

Naomi Mitchison, the Naomi who spoke at the Conference, had every reason to speak about a woman writer's problems with less detachment some years later.

Sunday, 12th August 1945

... the girls and I and Joan discussing this business of babies. It really is doing in both Joan and to a lesser extent Ruth. And the same thing has happened to me. I can no longer concentrate myself; feel I ought to be doing something else, at any rate I ought to be in half an hour.

One is listening for the telephone or for a child. Even if I want to join in a conversation I feel myself impelled to distract myself, not to give full concentration, to read a book at the same time. I *can't* now think in a pointed way about *anything*. I can rather more easily concentrate when writing. But it is rare to have an hour undistracted. Because of this I know I can never be first class at anything. The mornings are slightly better, but are more occupied by other things. By the evening I am too tired to do anything. I cannot even read a serious book now ... What we might do is lost except in so far as we can pass it on to our children in our chromosomes. The fact that our children are voluntarily begotten makes it all the more difficult. We cannot just say they are something that has happened to us, an act of God or however it should be expressed. We deliberately took on this burden. Yet we didn't know beforehand how crippling it would be. Ruth thought she could combine her work as a doctor with having children. But she may yet be able to. I am more doubtful about Joan. She is almost deliberately sacrificing herself now. She is facing the practical problems, rather than the emotional or moral ones, of combining career with marriage and children.

Those, of course, are the problems which were there from the beginning and will probably be there until the end. After five children (of her eventual ten) in eight years, they must have plagued the Quaker reformer Elizabeth Fry:

Earlham, Eighth Month 20th 1808

I have married eight years yesterday: various trials of faith and patience have been permitted me; my course has been very different to what I had expected; instead of being, as I had hoped, a useful instrument in the Church Militant, here I am a care-worn wife and mother, outwardly, nearly devoted to the things of this life: though at times this difference in my destination has been trying to me; yet, I believe those trials (which have certainly been very pinching), that I have had to go through, have been very useful, and brought me to a feeling sense of what I am...

But if she is a woman suffering the inhibiting—not to say exhausting —effects of marriage in an age when it was close on compulsory, here is another famously working woman, Barbara Castle, touching on the benefits in an age when it is not:

Wednesday, 24th December to Sunday, 28th December 1969

I dread to think that anything might happen to Ted. How could I ever face life if I lived a solitary self-contained widow's life? Politics is only tolerable if one has human interludes like this. [Christmas]

There is another side to the coin, it must be said. Problems of the energy levels:

Friday, 29th July

Down to the cottage, housekeeperless, to a weekend of hard domestic work and cooking. No one has any idea of the problems of a woman Minister!

And problems of the ego. Does her conspicuous success make his failures seem worse?

Friday, 17 April [1970]

A good day at Wakefield, opening a new government training centre. I love these sallies into the field. But I returned home to disaster. Ted had just learned from one of his sponsors that he had not been rechosen as an alderman of the GLC. I have never seen him in a more desperate state. He was knocking back whiskies when I arrived and almost shouting aloud with the pain of his humiliation. 'Everywhere and by everybody I am rejected. Why? I am arrogant enough to believe that I am as good as, or better than, the dozens of people I have helped, yet no one—absolutely no one—helps me. At every stage of my life I have failed. Why? I ask myself. Why? Why?' There were tears of sheer despair in his eyes. 'You can't possibly understand. How could you? You have gone on from success to success. I have gone from rejection to rejection. What am I to do with myself? I go back to London with you. How am I to fill my time? You've no time to spare for me: how could you have?...'

I lay in the dark, the tears running down my cheeks. Everything turns to ashes when he is hurt in this dreadful way: Hell Corner, my job—everything. 'April 17th,' he had said. 'Make a note of it. This day I died: here inside me.' Shouting: 'I am dead, do you hear? Dead inside. And

I hope tomorrow I don't wake up.' When at last he slept I dedicated myself to getting him the recognition he deserves. I'll see Harold, Reg Goodwin, anyone. I will not have Ted destroyed in this way.

That is a problem Beatrice Webb chose never to provoke, stressing even to her diary her status as Sidney's assistant, more than partner. And, apropos of a meditation on 'womanhood—and the perfection of it', she wrote:

> From the first I would impress on her the holiness of motherhood, its infinite superiority over any other occupation that a woman may take to. I do not much believe in the productive power of woman's intellect; strain herself as much as she may, the output is small, the ideas thin and wire-drawn from lack of matter and wide experience. Neither do I believe that mere training will give her that fullness of intellectual life which distinguishes the really able man.

Not that she practised what she preached. From the same entry:

> I myself—or rather we—chose this course (of deliberate childlessness) on our marriage, but then I had passed the age when it is easy and natural for a woman to become a child-bearer; my physical nature was to some extent dried up at thirty-five after ten years' stress and strain of a pure brainworking and sexless life.

It is an ironic case of the fallible practice being far more sympathetic to us now than the inflexible theory. We can sympathise with her racking anxieties, often repeated in the first months after the wedding, about what marriage is doing to her mind:

> Somehow or another my intellect is becoming less strenuous than before my marriage. I must wrestle with this tendency to become parasitic on Sidney's efforts. I must do myself an *honest day's work* and not give way to this desire to shirk my share of the hard labour . . .

We can rejoice with her when, only three weeks later, these anxieties are judged unfounded:

> What light love brings to the daily task: it turns that black despair of the over-strained brainworker into calm quiescence. When first I was married, I feared that my happiness would dull my energies and make me intellectually dependent. I no longer feel that; the old fervour for work has returned without the old restlessness. Of course my life in London, with its other claims, leaves me with less physical energy, but this I think is almost counterbalanced by the absence of any waste through mental misery. On the whole, then, I would advise the brainworking woman to marry—if only she can find her Sidney!

A happy answer—if only a very conditional one! And if any doubt is left on the subject, here is a postscript in the same decade, from a lady, the Viscountess Monkswell, who had chosen the path of marriage pure and simple and though happy in it, is yet aware that something may be lost:

Tuesday, 13th June 1890

On June 7 Miss Fawcett came out *above* the Senior Wrangler in the Cambridge mathematical Tripos. This caused a great stir throughout the cultivated world. I never saw Bob more moved as one of his most intimate beliefs is the inferiority of the female brain where mathematics are concerned. He has a perfect right to this belief after having been married to me for 17 years, for I can just get through the household accounts & the yearly budget and *no more*.

This success of Miss Fawcett's awakened old memories in me before I learnt that only the *one talent* had been committed to my charge, & my very unimportant business was to see that I did not hide it in a napkin. I used to care so very much for the 'Women's Cause'. Whether it is that the women who endeavour to lead it sicken me, or that my interests and joys are bound up in one man and three boys I do not know ... The real reason why I have ceased to care for it is that I have lived, surrounded by stronger characters than myself who have not cared, &, being reduced for so many years to less than half rations of health & strength, I have kept any small energy I might possess for more immediate use. Every woman feels 2 inches taller for this success of Miss Fawcett, aged 22.

Chapter 7
- Sex

'*Men, some to business, some to pleasure take; But every woman is at heart a rake.*'—Alexander Pope, *Moray Essay to Lord Cobham*

'*Males have made asses of themselves writing about the female sexual experience.*'—William H. Masters, American sexologist

The best film title in the world, said an American producer once, would be *The Diary of a Rape*. There has, after all, to be a reason why *9½ Weeks*, the recently filmed story of a sado-masochistic affair, was first written as a book—in diary form. Having said which there is bad news for voyeurs—women's diary extracts on the matter of sex are more a matter of quality than of quantity. There are a good many exceptions in our own century, but before that, even if a virtuous woman had the mental freedom and the vocabulary to describe her sexual life, it is unlikely that either she herself or her husband, brother, daughter, who preserved and edited her diary for posterity, would have left much of the material to prying eyes.

The exceptions, however, *are* many—sometimes glorious, sometimes grim. They tend not to come from the happily (or even unhappily) married woman doing a regular Saturday night session but from those who were consciously pushing at the barriers of their society—the professional, the adventurous, the gay... or, of course, the young, to whom the whole business is both daring and exciting anyway.

And on that tack, you are about to see, truth is *much* stranger than the ever-popular fiction...

Discovery

In the 'semi-rare' section of a university library (Cambridge) I found a book entitled *Diary of a Virgin* by Cindy Peach. It is not rare in the antiquarian sense, being published by Hamish Hamilton in 1978, but ranks there, presumably, in the sense that 'rare' is occasionally used as a euphemism for pornographic. Here is an extract:

> If I buy a paper, it's the *Sun*, because of the sex, in the week, and the *News of the World*, because of the sex, on Sunday. When I'm abroad I buy filthy magazines because they help to broaden my outlook, which is really very narrow, I find, when I look at these magazines. I don't buy them in England because I'm very, very shy. I look clean, and pure, and the man behind the counter always embarrasses me by giving me funny looks. Once, one of them put his hand up between my legs when no one was looking and touched me where it felt super. It was so super that I didn't stop him, and when he took his hand away again he looked quite pale, and he told me I was a 'natural'. I've often wondered what he meant.

The book was published without introduction or explanation, but without further research I would stake a lot of money that it is fiction, not fact. It has the fake innocence of a *Playboy* picture. It reads like a man's fantasy of young female experience. The reality, surprisingly, is often more explicit, if you take the evidence of the girls who wrote to Valerie Grove. But their confessions have a genuine ring of candour about them:

> I had an odd dream last night. I think I'm changing. I think I want to be loved physically and hang it I'm only 13. I think I want to be fused/joined/shared with/involved in one of the other side (ie. males). Someone who can handle me carefully and understands me.... I think I'm possibly passionate but I've nothing to practise on.

> Have to be someone worthwhile 'cos the first time is meant to be the most painful and wonderful—must be worth it! Yes, I would like to do it!... Perhaps not *all* the way—whoops—my body is shaking—out of control. Oh, but it would be a new life—a new dimension, gorgeously painful and satisfying! I want to get out of control—I want—*it*!

> I think that virginity is easy to lose but an achievement to keep, therefore I'm proud of mine... He's not entirely my type and I don't care how many contraceptives he uses, I don't want to have his baby. What shall I do?... We want to do it beautifully and with a night to sleep—I want it to be beautiful.

> If I become either a nun or a prostitute in both cases I will become immune to men. Either way, I won't have to understand them.

I think to be married, and to be able to tumble about in bed, legally with one's husband, naked, must be great! Such feeling and freedom!

Today at work when I was washing a basin one of the waiters with a face like a chimpanzee came in and managed to put his hand on my left breast. Boy, did it make me feel good—I glowed from inside for the rest of the day, it's amazing what a fondle can do in the right place. In fact I've been sexually appreciated—always a big boost for a girl.

A girl's final entry in her diary, at the age of 17: 'First orgasm of my life and I love him.'

Not all the young diarists who write about the dawn of sexual experience have got that far down the line, of course. Take Anne Frank:

Monday, 17th April 1944

Dear Kitty,

Do you think that Daddy and Mummy would approve of my sitting and kissing a boy on a divan—a boy of seventeen and a half and a girl of just under fifteen? I don't really think they would, but I must rely on myself over this. It is so quiet and peaceful to lie in his arms and to dream, it is so thrilling to feel his cheek against mine, it is so lovely to know that there is someone waiting for me. But there is indeed a big 'but', because will Peter be content to leave it at this? I haven't forgotten his promise already, but ... he is a boy!

I know myself that I'm starting very soon, not even fifteen, and so independent already! It's certainly hard for other people to understand. I know almost for certain that Margot would never kiss a boy unless there had been some talk of an engagement or marriage, but neither Peter nor I have anything like that in mind. I'm sure, too, that Mummy never touched a man before Daddy. What would my girlfriends say about it if they knew that I lay in Peter's arms, my heart against his chest, my head on his shoulder and with his head against mine!

Oh, Anne, how scandalous! But honestly, I don't think it is; we are shut up here, shut away from the world, in fear and anxiety, especially just lately. Why, then, should we who love each other remain apart? Why should we wait until we have reached a suitable age? Why should we bother?

Three months earlier she had written:

I already had these kind of feelings subconsciously before I came here, because I remember that once when I slept with a girlfriend I had a strong desire to kiss her, and that I did do so. I could not help being terribly inquisitive about her body, for she had always kept it hidden from me. I asked her whether, as a proof of our friendship, we should feel one another's breasts, but she refused. I go into ecstacies every time I see the naked figure of a woman, such as Venus for example. It strikes me as so wonderful and exquisite that I have difficulty in stopping the tears rolling down my cheeks.

If only I had a girlfriend!

Yours, Anne.

That the first sexual feelings are often sparked by another woman is something that is evidenced elsewhere—in Katherine Mansfield, in Joan Wyndham. 'Laura and I,' the latter writes near the beginning of the aptly-named *Love Lessons*, her wartime journal, 'are enjoying a gentle lesbianism of the mind.' She was nearly seventeen at the time, and the first of her 'lessons' is chronicled in the chapter on love. But soon they took a different tack:

> 'By the way,' asked Rupert, as we sat in the cafeteria and ate a Lyon's fresh cream sandwich for tea, 'why are you a virgin?'
>
> 'I don't really know,' I said. 'It's never occurred to me to be anything else.' ...

Is she fond of her virginity, Rupert asks her a few days later.

> Inside me I could feel every moral code I had ever believed in since childhood begin to crumble away. 'Yes and no,' I said, 'I don't think I shall regret it, although being a virgin in Chelsea gives you a certain cachet!'

Cachet or—as Rupert puts it—stigma, the fact is that Joan Wyndham was moving in an bohemian and more experienced circle where her virginity and the probable loss of it was a matter for public and almost daily comment. Joan, encouraged by her friends ('God, Joan, you don't know what you're missing'), enjoys a certain pleasurable self-consciousness: 'What a life,' I said, 'never knowing if you're going to be bombed or seduced from one moment to the next!' Rupert claims her deflowering as a public duty: 'I suppose I shall have to get one of those French letters—dreadful things. You know this business is going to half kill me!'

A few weeks later:

> Taking advantage of this opportunity, I asked R. a few more questions.
>
> 'Well,' he said, humouring me, 'you-er-stick it in—and wiggle it around, up and down, in and out, and so on—then you get thoroughly excited, and—well—you have an orgasm! Only'—his face took on an expression of intense gloom—'with a virgin you *can't* stick it in, that is, not without an awful lot of hard work. And as for the virgin, you can only hope she gets sufficiently excited not to think it's like being at the dentist, which it probably is.'

A few days after that, it proved to be a not inaccurate description of the event, at least from Joan's point of view:

I thought, 'Well, that's done, and I'm glad it's over! If that's really all there is to it I'd rather have a good smoke or go to the pictures.'

That isn't the end of the story, of course. It continued through a good many more pages, into another book (*Love is Blue*) with the discovery that having had sex doesn't really change a recurring situation.

> The crunch!
> Well, I was drunk, weak and I could see no real reason for saying no...
> Also I knew he would leave me if I didn't.

Through the continued elusiveness of the 'big O', she visits a shady doctor who prescribes a cream to produce a clitoris 'long enough and strong enough to hang a copper kettle on.'

> Meanwhile, I have to report that Oscar (another girl) and I had been rubbing away like mad with the magic cream for over a week now. She does it when I'm in the bath, and vice-versa. Neither of us has noticed any appreciable difference in the length of our clitorises (clitori?) but we're certainly having plenty of orgasms! In fact we find orgasms are quite easy to have provided there aren't any men around, doing all the wrong things... We plan to do a little practical field work soon with the Norwegians.

But nothing comes quite when you expect it. Experiments with the Norwegians prove unavailing, but almost a year later Joan is with another man, one with whom she has been the eager partner:

> I knew, of course, that ultimately it would be disappointing—there would come a point when I would go dead and nothing would happen—so what happened next was a complete surprise.
> He was inside me and kissing my breasts at the same time when I suddenly felt the most extraordinary sensation as if an electric current had been switched on, turning my whole body into a radiant powerhouse of sexual expectation. It was as though someone had mended a fuse in a dark room and all the lights had blazed on. For the first time I felt totally at home inside my own skin—not watching myself any longer from the outside, I was really there, relaxed and letting go. My mind went dead, but my body was running away with me, and as our movements became faster and stronger it was like the long ride down from Flichity Inn, freewheeling all the way—look, no hands!—laughing and shouting with surprise and pleasure as I finally relaxed into joy.

After that, you feel, there is nowhere else to go—except to touch on a few other writers coming to grips with sex. Here is Sylvia Plath in the 1950s, formally assessing her needs:

> *September 1951*
> Looking at myself, in the past years, I have come to the conclusion that I must have a passionate physical relationship with someone—or combat the

great sex urge in me by chastic means. I chose the former answer. I also admitted that I am obligated in a way to my family and to society (damn society anyway) to follow certain absurd and traditional customs—for my own security, they tell me. I must therefore confine the major part of my life to one human being of the opposite sex.... That is a necessity because:

(1) I choose the physical relationship of intercourse as an animal and releasing part of life.

(2) I cannot gratify myself promiscuously and retain the respect and support of society (which is my pet devil)—and because I am a woman: ergo: one root of envy for male freedom.

(3) Still being a woman, I must be clever and obtain as full a measure of security for those approaching ineligible and aging years wherein I will not have the chance to capture a new mate—in all probability. So, resolved: I shall proceed to obtain a mate through the customary procedure: namely, marriage.

Her words, a little later, are hot:

May 1952

... I remember a cool river beach and a May night full of rain held in far clouds, moonly sparks saying on the water, and the close, dank, heavy wetness of green vegetation. The water was cold to my bare feet, and the mud oozed up between my toes. He ran then, on the sand, and I ran after him, my hair long and damp, blowing free across my mouth. I could feel the inevitable magnetic polar forces in us, and the tidal blood beat loud, loud, roaring in my ears, slowing and rhythmic. He paused then, I behind him, arms locked around the powerful ribs, fingers caressing him. To lie, with him, to lie with him, burning forgetful in the delicious animal fire. Locked first upright, thighs ground together, shuddering mouth to mouth, breast to breast, legs enmeshed, then lying full length, with the good heavy weight of body upon body, arching, undulating, blind, growing together, force fighting force: to kill? To drive into burning dark of oblivion? To lose identity? Not love, this, quite. But something else rather. *A refined hedonism.* Hedonism: because of the blind sucking mouthing fingering quest for physical gratification. Refined: because of the desire to stimulate another in return, not being quite only concerned for self alone, but mostly so. An easy end to arguments on the mouth: a warm meeting of mouths, tongues quivering, licking, tasting. An easy substitute for bad slashing with angry hating teeth and nails and voice: the curious musical tempo of hands lifting under breasts, caressing throat, shoulders, knees, thighs. And giving up to the corrosive black whirlpool of mutual necessary destruction. Once there is the first kiss, then the cycle becomes inevitable. Training, conditioning, make a hunger burn in breasts and secret fluid in vagina, driving blindly for destruction. What is it but destruction? Some mystic desire to beat to sensual annihilation—to snuff out one's identity on the identity of the other—a mingling and mangling of identities? A death of one? Or both? A devouring and subordination? No, no. A polarization rather—a balance of two integrities, charging, electrically, one with the other, yet with centers of coolness, like stars.

But the assessment, one can't but feel, is too cold with the artificial distance of youth (she was still at college). 'I was trying to be like a man,' she wrote later, in therapy, 'able to take or leave sex, with this one and that. I got even. But really wasn't meant for it.'

Any more than fifteen-year-old Alice, on drugs and on the run, was doing what she was meant for—'Another day, another blow job.' There is a pathetic bravura about her entry. Sex *has* been wonderful to her, but only because she was high on drugs at the time, and she knows that something has been missing:

> It's strange how much sex I've had and yet I don't feel as though I've had any. I still want somebody to be nice and just kiss me goodnight at the door. That's a laugh!

On the surface it is a world away from Alice in the 1960s to Henriette Dessaulles in the 1880s facing marriage, about to begin a new life:

> ... a life partly hidden by a mysterious veil that no one lifts for me. I'll discover it with him, my beloved who will be my husband. How strange it is to be entering an unknown world that everyone seems to be familiar with and yet no one speaks to me about...

> *January 15, 1881*
> I suppose Jos doesn't know any more about it than I do, but her words 'I hope...' imply that people only have children when they really want to. That does make sense, but on the other hand, the way things happen in poor families makes me wonder if this is so. Last week at the X's, the mother and father were down in the dumps because they are going to have a sixth child, while the other five already don't have enough to eat. Surely, when there is no work, that is too many children for their means. But isn't it up to them, then, to decide not to have any more?

That is the voice of innocence. But is Alice's voice really the voice of experience? Earlier in her teens Henriette shows a refreshing independence of spirit over her first mild sexual adventure:

> *September 8, 1875*
> I'm thinking about last night—he kissed me. What would Monsieur Prince say? He'd explode! But I wonder why. I let Maurice do it because he asked me, because he was sad, I wouldn't have wanted to make him even sadder, especially not by refusing him such a tiny thing.
> As far as I am concerned, well, between him kissing me and him telling me tenderly that he loves me, I'd rather hear him say he loves me. Besides, letting yourself be kissed by a man isn't done, so I won't allow Maurice to do it often. I'm preoccupied with all of this now, but yesterday it was much

simpler. He asked me and I said yes, because I would have hated to disappoint him. That's all. And that the Good Lord and all His angels may have seen us doesn't bother me one bit. I couldn't feel less guilty.

Could it be that, to a degree at least, women and girls, whatever the shibboleths of their time, have always made their own sexual morality?

Morality

'There is a sort of morality I can never comprehend,' wrote Lady Holland in 1800, chronicling Society's somewhat inconsistent attitudes toward Mrs Fitzherbert, the Prince Regent's amour.

It is all too easy to assume that women discovered sex—or at least the joy thereof—circa 1970. There have at various times in the past been cultural inhibitions on their expressing or exploring their enjoyment of it . . . but sexual morality may not always have been as restrictive as it looks. 'God knows celibacy is as painful to a woman (even from a physical standpoint) as it is to a man,' wrote Beatrice Webb in 1889. Or rather, the morality we see may have been essentially a middle and upper middle-class one, with the diary-keeping upper-classes, like the largely silent lower ones, tacitly exempt. The Duchess of Northumberland, travelling in Bonn in the late eighteenth century, records without visible disapproval that:

A virtuous woman is here almost as rare a Bird as a Black Swan. All have their Lovers and too often those of their own Family. The Comtesse Fugger who is not reckon'd one of the worst told Mrs Gressener that the Grand Ecuyer by whom she is now kept (or rather I believe she keeps him), was her 49th Gallant.

While at home:

Poor Lady Craven who had hitherto behaved herself very prudently and made a very good Wife began about this Time to expose herself prodigiously by suffering Ld. Cholmondely to be for ever at her Ear. But Ld. Berkeley, who was very fond of her, acted upon this occasion with so becoming a spirit that he quite broke off the Connection, and at the same time proceeded with so much discretion that the Affair I believe never came to L -d C-'s knowledge.

More than a century later, in 1891, eighteen-year-old Daisy, the upper-class English girl who became Princess of Pless, drove off to Silesia with her new husband. 'I began my married life totally unprepared for any of its experiences, duties or responsibilities. Literally, I knew nothing.' She learnt. In 1903:

I lunched with Alice Keppel (Prince Edward's mistress) before leaving for Berlin; three or four of the women present had had several lovers, and did not mind saying so, but I can generally *placer* myself in any *milieu*. Alice is fascinating.

Yes—but between the Georgian and the Edwardian eras, the Victorian intervened. So what of the years when even pianos had to be dressed to hide their legs? Did prudery descend the day Victoria came to the throne? Perhaps not. Two years later, in 1839, the young Queen's reign was marred by a nasty Court scandal which dented her popularity and showed her in an unflattering light. When Lady Flora Hastings, both personally and politically antipathetic to the Queen, complained of pain and swelling in the stomach, Victoria's pious horror was only less noticeable than her readiness to jump to conclusions about the nature of Lady Flora's complaint:

> *2nd February 1839*
>
> Lady Flora had not been above two days in the house before Lehzen and I discovered how exceedingly suspicious her figure looked—more have since observed this and we have no doubt that she is—to use the plain words—with child!! Clark cannot deny the suspicion; the horrid cause of all this is the Monster and Demon Incarnate whose name I forbear to mention but which is the first word of the 2nd line of this page [Conroy]. Lady Tavistock accordingly with Lehzen's concurrence told Lord Melbourne of it, as it was a matter of serious importance. He accordingly replied to me this evening without—very properly—mentioning names, that 'The only way is to be quiet and watch it'. That it was a very ticklish thing for a physician to declare what might not be true, as so many deceptions had been practised upon physicians.... Here ended this disgraceful subject which makes one loathe one's own sex. When they are bad how disgracefully and disgustingly servile and low women are!! I don't wonder at men considering the sex despicable.

Lady Flora was medically examined and pronounced a virgin, but the Queen remained sceptical.

> *22nd June 1839*
>
> Lord M. asked how Lady Flora was; not so well, I said; that her own family were very fearful she would die, as they knew it would be said that she had died lying-in. Lord M. said, 'Exactly so'. Talked of the dreadful fuss they had made about it—and Lord M. said Lord Hastings made such a piece of work about it—as if there was no other family in the world but the Hastings. 'I don't see,' said Lord M., 'if she was to die, that it's of such great importance if they say she was so (pregnant) or not; they make such a fuss about it; it is a very shocking thing and a very wrong thing, but such things have happened in families; it isn't unprecedented'; which is true enough.

Victoria's pragmatism soon gave way to qualms about her own position in the matter; Lady Flora did die ('The poor thing died without a struggle and only just raised her hands and gave one gasp') and was found to have been suffering from nothing more sinful than a growth on the liver. But the point of interest is that the girl who gave her name to the age of restriction herself reacted with the assumptions and attitudes of a more adventurous age.

Towards the end of the century Ellen Peel, despite having been brought up in the most sheltered environment, finds herself travelling with, and to all intents and purposes in charge of, a brother whose mental abstractions lead him into a stream of sexual misadventures. Her reaction is both pragmatic and—in its absence of blame— broadminded:

Sunday, 6th May

Mr Foster told me that Willy has begun again. It is too annoying, an actress in the second class. Must watch him like cats.

Friday, 11th May

Fresh bothers. Willy has actually insulted a lady here, a Mrs Smerdon. Mr Foster talked to him but the thing itself makes no impression on him, only the consequences. It will be so hard when we get home.

Saturday, 12th May

Willy won't apologise to Mrs Smerdon so I did, but it was disagreeable as I had hardly spoken to her before. They all think him off his head and he has such a bad name. It is very, very hard, especially on him.

It was, when you think of it, an extraordinary position for an unmarried woman of the period to be placed in. But theory as applied to others and practice as applied to yourself are still a long way apart, as Ellen found on her engagement:

I was awfully frightened and nearly fainted after dinner. He was too nice.

Can you disentangle the various moralities behind Margaret Fountaine's relationship with Khalil Neimy? They are beyond me:

1901

Those first days at Baalbek were fraught with blind entreaties and mad infatuation, till I began to think that I had made a mistake in engaging Neimy as my courier for the summer. I had longed sometimes to have once more a lover, but after this, never again. It was only the day after our arrival that he suddenly threw his arms round me and tried to kiss me on my face by force. I was furious at his assurance, and for fully half a minute I struggled to free myself from his grasp. I had never felt in such a rage before; I trembled from head to foot in my fury, till at last he crouched before me imploring my forgiveness. But alas for the weakness of human nature, only the very next day on the mountain side under the shadow of some huge rocks in one of the quarries in the neighbourhood of Baalbek, I sank lower than I had ever sank before; the very audacity of the man overcame my sense of all that was right and proper. Why are men such animals? I sometimes almost forget the vile depravity of human nature till I find myself confronted with it again, the selfish lust which men mistake for love.

However, I still meant to make an effort to rise again, for I had not sunk to the lowest level of all. So I turned upon my lover and scorned him for what he had done, and when on the day following after this we were going over those marvellous Baalbek ruins I refused to speak to him, listening only to the guide, and if he held out his hand to help me over the huge, fallen stones and columns, I declined to take it.

Later that afternoon I found myself talking with Miss Stowell, the English missionary here at Baalbek, and for the first time I began acting that double part which I kept up so well during the whole rest of the time I was in this country. It has been said that all women are born actresses, which is, I think, quite true. And as I sat talking to Miss Stowell I was again a high-minded, honourable Englishwoman; the thought that on the previous day I had almost sunk to the level of being the mistress of my dragoman could not live in the pure atmosphere of the British Syrian School House.

... I could often have wished he was not quite so coarse in his words and actions—one thing he would always say was, 'I love very much your legs'. However, I did my best to raise the tone of his mind; though it seemed difficult to make him see that the animal side of human nature was not all we had to live for....

If the world of Victorian sexuality seems sometimes full of contrasts, unnatural light and rather suspicious shade, then the relationship between Hannah Cullwick and her Massa looks like an extreme example. For years at a time she wore around her neck a chain and padlock to which only he had the key. For him she 'blacked up' to show herself his slave (her name for him of Massa was in imitation of Negro speech). She literally licked his boots (and not only new ones, for which saliva was a recognised treatment). The implications of sado-masochistic sexuality—as well as of goodness knows what else—are obvious. Yet, side by side with the alarming evidence of practices we cannot find easy to accept, Liz Stanley, who edited Hannah Cullwick's diaries, finds evidence for another unexepectedly acceptable side of Victorian (and pre-Victorian) sexuality: 'For Hannah and many other entirely respectable working-class women, kissing'—in this case with a fellow servant—'was something to be engaged in as often as possible, was understood to involve nothing more than harmless pleasure and was seen as a good way of meeting potential marriage partners', through traditional games like kiss-in-the-ring. Even the other side of the story, the one that seems to show Hannah as the degraded victim, is not, in Liz Stanley's opinion, as simple as it seems.

The message seems to be one of the oldest in the book—that with sexual morality, you never quite know where you are. Look at Mary Astor, scandalously divorced in 1936 with a court order to burn the 'obscene' diaries which had been produced as evidence. And then look at the *Castaway* diaries Lucy Irvine kept on Tuin when her refusal to sleep with her desert island husband had already become a problem:

> Never have I used my body for sex without wanting the man. In a world of choice, that mattered. Now, here, not even it's not mattering matters.
> 'It wouldn't hurt you.'
> 'What's so sacred about that thing between your legs anyway?'
> Yes yes. But looking apart from, beyond all that, which after all is only talk, gross words spoken through pain, there is the issue of genuine care, for I do believe that as I care for him and about him, G cares for me. The trouble is that it is not in the same way at all. His love is man to woman in all respects. Mine, and I will not quibble about calling it love, is a warmth born of a shared struggle, a thing that growing slowly, catching me unawares, at odd moments, despite and because of all that has happened between us, has sat down firmly in my being and I do not believe it will ever go away. How brutally unfortunate that it is not the love of a woman for her man.
> And what of those days in London when I slept with him and there was sex? It is Tuin that has entered my body. It was Tuin, any Tuin, that was in my mind when I looked at G's red hair on the pillow and knew that we were going to go to an island together. If only he had wanted the island as badly as he wanted a woman. If only I had wanted him as badly as I wanted the island. Oh, to hell with ifs. It is no wonder he has called me a little whore. Woman is a vessel. Good luck to all who sail in her.

You are damned if you do, apparently—and you are damned if you don't.

Breaking the Rules

In any age, whatever the prevailing rules, there have always been those who made their own. One such was Anne Lister, the upper-class woman who lived in Yorkshire between 1791 and 1840. Within the world of her diaries, her lesbianism was no secret; to the outer world, she picked a precarious path, refusing (rather to the contempt of one more militant female) to 'come out', but so conspicious a figure that even her sexual identity was in question:

Sunday, 28th June 1818

The people generally remark, as I pass along, how much I am like a man. I think they did it more than usual this evening. At the top of Cunnery Lane, as I went, three men said, as usual, 'That's a man' & one axed [sic] 'Does your cock stand?' I know not how it is but I feel low this evening...

She happily adopted the conventionally male role of the pursuer in her flirtations and amours:

... She seems determined to let all the notice come first from me. Sensible girl. She knows how to play her part.

Even in its less attractive aspects:

... She seems innocent & unknowing as to the ways of the world. I wonder if I can ever, or shall ever, mould her to my purpose.

Like the conventional male seducer, Anne was prepared to differentiate between lust and love—a place for one, a place for the other:

... She is not exactly the woman of all hours for me. She suits me best at night. In bed she is excellent.

There is, in fact, a good deal in Anne Lister's diaries which make her sound as unacceptable in our day, though for different reasons, as she must have been in her own. There is, in particular, the remorseless class consciousness which made her steadfastly refuse to call on a woman she was trying to court. But we can welcome her frank avowal of the pleasures of the bed:

Thursday, 22nd July 1824

Two last night. M— spoke in the very act. 'Ah,' said she, 'Can you ever love anyone else?' She knows how to heighten the pleasure of our intercourse. She often murmurs, 'Oh, how delicious,' just at the very moment. All her kisses* are good ones...

Another who was learning all about pleasure was the 'virgin prostitute', as she called herself, Anaïs Nin. The original publication of Nin's diaries in six volumes, exhaustive though these seemed at the time, proved to be anything but the full story. (The full story, in the University of California archives, runs to *35,000* handwritten pages.) Edited out of the Volume 1, which covered the early 1930s, was not only a live and present husband but a remarkable complete love affair, only now come to light in the recently published *Henry and June*.

In 1931, after meeting the American writer Henry Miller and his wife June, Anaïs embarked on a voyage of sexual discovery. It was to involve, beyond those three, Anaïs' husband Hugo, her cousin

---

*a contemporary euphemism for intercourse

Eduardo, and her psychiatrist Allendy. It was to be the kind of voyage from which there is no real return:

> I asked Eduardo, 'Is the desire for orgies one of those experiences one must live through? And once lived, can one pass on, without return of the same desires?' 'No,' he answered, sensibly enough, and so it proves.

It is June who first arouses Anaïs' passion: 'As she came towards me from the darkness of my garden into the light of the doorway I saw for the first time the most beautiful woman on earth.' It grows to an obsession—'I must kiss her, I must kiss her'—but June goes away and it is Henry who is left, Henry with whom Anaïs goes to watch an exhibition of two women together in a bardello, and with whom she embarks on an affair which unlocks the door to a whole world of sexuality and of sensuality:

> I masturbate often, luxuriously, without remorse or after distaste. For the first time I know what it is to eat. I have gained four pounds. I get frantically hungry, and the food I eat gives me a lingering pleasure. I never ate before in this deep carnal way. I have only three desires now, to eat, to sleep, and to fuck. The cabarets excite me. I want to hear raucous music, to see faces, to brush against bodies, to drink fiery Benedictine. Beautiful women and handsome men arouse fierce desires in me. I want to dance. I want drugs. I want to know perverse people, to be intimate with them. I never look at naive faces. I want to bite into life, and to be torn by it. Henry does not give me all this. I have aroused his love. Curse his love. He can fuck me as no one else can, but I want more than that. I'm going to hell, to hell, to hell. Wild, wild, wild.

The situation becomes complicated: 'Hugo is coming home in a few hours, and so life goes on like this in contradictory patterns'.... 'I love Hugo passionately, but tenderness is a strong tie too....' 'Are you ever dry?' he (Henry) teases me. I confess that Hugo has to use Vaseline. Then I realize the full significance of this confession and I am overwhelmed.'... 'Henry and I are one, lying soldered for four days. Not with bodies but with flames. God let me thank somebody. No drug could be more potent. Such a man.'

> I feel a powerful sense of life unimaginable to either Hugo or Eduardo. My breasts are swollen. I hold my legs wide apart in love-making instead of, as before, closed. I have enjoyed sucking to the point of almost coming to a climax while doing it. I have finally eliminated my childish self.

The situation becomes more complicated still, incestuous in every possible sense of the word:

> I have remained the woman who loves incest. I still practise the most incestuous crimes with a sacred religious fervour. I am the most corrupt of

all women, for I seek a refinement in my incest, the accompaniment of beautiful chants, music, so that everyone believes in my soul. With a madonna face, I still swallow God and sperm, and my orgasm resembles a mystical climax. The men I love, Hugo loves, and I let them act like brothers. Eduardo confesses his love to Allendy, Allendy is going to be my lover. Now I send Hugo to Allendy so that Allendy will teach him to be less dependent on me for his happiness.

When I immolated my childhood to my mother, when I give away all I own, when I help, understand, serve, what tremendous crimes I am expiating—strange, insidious joys, like my love for Eduardo, my own blood; for Hugo's spiritual father, John; for June, a woman; for June's husband; for Eduardo's spiritual father, Allendy, who is now Hugo's guide. It only remains for me now to go to my own father and enjoy to the full the experience of our sensual sameness, to hear from his lips the obscenities, the brutal language I have never formulated, but which I love in Henry.

Am I hypnotized, fascinated by evil because I have none in me? Or is there in me the greatest secret evil?

Where next? Back to June, it seems. 'I am rushing again into June's chaos. It is June I want and not Allendy's wisdom, not even Henry's love of aggressivity. I want eroticism, I want those moist dreams I dream at night...' Back first in thought and then, as June returns to Paris, in actuality. Whether in actual physicality or not one cannot be certain because the 'unexpurgated' *Henry and June* ends here ('So Henry is coming this afternoon, and tomorrow I am going out with June') and we are back to playing jigsaw puzzles with the censored diaries again, diaries which, contrary to appearances, conceal at least as much as they reveal.

Liane de Pougy is a more predictable figure than Anaïs Nin to find sailing these erotic seas. She had, after all, become a courtesan, a professional seductress, after the brief marriage of her early youth and the escape to Paris. When her *Blue Notebooks* begin she is fifty, married to Prince Georges Ghika, with her professional life behind her and the subject only for high-flown romantic reminiscences. When sexual episodes do begin to reappear in Liane's life, they are with women:

March 20 1922

At about three o'clock my Flossie arrived. We lay down to rest in the overwhelming scent of flowers. She took me in her arms and caressingly... we were both equally stupefied by tenderness. The Countess de la Bérandière looked in for a moment to throw a charm on our voluptuous stupor with her caressing, slightly purring voice.'

Nothing overt. But in describing the consolation she found when Georges had run off with another woman, she gets closer to it:

October 25 1926

Mimy's love is ardent, impassioned, whole, jealous. Love in the Italian style! It sings, it shouts, it howls in keeping with her beauty, her gestures, her fiery glance. Mimy is a creature of excess.

We stay in bed late of a morning; we have breakfast; we tease, we laugh; we kiss. We open our letters. She gives me an Italian lesson: verbs, vocabulary, dictation, translation. We have a very good time.

With women, Liane presents herself as much tempted by as tempting a series of charmers. While she wrote in her later and more religious life of lesbianism as 'that vice', she earlier cherished fantasies of Sappho's '... happy, flowery island'. With men, she seems interested chiefly in her power to tempt. In her notebooks she copies another's words:

November 21 1925

Le Figaro littéraire has devoted an issue to Courteline. I was much taken by an unpublished fragment of Boubouroche which someone found by chance in a café blotter: 'I am a bad adviser in matters of love because my way of understanding and practising love is rather special. No one in the world has loved more than I have; I have spent my life at it. When this little accident befalls me I play my part stoutly and I let things happen without doing anything to speed them up, *seeing that there is more delight in wanting a woman than in getting her, that a woman's power lies wholly in the desire you feel for her and that the intoxication of possession is always inferior to the dream one had of it.'* I underline the part which I feel and understand as a way of showing the opinion I share. The fever drops, the thing is seen for what it is and beauty is rare in this world ...

After her husband, Georges-Gilles, returned to her, beauty in sex was certainly thin on the ground:

April 9 1927

Moral collapse of Gilles: his idea—he confessed it to me—is to go out and solicit women wherever he see them— unknown women—and do it very fast! 'Because if I have to talk to a woman for twenty minutes I stop wanting her.' He would like to bring them back to me, to go in for the most obscene and lewd games. So now what! I am going to consult my confessor and Father Sanson. I asked my dear Pinard for his advice, and according to him the calm and dignity of my household depends on soothing baths and doses of cascara. Dear God, I have no one but You!

When her husband's syphilis becomes apparent and is diagnosed, she writes: 'So here I am at last, delivered from those desolatingly loveless embraces.'

Sale

When Liane de Pougy became old and unhappy she sought comfort in religion, forgiveness through repentance. And what she repented in the watches of the night seems to have been less her sexual acts than the absence of love she might have put into them. 'I was a deranged little Messalina, cerebral, woefully vain':

> You had mercy on no-one [she accuses herself].
>   Not one of those who came near you found grace in your eyes. You never loved even the most magnificent of your lovers. Kings, great financiers, poets, children, old men, scholars—they all clustered round you and you defiled them all. You sold yourself—

She did, of course, though never for too low a price. (One of her more cherishable reminiscences concerns the lover—'impotent and a terrible masochist' who summoned a jeweller to show her some rings. The jeweller spread 'a million and a half's worth' on the table; the lover, seeing her unable to decide, told her to take the lot.)

This isn't the place to start speculating on how many women have sold their sexual services in one way or another (including marriage) with the same 'excuses' Liane offers herself—'my youth, my foolishness, temptation, my poverty'—the last named doubtless being often the most powerful. Those who sold themselves most directly and crudely, the streetwalkers, didn't belong to the diary-keeping classes. But there are other currencies than cash, and more than one woman has traded sex for a favour (i.e. the director's casting couch), with no doubts as to what she was doing or why.

But it is back to clergyman's daughter Margaret Fountaine for the last words on sale and sex:

> When Khalil came in next morning and folded me in his arms—while I feebly expostulated, because I was still only in my nightgown and dressing-gown—my whole heart went out to him. He carried me in his arms across the room, and laid me on my bed, and when he lay over me the weight of his body was sweet to me now, because I loved him. We went very near the brink, but I knew that if I gave him all he asked, all I now longed to give him, I might find myself in a condition which would compel me to implore him to marry me; for my power was infinite only so long as I witheld from him what he most desired. I longed to give him the delight he sought from me and which he had every right to ask, but I forced myself to say: 'Now go away please. It's too hot.' And my voice was calm and collected, so he never could have known the struggle within me.

Part *III*
Looking Outwards

Chapter 8
- Work

'Give a woman a job and she grows balls.'—Jack Gelber

'A woman's work is never done.'—Proverb

'They have the right to work whenever they want to—as long as they have dinner ready when you get home.'—John Wayne

I: OUTSIDE THE HOME

Florence Nightingale, approaching the age of eighty, thanked God for giving her 'work, constant work, work with Sidney Herbert, work with Lord Lawrence, and never out of work still'. But work, apart from the domestic sort, doesn't get too much space in the pages of women's diaries, for the obvious reason that until recently it applied to fairly few women, especially of the diary-writing classes. Exclude the artist or thinker, writing about her inspiration or opinions, stick to work in the sense of paid employment outside the home, and the options are cut down even further.

There are the exceptions—like the seventeenth-century London midwife who left her professional diary behind her, and like Abigail Gawthern of Nottingham (1757-1810) who married a white-lead manufacturer and, when he died in 1791, continued to run his works. But if that is at all surprising, this is more so: the brief entries of her diary record the races, the assizes, the births and deaths of the neighbours and the early spring but give scarcely a line to the business. Women of affairs, perhaps, were thinking less in terms of structuring a career than of doing their duty in the estate to which God had called them—like Queen Victoria, aged twenty-one and settling into her reign:

Talked to Lord M. of my growing disinclination to business: 'You must conquer that,' he said, 'it isn't unnatural when the first novelty is over, but you mustn't let that feeling get the better, you must fight against it.' I had said it was unnatural for a young woman to like business.

Recently published under the title of *Dear Girl* were the letters and diaries of two 'working girls' in the early years of this century. Ruth Slate was a clerk in a grocery firm in the City, Eva Slawson was a secretary in a solicitor's office in Walthamstow. Writing in, and most directly aware of, a time which saw the dawn of feminism and by consequence of the 'career woman', they were probably more prepared than their predecessors would have been to 'like business', as Queen Victoria put it. But all business seemed to offer were unattractive ethics and few opportunities, so that in the end the office plays a comparatively minor part even in *Dear Girl*, as Ruth in this rare entry points out:

Thursday, 2nd May 1907

I have written very little, or nothing, in my diary, about business, but a climax has come, and the course of my life may be altered by it. I have not written previously, because I knew if I started I should want to say so much, moreover it would be difficult to express the disgust and indignation I daily feel. The whole system is so abominable, and so unjust—its influence so crushing—that I wonder it does not bring about revolt; but the crushing, I suppose, prevents that. The most terrible instance of the effect this slave-driving process has, is the case of the Brentwood manager, who threw himself under a train and was decapitated; and of another, who went mad. The firm is universally spoken of as a firm of 'sweaters', and the experience proves the name truly given.

Numbers and numbers of office staff, male and female, have been trying to get the small increase in salary which in most cases, including my own, has long been overdue. Yesterday we were told it is vain to ask and that if we are not satisfied we had better look for something else. It is only the thought of the home folk which has kept me there so long, and prevents me leaving on Saturday, but I have finally determined to do as they suggest and 'look out for something else'.

In addition to the unjust treatment, there is the terrible depression to which I so often fall a prey, in consequence of being in the department for dealing with all questions of competition. The meanness of tactics adopted for the baffling of tradesmen and their ultimate undoing, is beyond description. The unfortunate managers, whose business it is to flog them up well, and be flogged themselves by Head Office for not being drastic enough, all come into our little office before Mr Bray, who is certainly a splendid 'bully'. But to listen to this bullying, day after day, makes the heart sick.

But the bitterest drop in my cup, I know, is the knowledge that whereas I might have been fitting myself for some higher order of work, I have drifted along, absorbed in my trouble over Wal, or in day-dreaming. I know myself to be ignorant and incompetent, and the knowledge *is very bitter*. What shall I now turn to?

But given that a woman under the necessity of earning her living was considered an object for compassion, it is remarkable how strong a dissenting voice runs through women's diaries even before Victoria's day. A voice which not only recognizes the agony of idleness, but which makes a vague bid after status and satisfaction outside the roles of wife, mother, daughter.. sister. Here, the playwright Sheridan's sister Betsy, in 1785, describes a party at which:

> ... I was the only person in the room who had not some consequence in life from fortune, rank or acknowledged abilities. There can be no true pleasure derived even from the most delightful society unless you feel you have a right to your place in it. I cannot make my Father feel the difference the world makes between a man of talents and the woman of his Family unless these are at least independent.

As Ellen Peel put it in 1887, recording a talk she had with her brother:

> He was thinking how one would feel when dying if one had never done anything but amuse oneself. He is about right. But what is one to do in the present circumstances? It is so different for a man.

Fifteen-year-old Helena Morley in 1895 was inspired by an encounter with a beggar to write:

(Tuesday, 24th December)

> I'm not sorry for anyone's being poor; I'm only sorry when they have no work. If anyone wants to punish me, it's to oblige me to stay without anything to do.

George Eliot, among a good many precise notes about the sums of money she made for her writing, and some indignation that the male pseudonym she adopted led to critics wrongly attributing authorship of her book elsewhere, is here grappling with the consciousness of fame:

March 16 1895

> Blackwood writes to say I am 'a popular author, as well as a great author'. They printed 2090 of 'Adam Bede', and have disposed of more than 1800, so that they are thinking about a second edition. A very feeling letter from Froude this morning. I happened this morning to be reading the 30th Ode, B. III. of Horace—'Non omnis moriar'.

Rachel Roberts, nearing the end of her life, looks back in despair at what she forfeited when she chose to put her work as an actress second and run away with Rex Harrison twenty years before:

November 19, 1980

I've written earlier that it wasn't a major mistake for me to go away with him, but despite the magic days, I think it was. It's too late to do more than speculate, but I had a need to act—have the discipine of that habit and to sublimate all my needs and emotions into the parts I was playing. I wanted to act. Always. But for my first marriage, I would have continued to do so with increasing confidence and flair—my personality and voice and instinct, powerful allies. I would never have sunk into this torpor. Never. Never have had a day like this. Never. Alone in someone else's house in Los Angeles. Yes, I loved Rex, passionately, and all our good larks. Yes, I adored walking up the Champs-Elysées with him. Yes, I adored Joseph's and the Berkeley and ice-cold, perfectly prepared dry Martinis and beautiful wine and brandy and potage and brains. Yes, I loved going back to the Lancaster and going to bed and making love. Yes, I loved the Rome Express and the adjoining *coupés* and snuggling up to Rex. Yes, I loved our love: it completely tallied with my adolescent fantasies. Yes, I loved the look of Rex's shoulders swaggering down the train corridors. Yes, I loved our walks past the donkey to San Fruttuosa. Yes, I loved the fires, the villa, the books, the cats, Homerino. I loved them passionately. And for all that, I forfeited my birthright inherited from Grandpa—my voice and Welsh emotionalism . . . my acting. It was all I ever knew or understood. Working in the theatre, I was easy with it. Understood it. Liked having my days structured by it. Really preferred rehearsing: I was with people. But I liked stalking the stage, too, I liked being told I was good. I liked controlling an audience *and could do it!*

I wish I could put the clock back. I wouldn't have known such empty days of solitude. I probably wouldn't have known Hollywood or New York. I wonder would I have drunk? Probably—but maybe not so much.

And the impulse to indulge in some sort of extra-mural activity can be seen, in a lighter context, in Lady Cynthia Asquith. Dissatisfied with what might be called her profession of society lady, she briefly tried nursing towards the end of the 1914-18 war, and immediately afterwards took the amorphous position of 'secretary' to an acquaintance, the writer James Barrie, creator of Peter Pan:

Thursday, 29th August 1918

Felt in a terrible breadwinning bustle merely because I had to be at Barrie's by eleven! Breakfasted downstairs punctually at nine and then tried to get letters and diary done before starting. More frantic recriminations from John's governess. Her last charge is that I used a phrase about her to which 'even Delysia' wouldn't have stooped—'the excrements of your brain!' She had misread excitements.

It takes me twenty minutes from door to door to get to Barrie by Underground. I found his favourite ward Michael with him—a delightful Eton boy. The work I did was easy enough—it is only socially rather difficult, because undefined. I don't quite know when to go, when to talk, when silently to work. There was not an over-formidable pile of letters. I devised my own method—opening them and giving them a precis of each: he either told me to destroy them or roughly intimated how they should be answered. In my own shorthand I scribbled notes on them, and then while he read his newspaper, I became C. Greene and wrote about twelve—taking such as were to be signed by him. I wrote one to George Robey. There were heart-rending ones from actresses, clamouring for engagements, sending photographs, etc. I got a blue flush from excitement, but all went well.

This was apparently the end of the working day. Lunch with friends was followed by more friends to tea, by a 5.30 pm caller and a dinner out. There can be no doubt that for that 9 am breakfast, Lady Cynthia did not have to boil her own egg. Some breadwinning bustle... but if we laugh, it is clear that she is laughing too.

Not All Joy

Not that many years earlier, on the other side of the green baize door which separated Upstairs from Downstairs, life was very different. A random day in the life of Hannah Cullwick, maidservant, is worth quoting in full:

Saturday, 7 March [1863]
Got up early, for they all went to Temple Bar to see the princess come through. They all got off in carriages before 9 o'clock—Mary the housemaid & Sarah as well & I was left, & it was a first rate chance for me to get some cleaning done. I black'd the grates & that & clean'd 3 pairs of boots. Took the breakfast up & Mr Garle came down & ask'd me to brush his trousers & I did 'em for him, kneeling on the floor & wi' him putting his foot on a chair for the bottoms. I stood in the hall & watch'd 'em off & then I had some breakfast. Clean'd away upstairs & wash'd the things up. Put coals on the fire. Went up & made all the beds & emptied the slops. Came down & swept the dining room all over & dusted it. Swept the hall & steps & shook the mats & then I had a mutton chop & some beer for my dinner. Clean'd the windows in the hall & passage & clean'd the hall & steps on my knees, the backstairs, then I was got the passage. I took the matting out & shook it. Swept the passage & took the things out of the hole under the stairs—Mary uses it for her dustpans & brushes. It's a dark hole & about 2 yards long & very low. I crawl'd in on my hands & knees & lay curl'd up in the dirt for a minute or so & then I got the handbrush & swept the walls down. The cobwebs & dust fell all over me & I had to poke my nose out o' the door to get breath, like a dog's out of a kennel. Then I swept the floor of

it & got' my pail & clean'd it out & put the things back in their places. I was
very black as I could be, but I didn't wash till I'd clean'd the passage &
'tatoe hole out & the shelves & back celar [sic], & then I finish'd in the
kitchen & made the fires up & wash'd my face & hands. Shut the shutters &
lit the lamp. Shut all the windows upstairs, for it began to rain & was
getting dusk, & I saw the people rushing home again as much as they did to
go & see the procession, & there was hundreds went past young & old &
some wi' children even.

The first part of the family came back at six & was ready for tea. The
Mistress said she was very glad to be at home again, it'd been such a hard
day for her. She said that as I carried umbrella over her from the front gate.
I carri'd the tea things up & all that & waited on them all they wanted,
& then a lot more came in & I wash'd up & took up fresh tea. Clean'd
away again & then laid the cloth for supper & cook'd the potatoes.
Carried the supper up & waited on them. Clean'd more knives & wash'd
plates. Clean'd away & laid the kitchen cloth for Mary & the
waiter & us all. Had supper. Put away & then I went to bed very tired
& in my dirt.

An extreme example? Not really. Liz Stanley, who edited Hannah's
diaries, suggests she may have been unusually conscientious, but
quotes the *Journal of Social History* to show that 'in the middle and late
Victorian period about a third of all females between fifteen and
twenty, and so about half of all working class females of that age, were
in service'. The experience, then, was far from being uncommon.

Long hours, far too many tasks with too little help... the comparison
could, obviously, be taken much too far, but the description could be
applied to an equally significant section of our own society—working
wives and mothers. This chapter should really be read in conjunction
with the one on marriage, where the 'Better to Marry than to Burn?'
section sees a group of women debating the problem (for problem it
seems to be). And though an undue proportion of the women there
seem to be writing at a time and from a class where servants took care of
many of the practical problems, later diaries giving the view from the
shop floor are hard to find. Lucy Gore's *Diary of a Working Mum*,
published in 1984, has a likely sounding title. But a freelance translator
with a teenage son didn't have to cope with the problems which faced
architect and mother of three Alison Smithson, one of the personal *and*
professional achievers—but not superwomen—interviewed by Valerie
Grove for her recent book *The Compleat Woman* (Chatto & Windus). In
1967 Alison Smithson kept a detailed diary for Rhona and Robert
Rapoport, sociologists who published an investigation into *Dual Career
Families*. It revealed, Valerie Grove writes:

How walking the baby to the shops could consume a large part of the morning, so that she is forever typing manuscripts into the night, or snatching time between children's homework to discuss a design with a colleague, or to produce children's party invitations, or to study the plans for the redevelopment of Stockholm....

Meal times were strictly regulated: lunch at 1 pm without fail. At weekends they would drive in their Citroen to Wiltshire and discuss their projects on route. Living-in students stayed at the Smithsons' in exchange for babysitting, and there was a daily housekeeper and a secretary who helped with shopping.

It sounds like the lifestyle of American sculptress Anne Truitt. 'If there were fifteen minutes between shopping and carpool, I used them,' she recalls in 1975:

24 January

I began working in sculpture in 1948. Married, I had to fit my own work into a schedule of shopping, cooking, housecleaning, entertaining, and—very often—moving from city to city. My first child was born in 1955, followed by two more in 1958 and 1960. By 1961, when all of a sudden my work took a quantum jump into a range I recognized as pre-emptive, demanding, undeniable, totally categorical for me, I had a large and complicated setup within which I had to operate.

My husband was an enterprising journalist, which in Washington means a lot of entertaining and being entertained—very time-consuming, and energy-consuming too. I was expected to enter into his life with commitment to his career. And, within the context of marriage as we had defined it without thinking too much about it, I felt I should do so. My husband and I were both hospitable. We had house guests continuously. Having been traditionally brought up, it did not occur to me to fight against this situation. I simply took it for granted that I had to fit what I wanted to do within it. My children were at that time six, three and one. Their care came first. Doctors' appointments, reading to them, rocking the baby to sleep, carpools—all that had to be done, and done as well as I could, before I could turn to myself....

Before I went to sleep, I loosely organized the following day's schedule—loosely because there were, of course, always unexpected events. But I tried to hold course in accordance with my values: first—husband, children, household; second—my work. The periods of time left over from my practical responsibilities were spent in the studio. If there were fifteen minutes between shopping and carpool, I used them. If I had an hour, or two hours, I rejoiced, but didn't waste time feeling happy, just worked.

Her counsel, in the end, is the demanding one of perfection. 'Doing my duty'—i.e. to her children—'as well as I can is essentially self-serving. It is only by attending to tasks and responsibilities as they arise that I can prevent myself from feeling angry that I cannot work in the studio as much as I want to....' Ouch.

A less detailed picture, but one broader in its implications, comes—oddly enough—from the reformer Elizabeth Fry more than 150 years before:

Tenth Month 15th, (1818)

My prison concerns truly flourishing: surely in that a blessing in a remarkable manner appears to attend me; more apparently, than in some of my house duties. Business pressed very hard upon me: the large family at Mildred's Court, so many to please there, and attend to—the various accounts—the dear children and their education—my husband poorly—the church—the poor—my poor infirm aunt whom I have undertaken to care for—my public business, and my numerous friends and correspondents.... I have felt helped, even He whom my soul loves has been near; but I have also had some perplexity and discouragement, thinking that some of those very dear, as well as others, are almost jealous over me, and ready to mistrust my various callings; and are open both to see my children's weaknesses, and almost to doubt the propriety of my many objects....'

If it's only 'almost' Fry was in a sense lucky—but the fascinating thing about her entry is that it makes one think how very slow opinions are to change. Even today, the idea that a working mother is a bad mother persists. Here are two extracts from Naomi Mitchison's diary, in the Second World War, to make the point:

Friday, 14th February 1941

...I asked what he (Jack W) thought of communal meals, he said he didn't hold with them, the only kind he wanted were big kitchens for a street, where women could go and cook; I said that wouldn't release the women. He said what for? to work in factories? I said to do all (or) anything they want to. He said if she has a nice home and a good wage and plenty to eat that's what a woman wants.... I said that it was possible for people to regard even their own families as respect-worthy individuals, not as objects of ownership. But of course it was no good. He just thinks I'm balmy, and that of course no real woman would believe any of that nonsense. He says of course if you'd ever been a working class wife.... Very odd, it's really this kind of thing that makes me furious. The common working class attitude, when the girls are expected to do the domestic chores, the women must even spend their evenings sewing and mending while the men have a paper or a game. It makes me feel murderous. And it can't be changed in a generation. Mrs W agrees with me, says Yorkshire men are all like that. They all really treat their women as dirt, they don't understand that you don't want to be cooking and washing all day.

If there is one point to be drawn from a look at women's diaries it is surely this one: there is nothing new under the sun. And here is Beatrice Webb unconsciously hammering the message home:

13th January 1891

Octavia Hill objected to my being asked to preside at a meeting because I tried to float myself and my work through my personal influence on men: and the same impression had reached Florence Nightingale.

Work ethics fit for the feminist late twentieth century—eighty years before their time!

Paper Tigers?

Situations *do* change, of course. Nella Last's rediscovery of herself through work in a canteen (see Chapter 6) was triggered by a world-wide upheaval, the Second World War, which performed the same service for many women. And (from the seventies) writer May Sarton is one optimistic voice cheering in the wilderness:

11th November

My father was theoretically a feminist, but when it came down to the nitty gritty of life he expected everything to be done for him, of course, by his wife. It was taken for granted that 'his work' must come before anything else. He was both a European bourgeois in upbringing and a man of the nineteenth century, so my mother didn't have a prayer. My father didn't like her to work and never gave her credit for it, even in some years when she was designing embroidered dresses for Belgart in Washington D.C., and made more money than he did. Her conflict—and it was acute—came from her deep belief in what he wanted to do and at the same time resentment of his attitude toward her and his total lack of understanding of what he asked of her. They simply could not discuss such matters. Here we have surely made enormous strides in my lifetime. Few young women today would not at least make a try at 'having it out' before marrying. Women are at last becoming persons first and wives second, and that is as it should be.

Her words open up another issue—the internal, as well as the external, battles women may have to fight before they can convince themselves, let alone their husband or boss, that their work is of importance. It is something that particularly applies to—or has been particularly well articulated by—women in the 'artistic' or intellectual fields. As the student Vera Brittain put it rather forcefully in 1915: 'Hard manual labour would be easier; truly my sort of work is difficult now, when so much of intellectual life seems at a standstill and the war cry drowns the purer voices of the upper air.'

Hidden in Sylvia Plath's tense lament is the tell-tale assumption that husband Ted Hughes' work is inevitably a greater priority:

Sunday morning, September 14 [1958]

Two weeks here have inexplicably withered away. Yesterday we both
bogged in a black depression—the late nights, listening sporadically to
Beethoven piano sonatas—ruining our mornings, the late afternoon sun too
bright and accusing for tired eyes, meals running all off schedule—and me
with my old panic fear sitting firm on my back—who am I? What shall I do?
The difficult time between twenty-five years of school routine and the fear of
dilatory, dilettante days. The city calls—experience and people call, and
must be shut out by a rule from within. Tomorrow, Monday, the schedule
must begin—regular meals, shopping, launderings—writing prose and
poems in the morning, studying German and French in the afternoon,
reading aloud an hour, reading in the evenings. Drawing and walking
excursions.... I must be happy first in my own work and struggle to that
end, so my life does not hang on Ted's. The novel would be best to begin this
next month. My *New Yorker* poems were a minor triumph. Who else in the
world could I live with and love? Nobody. I picked a hard way which has to
be all self-mapped out and must not nag [omission] ... (anything Ted
doesn't like: this is nagging); he, of course, can nag me about light meals,
straight-necks, writing exercises, from his superior seat. The famed and
fatal jealousy of professionals—luckily he is ahead of me so far I never need
fear the old superiority heel-grinding—in weak-neck impulse. Perhaps
fame will make him insufferable. I will work for its not doing so. Must work
and get out of paralysis—write and show him nothing: novel, stories and
poems.

Anne Truitt explores the reverse side of the same coin—what author
Colette Dowling wrote of as *The Cinderella Complex*: women's hidden fear
of independence:

28 March [1975]

... The fact leads me to the uncomfortable hypothesis that some part of me
wants me to fail, to reveal my anxiety, actually to wave it like a flag....

While driving through the palm trees on the way back from the beach in
Puerto Rico in January 1963, just a week or so before my first New York
exhibit was due to open, I had a moment of purest panic. I saw clearly that I
could have lain low, snug in my marriage and motherhood, and I most
profoundly wished that I had. No one would have faulted me. There would
not even have been much loss of face, as I had rarely let on that I was doing
anything beyond being a housewife. As I eased the car over the sandy ruts, I
thought to myself how pushy I had been in aiming to do anything more. It
seemed incredible to me that in a short while I would have to face the public
gaze. Every fiber shrank.

Anne Truitt's *Daybook*, a journal written over seven years, was kept
with the avowed purpose of coming to terms with the artist within
herself. An articulate lot, artists, and not only those whose trade is
words. Think of the pages that have been written on the difficulties of

Creation (with a capital C)—the agonies as well as the ecstasies. It is Virginia Woolf, with enough entries on or around work in her diaries to make the 300+ page compilation *A Writer's Diary*. It is Anaïs Nin, with discussions of her own writing sufficient in number and, goodness knows, in length, to make not one volume but several. It is Barbara Pym, more self-aware than most:

Sunday, 7th April 1940

Today I have been reading *Of No Importance*—Rom Landau's diary of February–October 1939. Many things in it I understand so well—the reluctance to sit down and begin writing so that one finds oneself doing all sorts of unnecessary tasks to postpone that moment of starting. And also the feeling that no day is really satisfactory if one hasn't done some sort of work—preferably a few pages of writing, but anyway something useful. Why is it that one is still surprised to discover that other people feel these things too?

And it is Katherine Mansfield in February 1916 urging herself to take up her pen: 'If only I have the courage to press against the stiff swollen gate, all that lies within mine; why do I linger for a moment?' Because she is idle, comes her own answer. Because she is locked into a love-hate relationship, comes the reader's. The month before, she had been lashing herself: 'Am I less of a writer than I used to be? Is the need to write less urgent? Does it still seem as natural to me to seek that form of expression?' Yes, is the answer. '... at bottom never has my desire been so ardent: ...'

22nd January 1916

Now—now I want to write recollections of my own country. Yes, I want to write about my own country till I simply exhaust my store. Not only because it is 'a sacred debt' that I pay to my country because my brother and I were born there, but also because in my thoughts I range with him over all the remembered places. I am never far away from them. I long to renew them in writing.

Ah, the people—the people we loved there—of them, too, I want to write. Another 'debt of love'. Oh, I want for one moment to make our undiscovered country leap into the eyes of the Old World. It must be mysterious, as though floating. It must take the breath. It must be 'one of those islands....' I shall tell everything, even of how the laundry basket squeaked at 75. But all must be told with a sense of mystery, a radiance, an afterglow, because you, my little sun of it, are set. You have dropped over the dazzling brim of the world. Now I must play my part.

Then I want to write poetry. I feel always trembling on the brink of poetry. The almond tree, the birds, the little wood where you are, the flowers you do not see, the open window out of which I lean and dream that you are against my shoulder, and the times that your photograph 'looks sad'. But especially I want to write a kind of long elegy to you ... perhaps not in poetry. Nor perhaps in prose. Almost certainly a kind of special prose.

And, lastly, I want to keep a kind of minute notebook, to be published some day. That's all. No novels, no problem stories, nothing that is not simple, open.

The love is there, passionate and demanding. It is only logical the hate should sometimes be there too. As the tuberculosis encroached on Mansfield's lungs, her desire to work was an enormous element in her desire to live.

What Toni Bentley writes of the ballet probably holds true for other artists as well:

21st November 1980

It's difficult, dancing, when the aim is to express beauty and joy, and the means to do it is work. The work must give the joy that must be the result. It's a vicious cycle. I think the joy misses out a lot.

The Best Narcotic

'Work,' wrote Beatrice Webb on 8 March 1885, 'is the best of narcotics, providing the patient be strong enough to take it.' It is impossible to write about work in women's diaries without repeated reference to her; almost impossible to contain the mass of material. Much of the later life work, engaged in with her husband, 'the socialist, Sidney Webb', was political in character but in those earliest, most fascinating years she did not seem to fit very happily into the 'political woman' bracket. So unhappily, in fact, that in 1889 she signed a notorious manifesto *against* the political enfranchisement of women—something she regretted almost immediately but did not publicly recant for almost twenty years. Her motives seem to have been 'dislike of the current Parliamentary politics', and a feeling that being a woman hadn't done her any harm ... 'Quite the contrary,' she wrote in *My Apprenticeship*, 'if I had been a man, self-respect, family pressure and the public opinion of my class would have pushed me into a money-making profession; as a mere woman I could carve out a career of disinterested research.' Not that the carving out of any career was a matter to be taken for granted:

15th September 1885

... Who would have thought it, we said constantly to one another, when we two as schoolgirls stood on the moorland near Bournemouth, watching the sunset and the trees against it, discussed our religious difficulties and gave vent to all our world-sorrow, and ended by prophesying we should in ten years be talking of cooks and baby linen, boys going to their first school and other matronly subjects, who would have thought of our real future? She, struggling for her livelihood with queer experiences of a working woman's life; of another with her cook and big establishment but also absorbed in work outside home duty; both passed through the misery of strong and useless feeling.... Who would have thought it! Will another ten years bring as great a change or have we settled down in the groove we are destined to run in?

The ambivalence about work continued. '... at times a working life is weary for a woman,' she wrote on 28 September 1886. 'The brain is worn and the heart unsatisfied, and in those intervals of exhaustion the old craving for love and devotion, given and taken, returns and an idealized life of love and sympathy passes before one's eyes.' Always the sense of either/or. That one could not have one's cake and eat it, that while certain women might reasonably demand (as she put it in a letter to her father) 'a masculine reward for masculine qualities', those qualities excluded then from the 'normal' life of women. Happily, she was to prove herself wrong.

Meanwhile, as she continued to take the 'narcotic' she had prescribed for herself against her long and fruitless passion for the radical politician Joseph Chamberlain, she had at least found the lines along which her work was to be directed—the 'accumulation of useful knowledge' towards an investigation into the life and condition of the poor. Her doubts did not die away—on 17 April 1889 she wryly quotes her 'old maid lodging-house keeper': 'See you are completely knocked up. You're only a woman: in spite of your *manly* brain, you're just as much of a woman as I am!' But they can't be taken without the other, direct proclamation: 'My work now utterly absorbs me...' and, incidentally, opens up to us the work of a very different class of woman.

In October 1888 Beatrice published *The Pages of a Workgirl's Diary*, the fruits of her own experience in passing herself off as a 'working', i.e. working-class girl, and taking employment as a seamstress in Stepney. It caused a sensation, not surprisingly, as much for Beatrice's initiative in undertaking such a project as for her vivid words. But they are colourful enough...

12th April 1888

Thursday morning I reappear at 198 Mile End Road. It is a long irregular-shaped room running backward from the retail shop to the kitchen. Two small tables by the gas jets (used for heating irons) serve for the two pressers. Then a long table with forms on either side and chairs at top and bottom, for the trouser finishers. Two other tables for machinists and vest hands and a high table for the trouser-basters complete the furniture of the room. It is barely 8.30 but the 30 girls are crowding in and taking their seats in front of their work and boxes on the tables. The 'missus' has not yet come down; the two pressers, English lads of about 22, saunter lazily into the room a little after the half-hour. The head woman calls for a pair of trousers and hands them to me. I look at them puzzled to know what to do; I have no materials wherewith to begin. The woman next to me explains: 'You will have to bring trimmings, but I'll lend you some to begin with.' 'What ought I to buy?' say I, feeling very helpless. At this moment the 'missus' bustles into the room. She is a big woman, enormously developed in the hips and legs, with strongly Jewish features and only one eye. Her hair is crisp and has been jet black; now in places it is quite grey. Her dress is stamped cotton velvet of a large flowery pattern; she has a heavy watch-chain, plentiful rings; and a spotlessly clean apron.

'Good morning to you,' she says good-temperedly to the whole assemblage. 'Esther, have you given that young person some work?'

'Yes,' replied Esther. '3½ trousers.'...

Sometimes the comments of the seamstress are obviously shocking—'Why bless you, that young woman just behind us has had three babies by her father, and another here has had one by her brother....' They also put a precise cash value on this finger-aching, back-breaking work: 'the trousers we are finishing for 3½ up to 5d are sold from 4s 6d up to 8s 6d....'

13th April 1888

I have my cup of tea. The pale weary girl is munching her bread and butter.

'Won't you have some?' she says, pushing the paper towards me.

'No, thank you,' I answer.

'Sure?' she says. And then, without more to-do, she lays a piece on my lap and turns away to avoid my thanks. A little bit of human kindness that goes to my heart and brings tears into my eyes. Work begins again. My friend has finished her trousers and is waiting for another pair. She covers her head with her hand and in her grey eyes there is an intense look of weariness, weariness of body and of mind. Another pair is handed to her and she begins again. She is a quick worker but, work as hard as she may, she cannot make much over a 1s a day, discounting trimmings. A shilling a day is about the price of unskilled woman's labour.

Another two hours and I say 'goodnight' to the mistress and leave this workshop and its inhabitants to work on its way day after day and to become to me only a memory...

'A nice-looking person like you ought to get married to a respectable man; you're more fit for that than to earn your living,' the 'shrewd Jewess' had said to her that afternoon. Loaded advice, indeed.

II: AT HOME

Early Accounts

The Diary of a Farmer's Wife 1796–97, which seemed to offer an unparalleled insight into the working life of a countrywoman in England before the Industrial Revolution, was proved five years ago to be a fake. But happily, there are other records, though not from quite the same strata of society, of whose authenticity there is no such doubt. Dorothy Wordsworth's *The Grasmere Journals*, for example, show an almost idyllic picture of the Good Life:

> *Saturday, 29th May, 1802*
>
> I made bread and a wee Rhubarb Tart and batter pudding for William. We sate in the orchard after dinner. Wiliam finished his poem on Going for Mary [published as *A Farewell*], I wrote it out. I wrote to Mary H., having received a letter from her in the evening. A sweet day. We nailed up the honeysuckle, and hoed the scarlet beans.

It may strike the feminist eye that while William is making poems Dorothy is rather often making giblet pie, but still.... The same mixture of culture and cultivation is to be seen in the lives of the Ladies of Llangollen. While Sarah Ponsonby kept the Receipt and Account Books (2nd July 1800 : Bread for the Harvest Supper 2s. To the Mother of the Boys whom we caught in our part of the Cufflymin, for Whipping them 1s.), Eleanor Butler kept the Journal:

> *Wednesday, 31st July, 1788*
>
> Gathered vegetables—pulled apples. Went to the Dressing-room— frizzing—powdering. The operation over read 'till twelve. Mr and Mrs Mytton arrived—brought Johnson's Letters published by Mrs Thrale now Mrs Lynch Piozzi. Went the Home circuit. Sprinkling rain.

A fairly random entry. But note—while the ladies may work in their own garden, or make repeated reference to the health of a favourite cow, there is no indication that they did much about scrubbing the garden produce or skimming the milk...

The diary of Lady Margaret Hoby two centuries earlier shows her similarly active in what you might call a managerial capacity. The diary entries for September 1599 include on various days: 'I took order for supper... did see my hunnie ordered... I wret some thinges touchinge Household matters... did order diverse thinges in the granirie.' She also 'dressed my patients'—stillroom or apothecary activities, of course, were standard for the county great lady. Mary Rich, Countess of Warwick, describes in 1668 offering palsy-balsam (and prayers!) for a poor woman's stroke.

Mary and Nancy Woodforde, respectively ancestress and niece/housekeeper to the famous diarist Parson Woodforde, kept journals which are a lot less domestic (as well as less interesting) than his own. And the diary of Abigail Gawthern, born in 1757, daughter of a superior grocer and wife of a manufacturer, makes little reference to household matters at all. This entry, which shows her in a trouble-shooting capacity (and a situation any home-owner wincingly recognizes) is an exception:

27th January 1795

> We were much alarmed by the water-closet cistern overflowing; it run down the wall of the staircase, the closet, the music room, and the kitchen; the waste pipe was froze (which) was the cause of it; the water was thrown out of the window; I had a waste pipe made for the waste water to go on Drury Hill so that the accident cannot happen again...

Socially, she must have been many steps below a Countess, or a Lady Hoby, an aristocratic Butler or Ponsonby. But the message is the same: until fairly recently *all* the diary-keeping classes could expect to have servants. And it is only the exceptional working-class day diary that has survived.

Servants

It is curiously apropos that Virginia Woolf's first diary, in 1915, should begin with a 'servant story'. A lady had written about a reference for a maid, who may or may not have been dismissed from her last place for what the Woolfs uncharitably assumed were 'the usual reasons', i.e. trouble with one of the game-keepers. It is apropos precisely because it is so unexpected. If 'the servant question' is at the forefront of Virginia Woolf's mind, one feels, who can be exempt? No one, perhaps.

Not that everyone feels the need to write about their household affairs, but the behind-scenes participants in those affairs do pervade some unexpected places.... They might have been expected to figure largely in the enclosed world of the Ladies of Llangollen, from the superior Mary, more friend than maid, who had assisted at their elopement, to a series of unsatisfactory men:

> ...told Richard we thought rolling four small Barrows full of gravel into the new kitchen garden was a very little morning's work. He gave us warning which (to his infinite surprise and evident regret) we immediately accepted, being determined never, while we retain our senses, to be imposed upon by a servant.

The world knows that Queen Victoria had a special friendship with John Brown, who figures particularly in the Highland journals; there was also a favoured Indian *munshi*. But isn't it a little surprising that those of her subjects who set out to brave a completely strange life in the still-wild colonies should take their preoccupations with them?

Not so surprising perhaps in the case of Anna Brownell Jameson. When she set sail in 1836 to join her husband in Upper Canada he was after all serving in Toronto as Attorney General. It was reasonable that they should employ a man-servant at eight dollars a month, a cook at six and a housemaid at four, and that 'the want of good servants'—most of those available being from 'the lower class of Irish emigrants'— should seem 'a serious evil'. But what of Anne Langton who, in 1837, plunged from a cultivated life in England into Canada's real pioneer territory? She and her mother had to acclimatize themselves to log walls with the wind whistling through instead of a well-hung Victorian parlour, to tallow dips and to having to act, for the first time, as their own butcher, baker, and even candlestick-maker (the making of tallow dips was Anne's special province). They could even stretch their limbs a little in new freedoms.

Tuesday, October 16th [1838]

How strangely one's ideas accommodate themselves to the ways and necessities of the country one is in! This summer, when our bustling household made a little help from the ladies often necessary, I used to be amused at myself going so composedly about my duties at the cooking stove, in full sight of Mr. Atthill, occupied in the joiner's shop. One would feel shocked at such observation in England.

Friday, March 20 [1840]

The details of today were anything but pleasant; the result, however, is very satisfactory. We got Sally Jordan to come and give her assistance, and we ladies were as busy as the servants, rubbing furniture, etc. Not, however, busier than we have been on a like occasion at Bootle. Here, indeed, we may make a comparison in favour of this much-abused country. You lose no respect by such exertions. In Mount Pleasant, where our establishment was very small, we used occasionally at busy times to make our beds. On one occasion a housemaid, receiving her dismissal, was inclined to retaliate by a little insolence and told us we were certainly no ladies, or we should not make beds. Here one of our domestics would be surprised, and perhaps think herself a little ill-used if, in any extra bustle, we should be sitting in our drawing-room. They are apt to think it quite right that we should be taking our due share, and are certainly our 'helps', though we do not call them so, as in the States. I cannot perceive that anything like disrespect is engendered by this relative position of mistress and maid.

Only so far, though. The servant problem, it would seem, is always with us ... 'The new girl will not do. I begin to think that those lead the easiest lives who keep no servant.' *Plus ça change*. Looking back over old letters from life in England recalls 'a tissue of domestic troubles' there. But sympathy is somewhat diminished when we realize that Kitty, the Langtons' mainstay in Canada, 'a capital scrubber, and so stout and strong that one did not feel a little hard-working occasionally would do her any harm', is only fourteen years old.

It is only occasionally that we realize how the difference between Them and Us was taken for granted. When you read of the advanced and reforming Vera Brittain, say, discovering her kitchenmaid has had a boyfriend to the house, you see clearly through her tolerance that the distinction of the green baize door is as alive to her as to her contemporaries. It is only occasionally that you realize how universal was help in the house: only when you read of the less privileged Nella Last having her own Gladys in one day a week. Vera Brittain was writing at the beginning of the 1930s, Nella Last in 1941... and it is hard not to feel that Nella, nearer to the kitchen floor herself, was by far the more human mistress!

Food

It was, of course, the Second World War which really saw the decline of the domestic servant in Britain. In diary terms, though, war and rationing served another domestic function—that of focusing everyone's mind on Food!

It took some time for restrictions to make their presence felt. Frances Partridge is still writing in May 1941 of 'delicious supper, asparagus, wine, chocolates' and, on the following day, 'home to a dream of a lunch—lamprey in a marvellous sauce, *foie gras* and champagne'. But by October 1942 she (like Anne Langton in different circumstances) has come face to face with the inside of a pig for the first time, 'pailfuls of strange marine-looking objects, pink and frilly, kept being carried into the larder. They seemed clean and not at all disgusting.' And with weekend visitors early in 1943, she writes:

> *February 19th*
> All through the weekend the stress was on Food—what we were going to eat next, or what a good meal we had just eaten, and I couldn't help feeling that sometimes too much attention is paid to this admittedly very important subject. However they went off saying they had never had such delicious *food*—so I hope they enjoyed themselves.

Rationing seems to have bitten different people at different times. In 1941 Naomi Mitchison (like Partridge, comparatively privileged as a country diarist) is anxiously totting up her resources:

Monday, 3 June 1940

Semple has started the ice-cream business; Val and I got some. They're as good as ever. Unfortunately all the rhubarb we'd been bottling is beginning to go. Everything seems to unless there is masses of sugar in it, which is so maddening. We have a certain amount of sugar saved, but of course it won't be easy after the present ration. The cut in butter will be no hardship, as nobody really knows the difference except me. I am trying to have cheese dishes etc, as much as possible. The meat isn't nearly as good as it used to be when Paterson killed and sold his own instead of having to take what he could get. We have bought about half a big jar full of eggs laid down in water-glass; I am getting smoked haddock once a week from Campbeltown which helps with that. The hens are not laying very well, and Eddie still hasn't cleaned out the hen house in the warren. Only I don't like to scold him too much when he's just going off. I have still a fair amount of last year's jam—or rather mostly jelly (red and white currant and gooseberry, all tasting exactly the same) but we use it fairly quickly between here and Mains. Few of us eat much sugar, but this week Jessie is making birthday cakes for both Lois and Murdoch. Have laid in some more soap, and coffee, which we can't get locally. Difficult to get Jessie to take the rationing seriously, though. She so enjoys cooking and longs for more material and more elaborate things to do! ...

But when it comes to wartime—or probably any other—cookery, Nella Last is queen:

Wednesday, 26th November, 1941

My bony mutton made a lovely casserole. I first fried it and then added onion, celery, carrot and turnip; I cooked it very slowly all morning by the dining-room fire, and added potatoes to it three quarters of an hour before lunch. On the other side of the fire, I had my big pan with the suet pudding in, and it was really one of the best puddings I've made for a long time. I minced the suet from the kidney I had bought with the meat, and also two slices of wholemeal bread and two strips of my candied peel, made by boiling orange peel till tender in a little honey and water. I added an egg beaten in hot water, to bring it up to the quantity of the two eggs that I used to use, and then a 5½d pot of sweetened bun flour and a tablespoon of sultanas. It made a very generous helping for the three of us, a helping for my husband to have tomorrow, and enough for a small portion each on Friday. The sauce was a problem—NO milk for it, not even a tiny drop, with so little being allowed. Finally, I made custard sauce with water, and added honey as a sweetener. I am trying to save my extra sugar to make marmalade after Christmas. At lunchtime my husband said, 'This is the nicest casserole we have had for a long time.' It had done so perfectly that there was no liquid—just tender, juicy vegetables and meat. When I served the pudding, I said carelessly, 'Oh, I've made clear honey sauce for a change'. I know that one, he doesn't like economy dishes—if he realises they are economy dodges! He said, 'By Gad, it's grand—and brings out the real flavour of the pudding.' Gladys and I laughed afterwards, but she said, 'If I'd not seen you make that pudding, I would never have believed it.'

The only better reading for a gourmet is her description of her sons' Saturday tea in schoolboy days—braised lambs' hearts 'with whole tiny onions and lots of hot toast' and a big dish of baked apples.

In the Secret Annexe where Anne Frank and her family were hiding, things were very different:

Monday, 3rd April, 1944

Dear Kitty,

Contrary to my usual custom, I will for once write more fully about the food because it has become a very difficult and important matter, not only here in the 'Secret Annexe' but in the whole of Holland, all Europe and even beyond.

In the twenty-one months that we've spent here we have been through a good many 'food cycles'—you'll understand what that means in a minute. When I talk of 'food cycles' I mean periods in which one has nothing else to eat but one particular dish or kind of vegetable. We had nothing but endive for a long time, day in, day out, endive with sand, endive without sand, stew with endive, boiled or *en casserole:* then it was spinach, and after that followed swedes, salsify, cucumbers, tomatoes, sauerkraut etc., etc.

For instance, it's really disagreeable to eat a lot of sauerkraut for lunch and supper every day, but you do it if you're hungry. However, we have the most delightful period of all now, because we don't get any fresh vegetables at all. Our weekly menu for supper consists of kidney beans, pea soup, potatoes with dumplings, potato-chalet and, by the grace of God, occasionally turnip-tops or rotten carrots, and then the kidney beans once again. We get potatoes at every meal, beginning with breakfast, because of the bread shortage. We make our soup from kidney or haricot beans, potatoes, Julienne soup in packets, French beans in packets, kidney beans in packets. Everything contains beans, not to mention the bread! . . .

'Our thoughts,' wrote Anne early in her Annexe confinement, 'go round and round like a roundabout—from Jesus to food and from food to politics.' That must be why there is a certain luxuriance about wartime writing on food. It is true that there is a link between the wartime housewife trying to extend the range of a limited diet and the American pioneer women (see Chapter 11 on Travel) seizing every chance to buy fish from the Indians or venture far enough from the wagon-train to pick berries. And, indeed, on to every shopper in the supermarket who cannot think what to buy for that night's meal. But there is another chain stretching forwards and backwards from the wartime writer. On to novelist Barbara Pym and the perpetual brief mentions of meals enjoyed—as well as the appropriateness of a food to a

character!— which show it is far from an indifferent matter to her. Back
to Katherine Mansfield in France, 1920:

> We bought figs for breakfast, immense thin skinned ones. They broke in
> one's fingers and tasted of wine and honey. Why is the northern fig such a
> chaste fair-haired virgin, such a *soprano?* The melting contraltos sing
> through the ages.

Or to Liane de Pougy in 1931:

> *September 20*
> So I had been invited to aioli. There were two kinds, one with lemon, the
> other without. In addition: a huge dish of cod, several dozen hard-boiled
> eggs, octopus stewed in wine, a multitude of snails, lots of bowls of fat
> winkles, a mountain of potatoes and carrots, beetroots, chick-peas, green
> beans, etc. More than a dozen dishes of aioli! A vast green melon as sweet as
> honey, an ice from Philippe, the best cake-shop, and champagne to follow
> the Clos Mayol wine and complete my tipsiness. The last beautiful grapes
> from the stripped vines, blue figs—their skin splitting as though
> wounded—peaches, pears, delicious coffee. 'A liqueur?' suggested Mayol.
> 'I have a little Marc which is not to be sniffed at.'—'Stop, stop!' I cried. 'I
> couldn't manage another mouthful.'

It is the kind of writing that makes you realize why descriptive cook
books are so popular. And that convinces you a cook's lot cannot be a
wholly unhappy one.

Chapter 9
– War

I: IN ANOTHER COUNTRY

In our own day, when women and the women's movement have become particularly associated with the issues of war and therefore of peace, it is easy to assume that they must always have had a lot to say about it. Not so—and for a reason that is sufficiently obvious when once you have thought about it. In England (not invaded since 1066, remember) until the arrival of the aeroplane, war was something that happened Somewhere Else. It was important news, of course—but it did not affect you personally, unless you had a lover or a brother who had gone to the fight. A brief entry from the journal of the thirteen-year-old who became Lady Frederick Cavendish, scion of a Victorian political family, unconsciously sums it up:

September 19th 1855

Oh, what a wretch I am! If I haven't forgotten to put in the grand news!! SEBASTOPOL HAS FALLEN! Yes, thank God, at last He has sent his much-prayed-for blessing.

Or as Beatrice Webb put it:

Kate Courtney remarked the other day that she always wondered, in reading the published diaries of confidential writings of private persons, why they seemed so little concerned with the great questions of peace and war—so infinitely more important than their own little doings or narrow range of interests, solemnly recorded in their diaries. And I bethought me that there is hardly a reference to the Russo-Japanese war in these pages. The answer I gave on the spur of the moment, is, I think, the true one—'The private person has no specialist knowledge, no particular or exceptional experience as to world politics. His thoughts and feelings would be a mere reflection of his morning newspaper and worthless both to him and to those who might some day read the story of his life.' And yet if one looks back on the past year and thinks how much one has brooded over the Far Eastern drama, how eagerly one has read each morning's news, how one has stumbled into foreshadowing the effect of the 'Rising Sun' on our western civilization, it is hardly fair to leave it unnoticed.

I take leave to doubt whether the answer she gives is true for everyone, but the question is as incapable of final answer as that old A-Level chestnut of English Literature students: Why does Jane Austen never mention the Napoleonic wars or the Battle of Waterloo? Either way, that state of affairs was drawing to its close.

The conflict about which Lady Frederick was writing was the Crimean War, which saw Florence Nightingale lead her band of nurses abroad. As Beatrice Webb wrote in 1904, the war was approaching that would not only see bombs fall on England, but see numbers of women diarists engage in war-work at home and abroad. With the First World War, the voices of women diarists rise from an occasional murmur to a chorus, albeit rather a ragged one. It is only with the Second World War that the chorus swells to a cacophany, and that it becomes impossible for any diary—sometimes any entry—written during those six years to be mistaken for anything written in time of peace.

From the journals of the Second World War, therefore, much has had to be left out. (As, on another tack, have several diaries from the American Civil War). With one exception, I have restricted this chapter to English writers, though that leaves out Anne Frank and Etty Hillesum, both watching events from the perspective of a Jew in a Nazi-controlled land. The exception is Marguerite Duras whose diary, reproduced in her book *La Douleur*, shows her waiting as so many other women all over the world must have done:

April

Opposite the fireplace and beside me, the telephone. To the right, the sitting-room door and the passage. At the end of the passage, the front door. He might come straight here and ring at the front door. 'Who's there?'

'Me.' Or he might phone from a transit center as soon as he got here. 'I'm back—I'm at the Lutetia to go through the formalities.' There wouldn't be any warning. He'd phone. He'd arrive. Such things are possible. He's coming back, anyway. He's not a special case. There's no particular reason why he shouldn't come back. There's no reason why he should. But it's possible. He'd ring. 'Who's there?' 'Me.' Lots of other things like this do happen. In the end they broke through at Avranches and in the end the Germans withdrew. In the end I survived till the end of the war. I must be careful; it wouldn't be so very extraordinary if he did come back—it would be normal. I must be careful not to turn it into something extraordinary. The extraordinary is unexpected. I must be sensible: I'm waiting for Robert L., expecting him, and he's coming back.

He came back from Dachau, a living skeleton—but he did come back.

Honourable Exceptions

They say that there are exceptions to every rule—but then, it was never meant to be a rule in the first place that the English weren't involved in war until this century. Some were—even to the extent of campaigning with the army abroad or sailing with the navy. Jane Austen's novels may not talk about Waterloo but the ladies who went with a large section of British Society to Brussels did. Irritatingly, like Fanny Burney, they seem to have done honour to the importance of the event by writing it up in formal style for their journals long afterwards, which is why, as a memento of the Napoleonic Wars, I prefer the account of Betsey Wynne (or Betsey Fremantle as she was then), whose husband sailed under Nelson:

Tuesday, July 25th 1797

The troops landed at two o'clock this morning. There was much firing in the Town, but from the ships it seemed as if the English had made themselves masters of it. Great was our mistake, this proved to be a shocking, unfortunate night. Fremantle returned at 4 this morning wounded in the arm, he was shot through the right arm the moment he had landed, came off in the first boat and stayed on board the *Zealous* till daylight, where his wound was dressed. Thank God as the ball only went through the flesh he will not lose his arm he managed it so well that I was not frightened, but I was not a little distressed and miserable when I heard what it was, and indeed he was in great pain and suffered cruelly all day but it was fortunate that he did get wounded at first, God knows if ever I should have seen him again had he stayed on shore. It was dreadful, poor Captain Bowen killed on the spot, The Admiral was wounded as he was getting out of the Boat and most unfortunately lost his arm. . . .

This is the most melancholy event. I can't help thinking of poor Captain Bowen's losing his life just at the end of a war in which he had been so fortunate. At the moment he was continually talking of the happy life he should lead when he returned home. His first lieutenant was likewise killed.

Fremantle was in great pain all day but I hope he will soon get well. All the ships were obliged to get underweigh this morning as the Spaniards fired at us and the shot went over us. A shot went through one of our sails, I would not go into the Cockpit tho Fleming asked me twice to go.

In a later war [the Crimean], it looks as though Mrs Henry Duberly (the wife of an officer) must have touched up her eye-witness account of the Charge of the Light Brigade with a little hindsight, but there is still the ring of authentic, unimproved experience about the beginning and ending of that day:

Wednesday 25th 1854

Feeling very far from well, I decided on remaining quietly on board ship today; but on looking through my stern cabin windows, at eight o'clock, I saw my horse saddled and waiting on the beach, in charge of our soldier-servant on the pony. A note was put into my hands from Henry, a moment after. It ran thus: 'The battle of Balaklava [Balaclava] has begun, and promises to be a hot one. I send you the horse. Lose no time, but come up as quickly as you can: do not wait for breakfast.'

Words full of meaning! I dressed in all haste, went ashore without delay, and, mounting my horse 'Bob,' started as fast as the narrow and crowded streets would permit. I was hardly clear of the town, before I met a commissariat officer, who told me that the Turks had abandoned all their batteries, and were running towards the town. He begged me to keep as much to the left as possible, and, of all things, to lose no time in getting amongst our own men, as the Russian force was pouring on us; adding, 'For God's sake, ride fast, or you may not reach the camp alive'. Captain Howard, whom I met a moment after, assured me that I might proceed; but added, 'lose no time'.

The 93rd and 42nd were drawn up on an eminence before the village of Balaklava. Our Cavalry were all retiring when I arrived, to take up a position in rear of their own lines.

Looking on the crest of the nearest hill, I saw it covered with running Turks, pursued by mounted Cossacks, who were all making straight for where I stood, superintending the striking of our tent and the packing of our valuables. Henry flung me on the old horse; and seizing a pair of laden saddle-bags, a great coat, and a few other loose packages, I made the best of my way over a ditch into a vineyard, and awaited the event. For a moment I lost sight of our pony, 'Whisker', who was being loaded; but Henry joined me just in time to ride a little to the left, to get clear of the shots, which now began to fly towards us. Presently came the Russian Cavalry charging, over the hillside and across the valley, right against the little line of Highlanders.

Ah, what a moment! Charging and surging onward, what could that little wall of men do against such numbers and such speed? There they stood. Sir Colin did not even form them into square. They waited until the horsemen were within range, and then poured a volley which for a moment hid everything in smoke.

The Scots Greys and Inniskillens then left the ranks of our Cavalry, and charged with all their weight and force upon them, cutting and hewing right and left.

A few minutes—moments as it seemed to me—and all that occupied that lately crowded spot were men and horses, lying strewn upon the ground. One poor horse galloped up to where we stood; a round shot had taken him in the haunch, and a gaping wound it made. Another, struck by a shell in the nostrils, staggered feebly up to 'Bob', suffocating from inability to breathe. He soon fell down. About this time reinforcements of Infantry, French Cavalry, and Infantry and Artillery, came down from the front, and proceeded to form in the valley on the other side of the hill over which the Russian Cavalry had come.

Now came the disaster of the day—our glorious and fatal charge. But so sick at heart am I that I can barely write of it even now. It has become a matter of world-history, deeply as at the time it was involved in mystery. I only know that I saw Captain Nolan galloping; that presently the Light Brigade, leaving their position, advanced by themselves, although in the face of the whole Russian force, and under a fire that seemed pouring from all sides, as though every bush was a musket, every stone in the hill-side a gun. Faster and faster they rode. How we watched them! They are out of sight; but presently come a few horsemen, staggling, galloping back. 'What can those skirmishers be doing? See, they form up together again. Good God! it is the Light Brigade!'

At five o'clock that evening Henry and I turned, and rode up to where these men had formed up in the rear.

I rode up trembling, for now the excitement was over. My nerves began to shake, and I had been, although almost unconsciously, very ill myself all day. Past the scene of the morning we rode slowly; round us were dead and dying horses, numberless; and near me lay a Russian soldier, very still, upon his face. In a vineyard a little to my right a Turkish soldier was also stretched out dead. The horses, mostly dead, were all unsaddled, and the attitudes of some betokened extreme pain. One poor cream-colour, with a bullet through his flank, lay dying, so patiently!

Colonel Shewell came up to me, looking flushed, and conscious of having fought like a brave and gallant soldier, and of having earned his laurels well. Many had a sad tale to tell. All had been struck with the exception of Colonel Shewell, either themselves or their horses. Poor Lord Fitzgibbon was dead. Of Captain Lockwood no tidings had been heard; none had seen him fall, and none had seen him since the action. Mr Clutterbuck was wounded in the foot; Mr Seager in the hand. Captain Tomkinson's horse had been shot under him; Major De Salis's horse wounded. Mr Mussenden showed me a grape-shot which had 'killed my poor mare'. Mr Clowes was a prisoner. Poor Captain Goad, of the 13th, is dead. Ah, what a catalogue!

And then the wounded soldiers crawling to the hills! One French soldier, of the Chasseurs d'Afrique, wounded slightly in the temple, but whose face was crimson with blood, which had dripped from his head to his shoulder, and splashed over his white horse's quarters, was regardless of pain, but rode to find a medical officer for two of his 'camarades', one shot through the arm, the other through the thigh.

Evening was closing in. I was faint and weary, so we turned our horses, and rode slowly to Balaklava. We passed Mr. Prendergast of the Scot's Greys, riding down to the harbour, wounded in the foot; the pluck with which an Englishman puts pain out of the question is as wonderful as it is admirable. Time would fail me to enumerate even the names of those whose gallantry reached my ears. Captain Morris, Captain Maude, both cut and shot to pieces, and who have earned for themselves an imperishable name!

What a lurid night I passed. Overcome with bodily pain and fatigue I slept, but even my closed eyelids were filled with the ruddy glare of blood.

Mrs Henry—Fanny—Duberly was an exception to a good many rules. In a lifetime of campaigning she stuck so closely to her officer husband that there was some ill-feeling (on her own part, at least) that she failed to get the Crimean service medal. Hers is one of those diary entries which prove women are not always exempt from what is credited as being the masculine pleasure in war:

> The impulse to accompany the cavalry was irresistible and I never shall forget the throbbing excitement of that gallop, when the horse beneath me, raging in fierce strength, mad with excitement, scarcely touched the ground. . . . We halted beyond the enemy cantonment, and underneath the grim walls of the fort.

It may not be such an uncommon excitement, either, as she seems to have recognized herself. Fanny was by this time campaigning in India, where she was taken to the women's quarters belonging to a native prince:

> One thing struck me: when in conversation with the ranee, she asked rather eagerly if I had ever been actually present at a battle. On being answered in the affirmative, she fell back in her chair and sighed. A whole lifetime of suppressed emotion seemed to be comprehended in that short sigh!

The 'War to End All Wars'—the First World War

A time was shortly coming when women's involvement in war would cease to be a matter for such comment. Women were working on the

Continent, running *cantines,* like Agnes M. Dixon ('ten times have I been up and down that platform today in this terrific heat! Miss Wilkinson and I both think we shall see it forever in our nightmares. I am *sure* it is worse than trenches!') or nursing, like the Viscountess d'Abernon:

August 31st, 1917

Today, when compassion had grown cold, and I began to feel as mechanical and metallic as the patched-up pump in our back yard an unexpected incident galvanized me once more into activity.

From out of a camion, closely packed with lightly wounded, a tall gaunt figure was led like a child into our shed. In spite of helplessness there was about him the indefinable air of a leader. The head was closely bandaged and the upper part of face concealed. On the field-card attached to his shoulder was written 'Complete lesion of both eyes'. Of our little group, I alone was on duty, and therefore able to lead him to a relatively quiet corner of the shed; the one in which we keep our stores, and where we have one chair and a table. He asked for black coffee, soap (an unprecedented request) and later for a post card. He explained that he wished to write a few words to his wife himself, fearing that news written in a strange hand would alarm her. It is not often that one sees tragic misfortune borne with self-forgetfulness in the first hours of shock and pain, and my whole heart went out to him in compassion and wonder. Nor did his blindness dull the swift understanding and confidence that passed like a live wire between us and lasted all the hours he was in camp. In spite of pain and loss of sight, he insisted on writing something on the post card himself. What he wrote was indecipherable and without saying anything I was about to supplement a few words of my own so as to make the message intelligible, when a rough soldier blurted out, 'No one can read that.' These unlucky words broke down his self control.

Some of those who were away from their own land when war struck didn't plan to be there, of course. Like Lady Harriet Jephson who was in Germany when it broke out:

August 9th 1914

No papers! No news! No letters! No money! All of us are more or less packed up ready to start. We are warned that no heavy luggage can go with us, and are limited to two small 'hand Gepack', which we can carry ourselves. I have presented my best hats to Kathchen, and it consoles me to think how comical she will look under them!—but 'flying canvas' is the order of the day.

Or, more poignantly, like English-born Daisy, Princess of Pless, who spent the war in her husband's land, her sons fighting against her native countrymen. In the long years of her marrige, of course, her roots in the Kaiser's empire had struck deep—but sometimes, as on this visit to a hospital near Caudry, her diary shows that she did not, could not, forget:

> Now I am just back. A charming old Oberleutnant came with us, a middle-aged man, who gave me a book of the Hospital and who took me round to see everything. He let me speak to the Englishman although it was all in a hurry, as our Head Doctor who accompanied us thought only of his stomach and wanted to get back for luncheon! But I had just time to slip into the hand of an officer called Major Craig a piece of paper quite small, which I had pinned ready into my blouse and on which I had written how I would give all the world to be lying ill amongst them, that I was a sister of the Duchess of Westminster, and that my heart was with them all and I wished them a quick return to health. He was sensible enough to take the paper, doubled up like a pill, and not open it. I only pray God he will keep it a secret and not show it to a soul, otherwise they will say the most devilish things against me because I wrote a kind word to a wounded Englishman. I should be shut up in Germany.
>
> The guns are booming; now they have announced that infernal lunch, so I must go and eat, but I do not wish to do so; and I must smile and say how marvellous that Hospital was; and no one knows what I felt—and wrote—and did—or of the little bit of paper I gave to Major Craig.

You could say hers was a peculiarly female situation. But that is true—and how much more often it happened—of every woman who had to watch and wait. Mary King Waddington (Madame Waddington) saw a troop train leaving in France:

> A pretty girl was saying good-bye to her soldier and crying. She was instantly taken to task by one of his comrades on our train. 'Voyons, petite, du courage; ne pleure pas; nous reviendrons!' She looked up at me through her tears, saying: 'Tous ne reviendront pas, Madame.' And that is what we all are saying in these awful days. Who will be missing at the final roll-call?

In England, of course, Vera Brittain was watching her Roland go off:

> *Friday, March 19th, 1915*
> I told him my peace of mind was gone from now until the end of the war; he said he could not be sorry that I cared, but he did want me to approve of his going. I told him I could not pretend to be glad, that I was no heroine who could pour forth set injunctions to do deeds of daring, or wear company manners because he was going to the front. Instead of this I was only a weak imperfect being, whose only interest in the war was through individuals concerned in it, and who, since his going to the front had become certain, had begun to pray again without believing in it much, just in case it did any good.

'I feel,' she continued:

Like one standing at the entrance of the Promised Land—or like one who has been permitted to gaze upon it from the mountain tops without being allowed to enter. Sometimes I have wished I had never met him—wished that he had not come to take away my impersonal attitude towards the war, and make it a cause of personal suffering to me as it is to thousands of others.

She never would enter it with Roland—he was, as anyone who has ever read her writing knows, one of those who would *not* return. (See Chapter 14 on Living and Dying). But meanwhile, there was running alongside her own life at Oxford, the life she led through his letters:

1915

He tells me that he has received my second letter, and that this one to me will have been carried under fire by the time it reaches me.

All these accounts of danger I can stand—with an aching apprehensive heart it is true, but all the time I feel I would rather know. But my courage gave way a little when he ended 'Do not worry on my account. Goodnight and much love. I have just been kissing your photograph.' My eyes filled with the most stinging tears, although I bit my lip to try and keep them back. Sometimes I think it is less the thought of his danger than the ardent desire for his presence which makes me so sorrowful, and when he writes such things as this—and he has never admitted so much before—I want him terribly badly, and the thought of what it may be if he returns, but is so likely never to be, is almost more than I can bear. At such moments I feel as if I were shut in a trap from which there is no escape, and that I am vainly beating my hands against the walls—a kind of fierce desperation, which renders me incapable of doing anything but feeling acutely conscious of inward suffering. Well, I asked for the big things of life and now I am up against them....

I had another violent fit of desperation this morning. I suppose I must get used to them, but they alarm me a little and make me wonder what I may do if Roland dies. At present my one desire in life is to see him. I think of how little there is of any tendency for the war to end, of how he is in the trenches day in and day out in momently danger, of the long long weary months ahead, and wonder how I shall ever bear them and get through them without any light, anything to look forward to, to carry me along. O glorious time of youth indeed! This is the part of my life when I ought to be living every moment to the full, tasting the sweetness of every joy, full of love and life and aspiration and hope, exulting in my own existence. Instead, I can only think how weary are the heavy hours, wonder how I can get through their aching suspense, wonder when they will end—and how.

'Don't mind describing the "horrors",' she wrote back to him—'women are no longer the sheltered darlings of men's playtime fit only for the nursery or the drawing-room.' All the same, she notes, as he tells her of the 'charnel house trenches' and the shooting of sentries who sleep on duty:

...no man can quite understand what it means to a woman, who know the trouble and pain the production of an individual costs, to hear of this light destruction of a human creature....

Not only through Roland's 'horrors' but through her own work in a hospital, destruction was something Vera Brittain got to know about. But it takes another diarist to remind us that this still didn't blot out the horizons all round. Virginia Woolf's brother-in-law was wounded in the fighting: she writes of him with kindness but without heat. Her diary for 1917, when she began to keep one regularly, makes comparatively little mention of the war at all. Towards the end of it she began to suffer from the air raids, but an extract, from January 1918, is a fair sample of her tone.... 'I don't know how much is fear, how much boredom; but the result is uncomfortable, most of all, I believe, because one must talk bold and jocular small-talk for four hours with the servants to ward off hysteria.' But then, look how she began her diary for 1918:

Friday, 4 January, 1918

There's no reason after all why one should expect special events for the first page of a new book; still one does: and so I may count three facts of different importance; our first use of the 17 Club; talk of peace; and the breaking of my tortoiseshell spectacles. This talk of peace (after all the most important of the three)....

II: AT HOME

The Second World War

However patchy or otherwise was the initial impact of the first 'war to end all wars', the second cast its shadow before it. Virtually all the diaries of the late 1930s seem to show the kind of consciousness Virginia Woolf reflects:

Monday, September 5th, 1938

It's odd to be sitting here, looking up little facts about Roger and the M.M. in New York, with a sparrow tapping on my roof this fine September morning when it may be 3rd August, 1914...What would war mean? Darkness, strain: I suppose conceivably death. Well, I can't spread my mind wide enough to take it in, intelligibly. If it were real, one could make something of it. But as it is, it merely grumbles, in an inarticulate way, behind reality. We may hear his mad voice vociferating tonight. Nuremberg rally begun: but it goes on for another week. And what will be happening this time ten days? Suppose we skim across, still at any moment an accident may suddenly bring out the uproar. But this time everyone's agog. That the difference. And as we're all equally in the dark we can't cluster and group: we are beginning to feel the herd impulse: everyone asks everyone Any news? What d'you think? The only answer is Wait and see.

Almost a year later: the enervating suspense is still a present factor in the diaries. But it is drawing to what must almost have been a merciful close:

Thursday, August 24th, 1939

Perhaps it is more interesting to describe 'the crisis' than R.'s love affairs. Yes we are in the very thick of it. Are we at war? At one I'm going to listen in.... But as a dress rehearsal it's complete. Museums shut. Searchlight on Rodmell Hill. Chamberlain says danger imminent. The Russian pact a disagreeable and unforeseen surprise. Rather like a herd of sheep we are. No enthusiasm. Patient bewilderment. I suspect some desire 'to get on with it'. Order double supplies and some coal. Aunt Violet in refuge at Charleston. Unreal. Whiffs of despair... One touch on the switch and we shall be at war.

Here is Naomi Mitchison waiting for the news to strike:

3rd September 1939

I listened to the 9 o'clock news, realizing fairly clearly what the next was to be. The others were mostly not down, but I had not slept well. Valentine went off to Mains to look after the Glasgow children; Dick and I discussed what was to be done about the education of Avrion and Valentine; the latter can go to school here for a term, but the former would learn nothing.

The maids hadn't wanted to come through; I told Annie, who was wonderfully cheerful and said she remembered the Boer War, and Bella who said Isn't that heartbreaking. After a bit she began to cry, a saucepan in her hands, said Think of all our men going, then to me, Of course you've got boys too. Dick said Think of the women in Germany all saying that too, but there was no response. Then she asked When will they send our men over? But none of us had much idea.

In the drawing room the big boys were writing and reading; I think perhaps writing poetry. I was feeling sick, and so were Stewart and Hank and I went over to Mains, but the teachers had just left—we followed them. Valentine had brought the Glasgow children over; they were talking happily but looked very white and thin and small. The village was empty; most people at church. It began to rain hard and we took shelter at the Galbraiths. Young Dick (Galbraith, one of the Carradale fishermen) said So it's come...

I'm a self-reliant kind of person, but today I've longed for a close woman friend—for the first time in my life. When I heard Mr Chamberlain's voice, so slow and solemn, I seemed to see Southsea Prom from the July before the last crisis. The Fleet came into Portsmouth from Weymouth and there were hundreds of extra ratings walking up and down. There was a sameness about them that was not due to their clothes alone, and it puzzled me. It was the look on their faces—a slightly brooding, faraway look. They all had it—even the jolly looking boys—and I felt I wanted to rush up and ask them what they could see that I could not. And now I know.

The wind got up and brought rain, but on the Walney shore men and boys worked filling sand-bags. I could tell by the dazed look on many faces that I had not been alone in my belief that 'something' would turn up to prevent war. The boys brought a friend in and insisted on my joining in a game, but I could not keep it up. I've tried deep breathing, relaxing, knitting and more aspirins than I can remember, but all I can see are those boys with their look of 'beyond'.

My younger boy will go in just over a week. His friend who has no mother and is like another son will go soon—he is twenty-six. My elder boy works in Manchester. As a tax inspector he is at present in a 'reserved occupation'.

The War was on—official. And for every one of the countless diarists who described it, it was to take a different form. Daily life went on, moulded to a new shape by the pressures all around but none the less engrossing for that. (Entries relevant to the Second World War can be found in other chapters too.)

Like Naomi Mitchison, Joan Wyndham, in London, also mentions feeling sick—it must have been a common enough reaction!—but seems to take things with something of the lightness of her sixteen years:

Sunday, 3rd September

This morning war was declared by the Prime Minister over the radio. Five minutes after the National Anthem, while we were still sitting around feeling rather sick, the air-raid warning went. For a moment we didn't believe our ears—we hadn't had time even to realize we were at war—then we went down to our gas room and began damping the blankets with pails of water.

When the room was ready we went and sat on the front doorstep waiting for the first gun. The balloon barrage looked too lovely in the sun against the blue sky, like iridescent silver fish swimming in blue water. After a bit the all-clear sounded. We heard afterwards that it had all been a mistake.

Nella Last records a measure of incredulity—but as the mother of sons of fighting age, it is no wonder that her thoughts turn to 'boys':

Sunday, 3rd September 1939
Bedtime

Well, we know the worst. Whether it was a kind of incredulous stubbornness or a faith in my old astrological friend who was right in the last crisis when he said 'No war', I never thought it would come. Looking back I think it was akin to a belief in a fairy's wand which was going to be waved.

Immediately after that announcement on 3rd September, certain special preoccupations began to make themselves felt. For Nella Last, as for another housewife, Clara Milburn, it was the question of evacuees—but her work merged with her personal preoccupations:

Wednesday, 6th September 1939

Today I was in the company of several women of my own age, and we talked of the beginning weeks of the last war—of the mad stampede of boys and men to rush to the Shipyard and get under 'Vickers Umbrella', making them indispensable on munitions so they wouldn't be called up. There is so little of that now that it is not heard of. Instead, there seems a kind of resignation—a 'Well, I'll get my turn I suppose', and a look on the faces of the lads who have joined the Territorials and Militia that was not there this time last week.

I looked at my own lad sitting with a paper, and noticed he did not turn a page often. It all came back with a rush—the boys who set off so gaily and lightly and did not come back—and I could have screamed aloud. I have laughed to myself sometimes, thinking what a surprise—shock too—my rather spoilt lad was to get, but it's not funny now. He has such a love of order and beauty, not to say cleanness, and I remember stories they used to tell of the last war, of the dirt and mud in France.

Talking of dirt, the country and village people have had the shock of their lives with the sample of children and mothers who have been billeted on them from Manchester and Salford. One little boy of eight, after assuring a woman that the dirt 'would not come off' his legs and neck, was forcibly bathed with hot water and carbolic and said balefully, 'Cor! I don't 'alf feel funny!' There is a run on Keating's and disinfectant and soap while children who arrived with a crop of curls look like shorn lambs—but have stopped scratching!

Clara Milburn was also concerned 'with the evacuee question': she was also a mother. Here she is wishing her son Alan goodbye:

Friday, 5th January

The last time we'd hear Alan's voice for who knew how long. That day we went to see The Corn Is Green, which we did not care for, and when the theatre orchestra played 'Wish Me Luck As You Wave Me Goodbye', I found myself saying out loud: 'Oh no, not that' and wishing I could bury my head somewhere and weep. However such feelings had to be severely repressed . . . All the evening went by and our spirits dropped lower and lower, till at last bedtime came and we went sadly upstairs. Then at 10.45 pm the telephone rang and, as I arrived breathless, a voice said: 'This is Alan.' He told us he was going early the next morning, and after the first six 'pips' we had a second call. Then I said: 'Well here's your father' and stood by wishing I could hear what he was saying, till Jack said: 'Well, goodbye old man—good luck!' And so I never really said my farewell, as he had rung off.

Nella Last was the luckier: in a few months Alan was missing. When news arrived that he was a prisoner, the first reaction was relief—'My darling dear, you are alive!'—but long term, it was a situation that couldn't but damp the strongest spirits:

Sunday, 6th October 1940

I wrote the 21st letter to Alan today, and just for a few moments this evening black depression flooded over me. This separation, for such a cause, and the prospect of a long war and consequent long separation, and not knowing where he is and what is happening to him, simply engulfed me. And the stifling, choking feeling of not being able to do anything. Oh, dear, it was dreadful! But 'Lift up your hearts' was said at church today and we replied: 'We lift them up unto the Lord'.

In general terms 'lift up your hearts'—or 'chin up' might be a different way of phrasing it—is Mrs Milburn's tone. Mrs Miniver, she might be called....'After a night in the Bunkhole, where we three slept soundly, I got up in time for church at 8.45....' 'Another good sleep in the Bunkhole....' Nella Last is more expressive:

Monday, 2nd September 1949

We are going to bed after the news at 9.30, to try and get some sleep before the planes or air-raid warnings come. I've averaged only three hours' sleep all week. I seem to be lying fully awake at 11.30, straining my ears for the sound of the planes. When they come they circle round and round and round over the fells and countryside, looking for us—like a dog trying to pick up a scent. I lie tense and still, expecting to hear the crash of bombs. When they have gone I still listen, listen; and if I doze, wake with a start and feeling of WHAT'S THAT? I don't want to start taking a lot of aspirin, and have tried chewing gum and a glucose sweet, breathing deep and counting. I think tonight I'll put cotton wool in my ears. Anything is worth trying.

One factor one tends to forget at this distance of time, when thinking about the bombing, is the difference location made. Barbara Pym didn't see much of it:

Put in some hyacinth bulbs. Reading a biography of Caroline Brunswick. *Band Waggon*. This is a war diary but this seems to be our life.

Neither did Naomi Mitchison in Kintyre:

5th September 1940

Most people who write from the south are well into the battle, doing things, and comparing notes about raids. Nobody seems much frightened...

Frances Partridge in the southern countryside starts out by feeling cut off from the worst of it. Of a visitor:

For someone living in the Blitz, who finds herself among four country-dwellers, Hester's tone was perfect. She discussed how to keep rabbits as if it were the most important thing in the world, but when she did start on her shelter stories they were fascinating.

But soon, it comes to her:

February 11th 1943

As I stood bung-eyed at the stove, over the breakfast frying-pan in came Wilde for the chicken pail and burst out, 'Newbury was bombed yesterday'. 'No! Was there much damage? Anyone killed?' 'Yes, quite a few. A school and a church were hit.' It turned out to be exactly true, and some eighteen people were killed. If this had happened earlier in the war people would have stopped sending their children in to school in Newbury. Now it's as if being bombed by the Germans was one of the normal hazards of life, like being run over by a motor car, and there was no use trying to avoid it. Probably it's more realistic than the earlier reaction.

Virginia Woolf at Rodmell could hardly be closer:

Friday, August 16th [1940]

Many air raids. One as I walked. A haystack was handy. But walked on, and so home....
... They came very close. We lay down under the tree. The sound was like someone sawing in the air just above us. We lay flat on our faces, hands behind head. Don't close your teeth, said L.

Except that it *was* worse in London, where their property and the houses of friends were being destroyed:

Sunday, October 20th 1940

The most—what?—impressive, no, that's not it—sight in London on Friday was the queue, mostly children with suitcases, outside Warren Street tube. This was about 11.30. We thought they were evacuees waiting for a bus. But there they were, in a much longer line, with women, men, more bags, blankets, sitting still at 3. Lining up for the shelter in the night's raid—which came of course. Thus, if they left the tube at 6 (a bad raid on Thursday) they were back again at 11. So to Tavistock Square. [Their house, No. 52, had been destroyed by a bomb.] With a sigh of relief saw a heap of ruins. Only relics an old basket chair (bought in Fitzroy Square days) and Penman's board To Let. Otherwise bricks and wood splinters. One glass door in the next house hanging. I could just see a piece of my studio wall standing: otherwise rubble where I wrote so many books. Open air where we sat so many nights, gave so many parties. The hotel not touched. So to Meck. [Their house, 37 Mecklenburgh Square, wrecked by a bomb.] All again. Litter, glass, black soft dust, plaster powder. Miss T. and Miss E. in trousers, overalls and turbans, sweeping. I noted the flutter of

Miss T.'s hands: the same as Miss Perkins'. Of course friendly and hospitable in the extreme. Jaunty jerky talk. Repetitions. So sorry we hadn't had her card...to save you the shock. It's awful...Upstairs she propped a leaning bookcase for us. Books all over dining room floor. In my sitting room glass all over Mrs Hunter's cabinet—and so on. Only the drawing room with windows almost whole. A wind blowing through. I began to hunt out diaries. What could we salvage in this little car? Darwin and the silver, and some glass and china.

Except, again, that Joan Wyndham living in London seems to be taking things more than calmly:

7th September 1940

The bombs are lovely, I think it is all thrilling. Nevertheless, as the opposite of death is life, I think I shall get seduced by Rupert tomorrow....

The next day being Sunday, they all went to church—'funny how devout people look after an air raid'. The raids go on:

The guns came nearer. We were in the back room when we heard a loud crash followed by an explosion that shook the room. Rupert, Agnes and I dived for the floor like three ninepins going down simultaneously. The doors rattled and I began to laugh hysterically.

Rupert was behind the bed with three pillows on his head and Agnes was saying the only prayer she could remember which was 'Gentle Jesus meek and mild, look upon a little child'. I felt quite thrilled and stimulated, but Agnes was petrified.

But three days later, on the 11th, the house where Rupert lived was hit and things really began to come home to her:

I hope I may never live through such a moment again. I turned faint and sick and my head buzzed. There was the green door with the three bells, and after that two flights of stairs leading up to doors that opened on to nowhere. Below the stairs I could make out the splintered remnants of broken-down floors, Prudey's gum tree wedged upside down with its leaves moving in the breeze, and the bed I was seduced on hanging out over the street with three foot of solid mortar where Rupert's head should have been. Leonard's studio was completely gone.

I rushed up to a warden and said, 'Where are all the people from that house?'

'Couldn't say miss, no bodies though, at least none that I've seen....' Choking back my sobs I ran down the street to my studio to see if Rupert might have gone there after the bomb. When I arrived I found I'd locked the door and hadn't got the key, but outside on the landing was deposited one guitar in a dented and dusty case, one un-neutered male ginger cat in a basket, very cross, and one gas mask inscribed 'RUPERT CHARLES AUSTIN DARROW, STILL LIVING BY THE GRACE OF HIS OWN

INGENUITY'. Arcana came out in her nightdress and said, 'Your friend came round with these in the middle of the night. He'd just been blown up, it was most extraordinary, he seemed to treat the whole thing as a joke. I couldn't believe him at first, he looked so cheerful.'

Thank you God, I thought, thank you for saving Rupert.

As the days wear on, first her Mother's nerve goes (Joan's assessment!) then Rupert's. Even she tires—but Rupert safe, her own nerve seems fairly secure. As a friend put it to her later: 'after all, what does the war matter when you've got a nice boyfriend?' Different dangers in the War seem to have been taken with different degrees of seriousness. Virginia Woolf, on September 13th and 14th (still 1940) is writing: 'A strong feeling of invasion in the air.' Frances Partridge certainly takes it seriously enough, but Joan Wyndham (predictably) makes only passing reference. Nella Last on the 12th was writing with surprising calm:

> I wonder if the reputed invasions of Britain—at Southend and district—is true, and why we have not been told. No doubt the Government have their reasons, but somehow I like to know the worst and find the 'silver lining' for myself. If things are kept from me, I always fear the worst.

But peace when it finally came—patchily, heralded by so many rumours that the effect was rather of the boy who cried 'wolf'—seems to have struck almost everyone in the same way: hollowly. Here's Nella Last:

> *May 1945*
>
> Steve pooh-poohed the idea that V.E. Day would come tonight. I said, 'It might have been announced in a programme' and I put the wireless on at five minutes to nine o'clock. We agreed that, if Stuart Hibberd said, 'The King will speak in approximately one minute's time', we would have missed an announcement—and smiled at each other when it proceeded normally. Then, when he said so unemotionally that tomorrow was to be the V.E. Day, and that Churchill was to speak at three o'clock, we just gazed at each other, and Steve said, 'WHAT a flop! What a FLOP!' We could none of us believe our hearing... I'd heard people say, 'I'll kneel down and pray if it's in the street when I hear it', 'I know I'll cry my eyes out', 'I'll rush for that bottle I've kept—open it and get tight for the first time in my life', and so on. I rose placidly and put on the kettle and went through to prepare the salad. I looked on my shelf and said, 'Well, dash it, we must celebrate somehow—I'll open this tin of pears', and I did.

Realizing that the Centre where she had worked for the duration of the war would shortly close, Nella Last was struck by a feeling of loss. As Joan Wyndham put it:

I think I was stunned, not so much because of the bomb (Hiroshima) as at the thought of the war ending. Later, when the meaning finally sank in, I felt the strangest mixture of elation and terror. It was as if my whole world had suddenly come to an end. Five years of security and happy comradeship, the feeling of being needed—and ahead a kind of uncharted wilderness, lonely and frightening.

At the same time there was a small but undeniable feeling of excitement, like the end of school term, the hols looming ahead. I was vividly aware of everything about me, the dusty golden ragwort, the blue sky, even the knots in the wooden gate under my hand.

And adds:

It's hard to explain but there has actually been a rather depressed feeling in the Mess over these last few days. Not at all like people who have just won a war.

Mrs Milburn's reaction on V.E. Day is initially pragmatic: 'My first thought was *bread*'—a first thought reputedly shared by half the housewives of England. But she goes on:

This morning's weather seemed symbolic. It was as if in the thunder one heard Nature's roll of drums for the fallen, then the one loud salvo of salute over our heads and the tears of the rain pouring for the sorrowing and suffering of the war. And then the end of the orgy of killing and victory symbolized as the sun came out and shed its brightness and warmth on the earth.

For her, the good news wasn't over yet: the next day, 'A Day of Days!', the best word of all came—Alan was on his way home. The day after that, he had arrived. The meeting is more British than can easily be imagined—such restraint after five years away—'we had a good hug and a kiss and then soon were speeding home, talking hard'. But there's no mistaking her joy when, two days later, the diary she kept for Mass Observation comes to an end:

I walk about in a half-dream and the long, bad years of war begin to fade a little as Alan's voice is heard, the M.G.'s 'voice', too, and the house is once more a real home. The intense relief at the ending of the European war is felt everywhere. No longer do we live under the strain of it, though we shall have it at the back of our mind, and its scars before our eyes, all our lives.

And here the 'Burleigh in War Time' Diary ends with Victory bells for
'O with hope and patience we have awaited for the day
When the tank is filled with petrol and the dust-sheet stowed away.
The engine's running smoothly—the M.G. free to roam
For Oflag's gates have opened wide and...
Alan John is home!'

Different though the two women must have been, it is Frances Partridge who most strongly echoes Clara Milburn's rejoicing. And very reasonably too....

> 'After all,' she writes, 'surely it's only logical that pacifists—of all people—should rejoice in the return to Peace?'

The last word on peace? Not quite. This must be left to Lady Cynthia Asquith, writing at the end of the First World War:

1918

I am beginning to rub my eyes at the prospect of peace. I think it will require more courage than anything that has gone before. It isn't until one leaves off spinning round that one realizes how giddy one is. One will have to look at long vistas again, instead of short ones, and one will at last fully recognize that the dead are not only dead for the duration of the war.

Chapter 10
– Politics and Public Affairs

'I am striving to take into public life what any man gets from his mother.'—
Lady Astor (Britain's first woman MP)

'The First Lady is an unpaid public servant elected by one person—her husband.'—Lady Bird Johnson

'There are two kinds of women: those who want power in the world, and those who want power in bed.'—Jacqueline Kennedy Onassis

'Positively I will again keep a diary,' wrote Beatrix Potter in 1893, 'I foresee larks, contingent on the opening of Parliament.' In 1893, of course, Parliament was strictly speaking none of women's affair. They couldn't sit in it, they couldn't vote for anyone else to...but they cared, sometimes passionately, what happened in it, even so.

But politics isn't just about Parliament, and neither is the history of women's political writing. Nor is it just about the public figures of the last hundred years: Barbara Castle, Vera Brittain campaigning for her husband or Beatrice Webb (more interested, she said, in claiming the right to smoke than the right to vote) with her socio-political concerns. It's about the women who proverbially stood behind great men, and the ones who fought for social reform in their own right. It's about suffragettes and court ladies, interested observers like Beatrix Potter, above—and reigning Queens, like Victoria, below:

20th June 1837

I was awoke at 6 o'clock by Mamma, who told me that the Archbishop of Canterbury (William Howley) and Lord Conyngham (the Lord Chamberlain) were here, and wished to see me. I got out of bed and went into my sitting-room (only in my dressing-gown), and alone, and saw them.

Lord Conyngham then acquainted me that my poor Uncle, the King, was no more, and had expired at 12 minutes p.2 this morning, and consequently that I am Queen. Lord Conyngham knelt down and kissed my hand, at the same time delivering to me the official announcement of the poor King's demise. The Archbishop then told me that the Queen (Adelaide) was desirous that he should come and tell me the details of the last moments of my poor, good Uncle; he said that he had directed his mind to religion and had died in a perfectly happy, quiet state of mind, and was quite prepared for his death. He added that the King's sufferings at the last were not very great but that there was a good deal of uneasiness. Lord Conyngham, who I charged to express my feelings of condolence and sorrow to the poor Queen, returned directly to Windsor. I then went to my room and dressed.

It is a prime example of the kind of thing women have written about in terms of politics and public affairs—what you might call insider dealing.

Insider Dealing

Saturday, 23rd January 1796

I forgot to mention yesterday that Clergy the ancient Valet de Chambre of the poor French King arrived here and dined with us. . . .He gave us many details on that unfortunate Royal family. Louis XVI died with great courage and never showed a moment's weakness. His neck being so fat his head did not fall at the first stroke and he was heard to scream. The Queen had been kept in such piggishness during a great while that she was quite an eskalleton when she was killed. All her members trembled. Mde. Elizabeth on the contrary was mild and calm and looked as fresh as a rose. (Betsey Wynne).

'Many details'—of the sort not available for just anybody—are meat and drink to certain diarists. Often they were involved—not precisely at first, but at secondhand, as daughter, cousin, wife. Sometimes they were an eye-witness observer to an event which shook the world: i.e Lady Bird Johnson's memorable entry:

Dallas, Friday 22nd November 1963

It all began so beautifully. After a drizzle in the morning, the sun came out bright and clear. We were driving into Dallas. In the lead car were President and Mrs Kennedy, John and Nellie Conally, a Secret Service car full of men, and then our car with Lyndon and me and Senator Ralph Yarborough. The streets were lined with people—lots and lots of people—the children all smiling, placards, confetti, people waving from windows. One last happy moment I had was looking up and seeing Mary Griffith leaning out of a window waving at me. (Mary for many years had been in charge of altering the clothes which I purchased at Neiman-Marcus.)

Then, almost at the edge of town, on our way to the Trade Mart for the Presidential luncheon, we were rounding a curve, going down a hill, and suddenly there was a sharp, loud report. It sounded like a shot. The sound seemed to me to come from a building on the right above my shoulder. A moment passed, and then two more shots rang out in rapid succession.

There had been such a gala air about the day that I thought the noise must come from firecrackers—part of the celebration. Then the Secret Service men were suddenly down in the lead car. Over the car radio system, I heard 'Let's get out of here!' and our Secret Service man, Rufus Youngblood, vaulted over the front seat on top of Lyndon, threw him to the floor, and said, 'Get down'.

Senator Yarborough and I ducked our heads. The car accelerated terrifically—faster and faster. Then, suddenly, the brakes were put on so hard that I wondered if we were going to make it as we wheeled left and went around the corner. We pulled up to a building. I looked up and saw a sign, 'HOSPITAL'. Only then did I believe that this might be what it was. Senator Yarborough kept saying in an excited voice, 'Have they shot the President? Have they shot the President?' I said something like, 'No, it can't be.'

As we ground to a halt—we were still the third car—Secret Servicemen began to pull, lead, guide, and hustle us out. I cast one last look over my shoulder and saw in the President's car a bundle of pink, just like a drift of blossoms, lying on the back seat. It was Mrs Kennedy lying over the President's body....'

A quarter of a century on, Kennedy's death still has the power to draw us, to bring us inside the circle of those to whom a public, peacetime event really *mattered*. The circle, in this case, was an exceptionally wide one. Many people in their thirties or older must have some milder version of the entry made by one of the teenagers who wrote to Valerie Grove, in the 1960s:

Friday Nov 22, 1963
Just about the most ghastly, hideous thing ever has happened—President Kennedy has been assassinated. I just don't know what to do. Can't think straight. It's awful awful awful awful awful awful awful awful awful awful.

Even so, on the following day the same teenager noted with 'astonishment and stupefaction' that 'everything seemed to be going on as usual. The people I passed were NOT all talking about Kennedy.'

When the event concerned is a less dramatic one, yesterday's news grows cold even more quickly. On a human level we can empathize with Fanny Burney's insider's account of the madness of King George III in 1788 and the sufferings of 'my poor royal mistress'—the Queen, to whom Fanny was lady-in-waiting. But the Prince Regent's take-over bid arouses no great concern and we have no very vivid sense of Fanny's

171

privilege. Royalty—unless romantic (like Mary Stuart) or personally impressive (like Elizabeth I)—seems less interesting a few centuries back.

It is still fascinating to read Lady Cynthia Asquith's account in 1915 of lunching with what then seemed 'the setting sun minister' who had just lost the Admiralty, one Winston Churchill:

27th May

I think his nature—though he may be unscrupulous and inclined to trample on susceptibilities of sailors, or whomever he may have to deal with, from eagerness—is absolutely devoid of vindictiveness....

Winston's chief consolation was in the reflection expressed in a glowing period of his extreme youth. Talking of the Cabinet of the morning: 'There was I after ten years in the Cabinet, and five years in the most important office, still by ten years the youngest member!' He said this with an attractively naive delight.

'Predestined to failure and vast ambition' was his successor's verdict on Churchill. No one can always be right.... But the point is, take the statesmen of a century back and we wouldn't be able to get the same kick out of the same kind of comment. We wouldn't know if the commentator proved right or wrong.

It is a pity—because comments on the Victorian statesmen, the Gladstones and the Disraelis, abound. References to Gladstone, for example, occur throughout the diaries of Beatrix Potter and her cousin Beatrice Webb (née Potter): (31 Dec. 1890: 'Gladstone totters to the grave grasping with senile persistency Home Rule for Ireland'); Lady Monkswell ('old Gladstone'); Queen Victoria (15 August 1892: 'It is rather trying and anxious work to have to take as Prime Minister a man of eighty-two and a half, who really seems no longer quite fitted to be at the head of a Government, and whose views and principles are somewhat dangerous'); Mary Gladstone, the PM's admiring daughter ('Papa's answer was one of the greatest that he ever made...'); and *her* cousin Lucy Cavendish. The ruling class was just that, and though women may have been debarred from direct participation (always excepting the Queen herself)—no one can doubt their hearts and minds were committed.

Crusaders

In fundamental matters women tend to be committed on the 'right' side. They may have been for or against 'old Gladstone' and various of his Bills, but just as the issue of nuclear disarmament has involved a great number of women who are in no sense politicians, so a high proportion of diarists in the nineteenth century seem to have been moved to comment upon slavery and the wider question of race. Eugenia Wynne in 1806, on being taken to view some of the 'Guinea-men' ships:

Friday, 22 August

'...my heart revolted at the relation of the cruelties practised upon the wretched negroes during their passage—the manner in which the ship is arranged for their accommodation is sufficient to make one commiserate their sufferings, were not additional barbarities executed towards these unhappy wretches—who has giv'n us the right thus to treat our fellow creatures?—God alone will show it on the great day when we are to account for our deeds.

Slave trading was banned by the UK in 1807: slavery in the British West Indies was abolished in 1833, but in 1838 Queen Victoria was still writing of a new Bill to ameliorate the conditions under which Negro apprentices were employed there:

13 March

...I must just observe that the necessity of this Act shows how shockingly cruel and cheating the masters of the Slaves are, attempting to evade in every possible way what they are told to do, and what, as the laws cannot be enforced on the spot, must be done by Act of Parliament here.

Two years later, Elizabeth Fry attended a meeting of the Anti-Slavery Society and wrote in her diary of the honour of appearing in such a cause. In America slavery was still common in the Southern States, as Barbara Leigh Smith Bodichon found as she sailed up the Mississippi in 1857. On 11 December she quotes a conversation on board ship the previous night:

Mrs B (who lives in Louisville and is evidently very kind to her slaves): 'Well, I say if they will run away, let them.' *Mr and Mrs H* (who, by the bye, are bringing south *a woman who leaves a husband and five children behind in Kentucky)*: 'Let them run away if they will! Why, every negro would run away if they could—people don't like to lose their servants.' Some said it makes the negroes unhappy to know how to read—what is the use of it to them? They are inferior to the whites and must be so always. BLS: 'But you say they improve and are better off every year, and that there is a wonderful difference between the African as he comes from Africa and the African after two or three generations in America. How can you tell where that improvement will stop?' *Mr C:* 'Yes, they improve, but that is no reason for giving them *much* instruction and us making them discontented—for they *never will be emancipated. We cannot consent to lose our property.'*

'If there is a creature living I hate, it is that Mrs Beecher,' said one of the slave-owning wives, 'with an expression of bitter feeling which distorted her good face'. The name of Harriet Beecher Stowe, author of the epoch-making anti-slavery novel *Uncle Tom's Cabin* and living proof that women were most actively involved in the anti-slavery crusade in the States as well as in England, occurs again among women diarists of the period. Here is Lady Frederick Cavendish visiting America after Lincoln's Abolition Bill to find for herself that legislation cannot quickly alter basic feelings:

> *Orange Valley, December 16th 1871*
>
> At dinner (which was very good) Mr Kerr broke into some excitement and much perspiration abt. Govr. Eyre: all the planters strongly side with him as far as we have seen; Mr Royes alone allowing with any candour that the violent measures went on too long. Mr K cd. say nothing to the query why 400 blacks were to be put to death in return for 20 whites and after the Govr.'s own official declaration that the rising was quelled: a pause ensued, and he cd. only repeat that the Govr. has saved all the white lives in the Colony. I can't help a creep at the evident implication that 400 blacks may well die in revenge for 20 whites: it reminds one of the expression of Legree in 'Uncle Tom's Cabin': 'After all, what a fuss for a dead nigger!'

The book, its characters and its author are seldom far from the thoughts of Mary Boyd Chesnut, herself the wife of a slave owner and writing in the years of the Civil War:

> *November 28th 1861*
>
> These Mrs Stowes have the plaudits of crowned heads; we take our chances, doing our duty as best we may among the woolly heads.

Horrifying though the reference to 'woolly heads' sounds now, Mary Boyd Chesnut's diary shows her no friend to slavery. It shows, too, the sense of wrong in many of the women around her—women who committed themselves to the American Civil War under the banner of Southern independence and bitterly resented the implication (right or wrong) that they were fighting to keep their slaves...Of her mother-in-law, tellingly, Mary writes: 'Ever since she came here sixty or seventy years ago, as a bride from Philadelphia, Mrs Chesnut has been trying to make it up to the Negroes for being slaves.'

'God forgive us, but ours is a monstrous system, a wrong and an iniquity!' Though Mary seems to be thinking predominantly of the sexual morality practised on the plantations:

> *August 27th 1861*
>
> I hate slavery. You say there are no more fallen women on a plantation than in London, in proportion to numbers; but what do you say to this? A magnate who runs a hideous black harem with its consequences under the

same roof with his lovely white wife, and his beautiful and accomplished daughters? He holds his head as high and poses as the model of all human virtues to these poor women whom God and the laws have given him. From the height of his awful majesty, he scolds and thunders at them, as if he never did wrong in his life...

The 'poor women', it would seem, are not the Black ones. Later, Mary Chesnut writes of 'African slaves'—to distinguish them from the white ones—'all married women, all children and girls who live on in their father's houses are slaves!' Aspects of Mary's morality look very unattractive now. The implications of the passage above are, to say the very least of it, mixed. But the connection between slavery and the position of women was one that would be made again.

Pushing Into Parliament

'There is evidently a feeling'—noted Barbara Leigh Smith Bodichon, in the course of the discussion quoted above—'that Abolition and Women's Rights are supported by the same people and the same arguments, and that both are allied to atheism.' If the question of Women's Rights and presumably by implication of suffrage was in the air in 1857, it hadn't gone away by 1884 when three consecutive pages, filled with social events, from the diary of Mary Gladstone who had just made her debut, include:

Tues. Mar. 25
Dined in Bry. Sq... very pleasant indeed, music evening. Sat betw. Messrs. Bryce and Gaskell, female suffrage the staple of our talk.

Mon. Mar. 31.
Mrs Earle to tea, joind by E. B. O.(ttley), funny talk on love in marriage and women's position and duties. The latter stayed on and we went on to morals.

Sun. Apl. 6
Over to 4 Carlton Gardens, between A. J. B. and A. Sidgwick—the latter most agreeable. He thinks people have wrongly formulated the characteristics which differentiate men and women—long novel talk, and also on our generation understanding another, on which he takes a hopeful view.

Thurs. May 29
The great Tod meeting at Chesham St., Lucy [the Lady Frederick Cavendish quoted above?] *v* Miss Tod on Women's Suffrage. I felt strongly what amateurs we were and how shallow seemed our arguments, as compared with her deep, wide whole-hearted study of the whole subject in all its bearings.

We could wish that she had recorded a few of the arguments, or better still her own opinions on the matter. But these briefly recorded references to suffrage, as an inevitable part of social intercourse, are in themselves significant, like the discussions on women's nature and capabilities quoted in Chapter 6 (Marriage), all bubbles which show the pot is coming to the boil. When it boils over, in the early years of the next century, two of the most vivid documents in the archive collection of suffragette papers held in the Museum of London's archives come in diary form.

Strictly speaking, in fact, Lady Constance Lytton's 'diary' of her imprisonment in Walton Gaol was written upon her release, on 31 Jan 1910, some few days after the first events mentioned. (She was sentenced on 15 January, giving a false name and refusing the option of a fine. She began her protest at once, writing slogans such as 'Only be ye strong and very courageous' on the walls of her cell.) But no one reading this account of her first brush with the horror that destroyed her health can doubt that the experience was still vivid:

At about 5 pm the Senior Medical officer returned with, I think, 4 wardresses and the feeding apparatus. The Doctor urged me to voluntarily take food—I told him that was absolutely out of the question. He did not examine my heart nor feel my pulse: he did not ask to do so, nor did I, directly or indirectly, say anything which could possibly induce him to think that I would refuse to be examined. I offered no resistance to being placed in position but lay down voluntarily on the plank bed on the floor. I shut my mouth and clenched my teeth. The Doctor offered me the choice of a wooden or steel gag. He explained elaborately, as he did on every subsequent occasion, that the steel gag would hurt and the wooden one not, and he urged me not to drive him to use the steel gag which however was the only one that could overcome my resistance. After failing to unlock my teeth with the wooden gag he used the steel. He seemed, not unnaturally, annoyed at my resistance. After being fed by the stomach tube I was much overcome and I vomited. As the Doctor left me he gave me a slap on the cheek, not violently but apparently to express his contemptuous disapproval: he seemed to take for granted that my distress was assumed. I said to him the next day 'Unless you consider it part of your duty, would you please not strike me (or I may have said *slap* me) when you have finished your odious job'.

He did not answer but never repeated the insult. The wardresses were kind and helped me to clean my clothes over which I had been sick, saying they would bring me others in the morning, but that it was too late to get a change then, and I passed the night in them as they were. Although after this first time, I took what precautions I could and always removed the coloured serge jacket, before being fed, yet my clothes frequently had to be changed, and the floor of my cell had invariably to be cleaned out after the feeding. Two or three times an ordinary prisoner was called in to do this when I was too much prostrated to do it myself, but on most occasions I did the washing up. I made no grievance of this—I could not bear to see a fellow prisoner given such a repulsive task, and I liked to make sure that the cleansing was thoroughly done. Of course the clothes of the Doctors and attendants suffered too. I frequently apologized for this and begged them to take more precautions to protect themselves.

I several times did my best to restore the Doctor's clothes. He made such remarks as:—

'Oh, never mind my clothes', or 'Oh! that's all in the day's work', or 'Really, you Suffragettes you ruin all my clothes'. I was removed from the punishment cell to my original cell the same evening after I was force fed, although my punishment had not expired.

The second time I was fed the vomiting was more excessive. It was a most revolting and exasperating business for the doctor and attendants as well as for the prisoner. I was sick all over the Doctor's clothes. He was angry and left my cell hastily, saying, 'You did that on purpose, if you do it again tomorrow I shall feed you twice'.

Olive Walton's diary—which *does* read with the real ring of a daily record—is in its way an even stronger testament. It begins on Wednesday, 27 March 1912 when she was sentenced to four months' imprisonment, to be served in Aylesbury Prison. On 11 April, the hunger strike began:

Wed 10th

I and the rest forcibly fed last night. Some of us very ill. I, personally, feel fairly fit.

Thurs 11th

Morn & eve we have that tube stuck down our throat and noses. This even: 7 of our number, who are very ill, were moved either to the hospital or else released.

Mon 15th

Unitarian Minister round today. News heard. Great fuss in the country over us being forcibly fed. Protest Meetings held—tomorrow influential deputation to wait on McKenna. This morning I had the stomach tube. Its after-results are worse than hard.

Tues 16th

The doct. begins to feed us three times a day. It is a shame. We have fine tussles before they get us tied into the chair! Feel very low-spirited today.

Wed 17th

. . . we have got our privileges back. What a victory! How lovely bread is!

Oddly enough, it is the not uncontented tone of the post-strike entries that really bring Olive Walton's diary alive.'All in all a most exciting game of rounders', she writes. Gardening—the official labour given to the suffragettes at Aylesbury—is 'jolly fine'. They christened the place the Simple Life Summer School: 27 May—'how young all we suffragettes seem'. 29 May—'I have felt most awfully "kiddish" here.'

Schoolgirlish indeed, the jumping games and obstacle races sound, but sterner life was only just around the corner. On 11 May there is an entry to the effect that 'Lady Constance Lytton has had a bad heart attack'—from the experiences described above. 'Hope the dear will soon be fit again.' A vain hope.... On hearing late in June that 'the Leaders'—Mrs Pankhurst and Mrs Pethick Lawrence—were being force-fed in Holloway, the Aylesbury group found the courage to embark on hunger strike a second time around. There is no conscious heroism in Olive Walton's diary, just this:

Thursday 27th June
What a vile thing this feeding is. The horror of having 6 to 7 wardresses going for one at once. This day has seemed an eternity.

Two days later, on 29 June, she was released. 'How heavenly to be free again', the diary ends.

How great a leap is it from the prison diaries of the suffragettes to the cabinet diaries of Barbara Castle, eight years a cabinet minister under a Labour government? In time, about sixty years. In the political position and experience of this one woman (though not necessarily for too many others) a gulf that could have taken far longer to bridge. And in style, a gulf as wide. *The Castle Diaries,* which run from 1964-70 and from 1974-76, are nothing if not a professional politician's account. Professional, in fact, to the point at which the daily grind of another negotiation, another Bill, makes fairly sticky going. For the lay reader, there is a strong temptation to skip through the diaries looking for the sentences that show the ordinary person under the politician's hat. 'My last free weekend before what may be an election and it is too bitterly cold to work in the garden, damn it!' When James Callaghan took over from Harold Wilson in 1976 and replaced her as Secretary of State for the Social Services, Barbara Castle was suddenly bereft of the official car, and wondered how she was going to manage, especially carrying food down to the country cottage at the weekends?

It is, hopefully, the human angle and not the 'woman's angle' you seek, but there is certainly a special interest in the entries which show Castle very much aware of the rare position she held. 'Having a woman minister,' she noted wryly in 1966, shortly after her appointment to the Department of Transport, 'certainly does help publicity.' In 1974, after a General Election:

Thursday, 28th March

Put on my best dress for the Cabinet official photo and hoped the tiredness wouldn't show too much. As it was cold the chairs had been set out in the upstairs reception room at No 10, instead of outside. We had all been given a set place and Shirley (Williams) and I found ourselves on the two outside seats of the semi-circle. 'You wait till the women of the movement learn about this', Shirley called out to Harold. 'Not to worry, Shirley', I called back. 'We can do a pincer movement on him. His days are doomed.' Harold just grinned but I hope he was a bit embarrassed.

With that, of course, you have to set the many, many words which just show sheer enjoyment of the political arena: 'I sat through Mike's speech, feeling like a truant but enjoying every minute of it...the delicious moment when the Tories climbed down ignominiously.' And, indeed, those of the career politician—*any* career politican, male or female—noting a few weeks earlier when the offer of the Social Services Ministry was made:

Monday, 4 March 1974

It is amusing how one can talk about terms before the event and when it comes to it everything melts away in the excitement and urgency of the moment. But if Harold is more self-assured this time, so am I. A year or two at Social Services and then it will be retirement—or a bigger bid. I am already scratching my head as to whom I can appoint my political 'cabinet'.

Yes, we have come a long way from the world of the suffragettes...in one sense. But in another, they dug a hole, planted and watered a tree, of which *The Castle Diaries*, more than the diaries of any of the other politically interested but non-Parliamentary women who came between them, are the logical fruit.

Chapter 11
~ Travel

ROSALIND: *'Well, this is the forest of Arden.'*
TOUCHSTONE: *'Ay, now am I in Arden, the more fool I:*
when I was at home I was in a better place:
but travellers must be content.'—William Shakespeare—*As You Like It*

Travelling For Pleasure?

Travellers, on the whole, have tended not to be content (or at least, not as content as they had hoped!), and it is probably just as well for the readability of their diaries. Anyone who has ever tried to write a travel article knows that they are among the hardest pieces of all to get right, and it is a sad fact that reading the raptures of certain travellers tends to be like being shown a very large number of someone else's holiday snaps—very, very slowly.

Happily, there are a great many exceptions to prove this particular 'rule'. Some diaries recount journeys that were of themselves extraordinary. Some were written under extraordinary circumstances. What can have prompted the already overtaxed pioneer women, crossing America by jolting wagon, to add to their duties by deciding to put pen to paper each day? Loneliness? Boredom? The burning desire that their efforts should not slip into oblivion, or the knowledge that they were making history?

Some of the diary extracts which follow are simply a vivid reflection of the individual writer's personality. Not all of them by any means are about the pains and penalties of travel. But some of the funniest are...

February 20 (02.00h) 1944

Peaceful night so far. Only one mild air raid. Have been reading a textbook on tropical diseases in preparation for my foreign draft, which is such a long time in coming. But the book rather puts me off! In India and China there's a disease called Kala-azar which sounds horrific. The unfortunate sufferer's limbs waste away, the spleen and liver become so enlarged that the abdomen extends to the size of a football. On top of all that the body is covered with nodules resembling leprosy. Eventually the victim dies of exhaustion. Then there is blackwater fever, a complication of Benign tertian malaria, which sounds particularly unpleasant—and there's no specific treatment. Delirium, profuse diarrhoea, persistent vomiting, black urine and a mortality rate of 10-15 per cent. In Africa there is a risk of trypanosomiasis—sleeping sickness. The blood is infected by the bite of the tsetse fly, causing enlargement of the lymphatic glands, thoracic pain, maniacal symptoms and coma—death is pretty certain.

We will be inoculated against cholera and yellow fever, so I hope to escape agonizing cramps, 'rice water' stools, collapse and death from the former; and convulsions, with a 25 per cent mortality from the latter.

But what about pneumonic plague? Fatal within a few days. Or typhus, which according to the book, is a disease not of hot climates, but of 'lousy populations', transmitted by lice or fleas. Having survived German bombs, how ironical it would be to be killed by a Chinese louse or an Indian flea.

Is a foreign draft really worth the risk?

And what *are* the advantages?

So far I've not got beyond sun, bananas—have not seen the latter for the last three years—and perhaps a wider outlook on life.

Not everyone has quite Nurse Eve Williams' professional expertise in finding reasons *not* to travel. (They didn't stop her—and when, in the course of her travels, she reached Hong Kong six years later and her diary became ecstatic, it also, she noted herself, became 'rather boring'.) But some of the amateurs do pretty well in the grumbling stakes. On 6 June 1869 Miss Julia Newberry, aged fifteen, from Chicago, having been dragged reluctantly on the version of the European 'Grand Tour' indulged in by wealthy Americans of the period, wrote that home is 'worth all London, Paris & New York put together'. She added, 'How much trash is talked, and enthusiasm wasted on travelling, when it is the greatest bore under the sun.'

Or as Virginia Woolf, ending a European holiday in 1933, puts it:

Now the draw of home, and freedom and no packing tells on us—oh to sit in an armchair; and read and not have to ask for Eau Mineral, with which to brush our teeth!

Not that she belonged to the anti-travel lobby: 'the dusting of our shoes and careering off tomorrow', she had written in Piacenza a few days earlier, are 'the price to be paid for the sweep and the freedom' of travel. Her travels gave rise to some memorable descriptions, but they are more of persons than of places:

Tuesday 9th May 1933

At Carpentras last night there was the little servant girl with honest eyes, hair brushed in a flop and one rather black tooth. I felt that life would crush her out inevitably. Perhaps 18, not more; yet on the wheel, without hope; poor, not weak but mastered—yet not enough mastered but to desire furiously travel, for a moment, a car. Ah but I am not rich, she said to me—which her cheap little stockings and shoes showed anyhow. Oh how I envy you, able to travel. You like Carpentras? But the wind blows ever so hard. You'll come again? That's the bell ringing. Never mind. Come over here and look at this. No, I've never seen anything like it. Ah, yes, she always likes the English. ('She' was the other maid, with hair like some cactus in erection.) Yes I always like the English, she said. The odd little honest face, with the black tooth, will stay on at Carpentras I suppose: will marry? will become one of those stout black women who sit in the door knitting? No: I foretell for her some tragedy: because she had enough mind to envy us the Lanchester.

What preoccupies her at home preoccupies her abroad; she *ought* to be describing the scenery, she writes in Italy, but somehow it is not long before a chance-met Italian steals the scene instead. Sweeping through Europe in her Lanchester, you feel Virginia Woolf must have remained unmistakeably herself. . . .

Beatrice Webb strikes a more militantly English note. (If the Americans were the most invincible travellers of the nineteenth and early twentieth centuries, the English must often have seemed to their hosts the most incalculable):

18th July 1882 (Murren)

The first three days were hardly pleasantly employed in suffering a nervous bilious attack . . . This air makes one feel rather lightheaded and excited. The inhabitants look wretchedly thin, pale and cadaverous and are mere beasts of burden, born to carry *Messieurs and Mesdames les voyageurs* and their requirements to this 'Pleasant Alpine Resort'. Father says, and I agree, that the Swiss do not seem endowed with a high moral nature. The wretched landlord, a most thriving one, actually refused to count our humble afternoon tea in with our *pension*. . . . However, we have done him, with the help of an Etna (patent stove), borrowed tea pot and milk and bread and butter for one. . . .

As for the scenery it is simply glorious. . . .

This was just one in a series of extended journeys Beatrice Webb (then Potter) was persuaded to undertake. And it was only much later, when her life's work was under way and her future with Sidney Webb in sight, that she really seems to have enjoyed them—a reflection which says quite a lot about the nature of the travel experience itself. Certainly the eye she cast on the early voyages was bleak enough:

4th June 1878

After three days' experience of the life, I decide in my own mind that it is very dull, and I am a wee bit sorry that I have left London town, but I console myself with the reflections that it is better for my bodily health and perhaps for my morale. The life is wanting in air, and I feel a long way on the road to absolute boredom....

So much for the 'broadens the mind' school of thought, though things did improve: (15 July: 'the last two or three days have been very amusing')—just as well since 'the life', on this occasion, was to last for five months. Eighteen months later and she is back in Italy on another extended trip. 22 January 1881: 'our stay in Rome up to now has hardly been very pleasant—due to weather, and to ill health.' The trip ends in April on an even more gloomy note: '...misery after a certain time consumes itself or its subject'. But Beatrice knew where the problem lay well enough—not with the 'enchantingly lovely place' but with the state of mind and body (and the companions) she took there....

Read Sylvia Plath's *Letters Home* as she travelled from the States to England and Europe, and you get all the bubbling enthusiasm you could hope for from the American abroad. Read the journals, and the picture is very different. It is 5 April 1956, she's in Paris, with an ex-boyfriend, Gordon Lameyer, and writing pages on end. But not about Paris—oh no. It is the state of play between Plath and her various men that seems from her journals to occupy her mind and affect her mood. Poor Paris gets hardly a look in.

Thursday, April 5

Yes, all the auguries are for departure: the Paris air grows cold and I shiver always and my white lingerie slowly turns gray and there is no bathtub; all gathers and with cold edges and blunt corners urges me to go; the train and the view will be a kind of solace; if only I can be civil to Gordon: why not? There is all that mess and scorn between us, and no bitterness ever entirely vanishes between the rejector and the rejected. I paid my complete train fare through from Paris to Rome in francs today and got that over; the plane ticket is formidable, and I shall pay part of that in England if he needs it. I feel used enough to having men pay for my food, and even hotels, and feel that Gordon chose to do this for my company, with the understanding it was to be merely friendly company.

In one sense, though, Sylvia Plath was treading a well-worn path—that of a stream of American visitors returning to Europe to claim the past—and sometimes to criticize the present. 'Ducks, dabbling in ditches, dribbling damps and dikes, dank dirty domiciles, dusty dams, disgusting dreary dullness and dolefully drowsy drouthy drinking dolts of Dutchmen!' (May 1837) is Fanny Appleton's (later Longfellow) alliterative and imitative summary of Holland. London comes off better:

May 4, 1837

...Sat all the morning at the window, amused with the constant panorama of passing objects. Curious cabs, with driver boxed up at one side; splendid equipages with every shade of livery—such neatness in their attire and such sleek glossy steeds; quaint vehicles, like trunks on wheels; ambulating *affiches*—blue-coat boys and 'London cues'—all from my childhood's picturebooks; Punches and wandering minstrels beyond number; an old lady in a genteel barouche buying cauliflowers at a grocery opposite; a damsel sauntering up and down in anxious expectation—'hi! ho! for somebody'—a romantic conjecture amuses me. 'Somebody' comes! after a hope deferred a half hour—a nice dapper youth. Ah! she smiles! she has his arm! and off they go 'happy as griggs'.—Now a dashing chariot drives up, the rattat-tat of the brass knocker on the green door bespeaking a visitor. Such beautiful horses! but such toilettes of the visitors! They enter, and in the doorway the spruce footman stands flirting with the buxom chambermaid. What scandal of mistress and master they are exchanging! The soldiers with their neat white pants and scarlet coats enliven the streets much. There goes a fair lady with a flamingo fellow at her heels carrying her purchases. What is the use of those formidable batons the footmen lean on the carriage roof? Dined so *à l'Americaine*—goose and apple sauce and gooseberry tart—that we thought ourselves at Aunt Sam's! How completely everything is changed from the Continent to the smallest minutiae of everyday life. But it comes naturally to us, as native customs. Took a stroll with Tom through St James Square and along the striking arcades to the Quadrant and the noble sidewalk of Regent Street....

But even London is not entirely unscathed:

'... *Quel spectacle* of horrible toilettes! No bad orchestra could jar my nerves with a more painful sensation of discord than such an array of monstrosities in the way of costume. Colors wedded together as inimical as vinegar and honey—all rules of 'the unities' disregarded—artificial flowers more fantastically garnishing these plain commonplace visages than Ophelia's mad garlands, and such ill-fitted, ill-made, tastelessly-designed robes! Alas for eyes fresh from Parisian elegance! What are splendid mansions and wealth if such taste masks fair forms and deforms all hidden fascination....'

Westminster Abbey (30 May) 'surpassed all my dreams', Shakespeare's birthplace (14 June), on the other hand, 'gave me a more startling evidence than I ever before thought of how genius entering into a man like a separate spirit ennobles and liberates him from lowness of condition....'

Uplift and romance (as exemplified by the pleasurably tragic figure of Mary Stuart) are what this particular American traveller prefers, though she can be sharply critical too: (21 June: 'No wonder Byron inhaled misanthropic notions, bred in such a dreary vicinity....') And sometimes it raises her to the point of prophecy:

June 28 1837

...Passed the entrance to Wordsworth's eyrie without entering as he is far away. Long afterwards, as his fame is waxing daily greater, and when he is dead, it will be one of the pilgrimages all will feel bound to make. However, all this vicinity is the mirror of his mind and all linked with him in love; he is the gentle interpreter which stamps these sweet lakes with fame eternal.

One cannot but think of another American traveller who came looking for 'the England of English literature' and found it—Helene Hanff, author of *84, Charing Cross Road*. After the book and the film, a lot of people already know the story. Of how a little-known American writer, a lover of old books and an Anglophile, began in 1949 a correspondence with a firm of antiquarian booksellers in the Charing Cross Road. Of how it was only in 1971, when her book had made her famous over here, that she could finally afford to visit the city she had fallen in love with at sight unseen. And of how, although the shop was gone and the man she wrote to dead, London lived up to her expectations even so:

Wednesday, July 14

Ann Edwards of the *Sunday Express* took me to lunch at the Savoy and refused to believe I wasn't disappointed in London.

'When I heard you were coming,' she said, 'I wanted to write you and say, "My dear, don't come. You're fifteen years too late."'

For what, Westminster Abbey?

I tried to tell her that if you've dreamed of seeing the Abbey and St Paul's and the Tower all your life, and one day you find yourself actually there, they can't disappoint you. I told her I was finally going to St Paul's when I left her and I could guarantee her it wouldn't disappoint me....

It was lovely to walk along the river with John Donne's cathedral looming ahead. Thought about him as I walked, he's the only man I ever heard of who actually *was* a rake reformed by the love of a good woman....

He was also a little batty. When Anne died, he had a stone shroud made for himself, and he slept with that shroud in bed with him for twenty years. If you write like an angel you're allowed to be a bit cracked.

I walked up the steps of St Paul's—finally, finally, after how many years?—and in through the doorway, and stood there looking up at the domed ceiling and down the broad aisles to the altar, and tried to imagine how Donne felt the night King James sent for him. And for at least that moment, I wouldn't have traded the hundreds of books I've read for the handful I know almost by heart. I haven't opened Walton's *Lives* in ten years, at least; and standing there in John Donne's cathedral the whole lovely passage was right there in my head:

> When his Majesty was sat down he said after his pleasant manner, 'Dr Donne, I have invited you to dinner and though you sit not down with me, yet will I carve to you a dish I know you love well. For knowing you love London I do hereby make you Dean of St Paul's and when I have dined, then do you take your beloved dish home with you to your study, say grace there to yourself and much good may it do you.'

And as Eliza Dolittle would say, I bet I got it right.

There were guides with large tourist parties in tow, each guide giving the standard lecture, some in English, one in French, one in German, the monotone voices jarring against each other. I got as far from them as I could and wandered around by myself. I went down a side aisle looking at all the plaques and busts, walked around the altar and started back up the other side looking at more plaques and busts. Even so, I almost missed it. It was an odd shape, it wasn't a bust and it wasn't a full-length statue, so I stopped and read the inscription. There in front of me, hanging on the wall of St Paul's Cathedral, was John Donne's shroud.

I touched it.

There's a small chapel just inside the door, with a sign that says: 'St Dunstan's Chapel. Reserved for Private Meditation'. I went in and gave thanks.

Fifteen years too late indeed.

Thirty-five years earlier, another American Helen (not Helene) was arriving in London:

12th November 1936

From Waterloo Station we took a taxi which, to my amazement, could carry our twelve pieces of baggage! I shall never forget the two trunks and three big cases of Braille notes I brought for literary work on the top of the taxi and the other seven stowed inside. I wondered if we should reach the Park Lane Hotel alive—I thought the trunks might fall through the roof, but soon I was convinced of our perfect safety. We drove through the usual London mist pierced by innumerable electric lights. With ripples of excitement in her fingers Polly enumerated the places we passed:

'Helen! The Houses of Parliament—you remember our dining there with Sir Ian Fraser when Teacher was here.'

'Westminster!...'

'The Mall!...'

'Now we have come to Piccadilly....'

'Oh, that's the Green Park opposite the Park Lane!'

A heartbreaking sense of emptiness swept over us because Teacher was not beside us to repeat those names in a voice full of happy memories and anticipation of another visit to the Park Lane where everything pleased and rested her.

Unlike Helene Hanff, Helen Keller never *saw* London. Her story is that of the deaf and blind girl who was educated by her beloved 'Teacher', Anne Sullivan, to the point of taking a full, even a pre-eminent, place in the world. 'Teacher' died in 1936: it was out of grief and loss that Helen, travelling with her companion Polly Thompson, began her journal. Blindness could not destroy her appreciation of what she encountered:

13th November

I was glad Polly's eyes were so full of charming sights. With my own senses I perceived the odours of fresh bread, wine-shops and passing motor buses. A whiff of enchanting single English violets made my heart give a little jump, and we went into the florist's to buy some.

I knew when I entered the Green Park by the smell of grass and burning leaves. It was a blessed corner to commune with nature away from the street traffic—men, women and children walking just for the pleasure of it, dogs gambolling without leash or muzzle, pigeons and gulls. I touched the noble plane-trees and oaks, and enjoyed the softness of the grass. The sparrows were very cocky and so fearless we almost stepped on them. We inquired why the plane leaves were being burned, and the reply was that it takes them five years to rot! Their ashes make a fine dressing for the soil.

What endless fascination there is for me in a gentle city like London where everything significant to the eye, ear and the touch is within reach!

The extent and pace of Helen Keller's travels took no account of her handicaps. On the contrary—because of them and of her achievements in overcoming them, she was in constant demand to visit, to speak, to organize and to be received all over the world. 'I have always by temperament been a citizen of the world,' she told her journal in 1937. 'My inner freedom from the limits of space and time is a precious possession.' She was at the time eight thousand miles out on the ocean, sailing towards Japan. Beginning the voyage, on 1st April, she wrote:

When we sailed through the Golden Gate a god plucked me by the ear, as the Romans would say, and winged memory bore me back twenty-two years to Mount Tamalpais where Teacher, Polly and I sat one heavenly day with San Franciso Bay gleaming, green-gold-blue, and the giant sequoia forest below us. Ned Holmes held us spellbound with romantic tales of the ships that entered the harbour, laden with jade, ivory, mahogany, myrrh and frankincense from the Far East. As we listened, Polly and I resolved (I did not then know our wish was simultaneous) that some time we would go the way of those ships from the Golden Gate to the Orient.

Wonder-smitten, I felt the *Asama-Maru* bearing us like a mighty genie at the command of Aladdin's lamp through that world gateway. In a mist of rain we moved slowly under the great Golden Gate Bridge, which is almost completed, and past the cliffs that rise sheer out of the sea. Then I had a sensation as if we dropped out of a life into another—into unknown vastitudes of experience. . . .

Yet I did not feel lost; rather I exulted in the thought of new horizons opening before my mind. Perhaps that was the beginning of my release from the torturing sense that a world had been burnt out with Teacher's passing. Certainly she seemed nearer than she had since she last kissed me. My purpose was revitalized, as if she had spoken from her celestial home encouraging me to go forth into the darkness and the silences yet untouched by hope. With her earthly presence is gone the dear familiar home atmosphere, and it may be that the task now required of me is to grow a new self out of the emotions and impressions I shall no doubt bring back to America. My heart is still like a house where friends come and go, but no one else can ever be Teacher or mother or father to me, and that means that one intimate chamber remains closed until I, too, depart. Since I have no husband or child, I do not know if other rooms will be opened for satisfying human relationships, but 'before me, as behind me, is God, and all is well.'

It is a true traveller talking. Ironically, it is also the woman who began her journal—aboard that other ship sailing to England—with these words:

The deepest sorrow knows no time—it seems an eternal night. Truly did Emerson say that when we travel we do not escape from ourselves, we carry with us the sadness which blurs all places and all days.

Beating The Boundaries

M. 10th October 1791

The Western Isles are inhabited by Portuguese who are fond of buying black cloathes whenever Ships call there, which they frequently do to take in water & which we should have done, had not the lateness of the Season in which we quitted England made it necessary not to lose an hour on the passage as we are doubtful of reaching Quebec before the St Lawrence is filled with Ice.

I should have liked to have gone on Shore here, as the Climate is said to be delightful & the Islands abounding in Grapes, Oranges, Melons, Chestnuts etc. No boats came to us with fruits & they rarely fish beyond their harbour on account of the heavy squalls to which the Coast is subject which endangers their being blown out to sea. From the description of the Islands I would like to make a voyage here instead of going to Tunbridge or other watering Places, where people frequently ennuyer themselves. The scheme would be more enlarged & I believe much more amusing. Being at Sea in good weather is delightful, & there is no occasion to execute such a voyage in the Equinoxial season.

If Mrs Simcoe could have looked forward some hundred and fifty years, or perhaps a little more, she might have been amused to see how many of her compatriots were to agree with her in preferring Mediterranean holidays to English resorts. But despite her advanced views Mrs Simcoe was not travelling for pleasure. She was accompanying her husband, the first Governor of Upper Canada, on a tour of duty which was to last five years. She was an early examplar of what Joanna Trollope in the title of her fascinating book was to call *Britannia's Daughters*, the women of the nineteenth and twentieth centuries who left their homeland in a steady stream. They went as wives to military or administrative men, as settlers and explorers, missionaries and medical workers, journalists and botonists, convicts and colonists, governesses and 'brides for hire'. Some categories cover sizeable numbers of women, others only the rare exceptions, but all were to some degree pushing outward the barriers enclosing their civilization or their sex.

The story of women's travel in the nineteenth and early twentieth centuries is an immense one, now beginning to get the coverage it deserves. It is not one necessarily best told through diary material. Women away from friends and family are obviously drawn towards the letter as a form of communication rather than the diary. (Often the two combined—Mrs Simcoe's diary was by no means unusual in being sent home in instalments to the lady who had charge of her four children while she was away. Is it for that reason that it is often so distinctly uninformative about her reactions to what she saw?) And then, those travellers aware that their journeys were extraordinary—look at the Virago Travellers list to see how many—often wrote up their travels as a public chronicle themselves. Fascinating the results often are. Diaries they are not.

And yet, there is often a particularly rich interest in those records that were kept (and released) in diary form. Take Freya Stark's record of *A Winter in Arabia* (kept as a diary while she and her two women companions, a scientist and an archaeologist, were stationary: she shifts to straight narrative when they take to the road again). The intimate tone is at least as revealing about Stark and her companions as it is about the Arabs:

25th November 1937
...The Archaeologist, under this first shock of genuine Arabia, is outraged to the very depths of her well-regulated heart. I have promised to keep her, as far as possible, separate from the inhabitants of this land; but alas! what will she make of a country whose chief if not only charm lies in its people? We cannot be completely isolated, like European delicacy in cold storage.

She herself has an appreciative but shrewd eye for the 'charm':

29th November

Qasim appeared today in the new *futah* (loincloth) I have given him for the feast, arranged like a ballet skirt with butterfly wings under his naked young torso, a sprig of sweet smelling *rihan* in his turban. He looked like an apparition of Youth in the frame of our dark stair.

He has a cheerful nature and an engaging liveliness in his opinions. The delicate shades of distance, whereby a servant is kept as a servant and not a family friend, are wasted on him: he emerges buoyant from every snub, with mere pity in his heart for us elderly irrational females. But Alinur he considers with affection, since she alone has some notions of cookery. On modern commodities such as camp-beds he looks with scorn—'comfortable for the dead', he says.

This is my week for housekeeping, and I usually find him and his assistant in a far corner of the kitchen squatting over a book of qasidas while the meat, boiling itself to toughness, bubbles in the middle of the floor. A servant in England would be abashed when surprised in literature, but Qasim leaps up delighted to show his poems, beautiful in red and black script. To have him and us in the same house, is like the Orient and Occident under one roof. The Orient does not get much done: it looks upon work as a part only—and not too important a part at that—of its varied existence, but enjoys with a free mind whatever happens besides. The Occident, busily building, has its eyes rigidly fixed on the future: Being and Doing, and civilization, a compromise between them. There is too little of the compromise now. Too much machinery in the West, too little in the East, have made a gap between the active and contemplative; they drift ever more apart. Woman hitherto has inclined to the eastern idea—the stress being laid on what she *is* rather than on what she does; and if we are going to change this, taking for our sole pattern the active energies of men, we are in danger of destroying a principle which contains one-half the ingredients of civilization. Before ceasing to *be*, it is to be hoped that our sex will at least make sure that what it *does* is worth the sacrifice.

Meanwhile I have just found Qasim straining the soup through an ancient turban that has seen better days. He says he washed it first.

In this record of her thoughts and feelings, not necessarily only of her travels, the 'women question' appears again and again.

27th December

'I have been waiting till you came,' the Mansab said presently, 'to decide whether to allow you to dig here, and meanwhile I have given those ladies four men. They asked for eight. I thought four was enough.'

Amused by this attitude towards female emancipation, I agreed with the Mansab's prudence, but suggested that the ratio might now be raised. The giving of labour would increase his prestige with the tribes around. The tribes are the perpetual thorn in the flesh of the Mansabs of Hureidha.

Female emancipation as a means of propaganda became comprehensible in his eyes and we parted friends. The Mansab, like any ordinary Englishman, appears to be afraid of the Strong-Minded Woman (whose mind, I sometimes think, is apt to be her weakest point). He had obviously imagined alarming things about us.

'I am glad,' he said, 'to find that you are Arabs like myself.'

European women, strong-minded or otherwise, seem to have been something with which the Arab races just had to cope. Around the turn of the century one of their strangest visitors was Isabelle Eberhardt, illegitimate daughter of a one-time pope of the Russian Orthodox Church, born near Geneva. Her extraordinary background offers a key to her no less extraordinary wanderings.

At the age of twenty she and her mother left the family home for North Africa: when her mother died, Isabelle set off towards the desert alone. She disguised herself as an Arab man, a double pretence which apparently fooled no one, but which no one was impolite enough to deny. To the jaundiced eye her progress there, combined with dangerously active political sympathies on behalf of French colonial rule, looks little short of disastrous, a passage of promiscuity and drugs which led her literally to beggary. But she sounds more like the last of the great Romantics:

Cagliari, 1st January 1900

Those silent nights again, those lazy rides on horseback through the salty plains of the Oued Righ's and the Oued Souf's white sand! That feeling, sad and blissful at once, that would fill my pariah's heart every time I struck camp surrounded by friends, among Spahis and nomads, none of whom ever considered me the despicable outcast I had so miserably become at the hands of fate.

Right now, I long for one thing only: to lead that life again in Africa . . . to sleep in the chilly silence of the night below stars that drop from great heights, with the sky's infinite expanse for a roof and the warm earth for a bed, in the knowledge that no one pines for me *anywhere on earth*, that there is no place where I am being missed or expected. To know that is to be free and unencumbered, a nomad in the great desert of life. . . .

Self usually wins out over Sahara as subject-matter for her journal. There are many such impassioned paens of praise to Africa and the life there. Her journal, found among her few possessions after she was killed by a flash flood at Aïn Sefra at the age of twenty-seven, is undoubtedly that of a traveller—a nomad even. But it is a traveller whose eyes turn ever to the inward landscape.

Turning from the diaries of Isabelle Eberhardt to those of Margaret Fountaine, you cannot but exclaim at a superficial connection—and celebrate a profound difference. Before and after her death in 1940, Margaret Fountaine was known as a lepidopterist of distinction, whose butterfly-hunting expeditions had led her across the globe. It was only in April 1978, at the first opportunity after the day, (15 April, her birthday) precisely specified in her will, that the sealed box left to the Castle Museum in Norwich was opened. In it were twelve volumes, kept from 1878 (when she was fifteen) to 1939. They had, it appeared, been written at regular intervals from notes made wherever she happened to be—deliberately written without benefit of hindsight, but transposed into continuous narrative, i.e. without the day-by-day breaks which usually constitute diary form.

The 'diaries' added a whole new dimension to the Margaret Fountaine story—one which almost overshadowed the public figure of the traveller and naturalist. *Love Among the Butterflies* was the title under which the first selection from them was published—and the assumption, whether on the part of the editor or of Miss Fountaine herself, was that of love and lepidoptery, most people would rather read about love.

Margaret's wanderings started circumspectly enough. A summer trip to Switzerland with her sister introduced her simultaneously to the delights of butterflies and the discovery of 'how beautiful was this earth'. Each subsequent trip, it seems, took her further afield: Italy, Corsica, Sicily, Germany, Hungary, Greece, Beirut, Damascus (where she was to meet Khalil Neimy, the married Syrian dragoman with whom she spent the next twenty-eight years), Algeria, Yugoslavia, South Africa, America, Cuba, Jamaica, Costa Rica, India, Ceylon, the Himalayas, Australia (where they tried to be farming settlers); everywhere on the way out and on the way back. And on—and on—and on. Pulling out passages of description from her prolific pages would be a hopeless and an unprofitable task: they are not what the reader feels the diaries are about. What they are about is the tantalizing combination of male admiration (unfailingly detected and commented upon) and female determination—one passage from Greece 1900, i.e. pre-Khalil, will do as well as twenty to illustrate this:

> Travelling with Mr Elwes entailed a good deal of luxury; he never took the trouble to do anything he could get his courier to do for him; he never ate bad food were it possible to procure better, and he never walked when a horse or mule was available to ride; in all of which I also scored.
> Unfortunately he was obliged to return almost at once to England, so he made an arrangement with Marcos to remain as my courier, while he should also spend his time catching butterflies for him. Mr Elwes was to give Marcos his salary and I was to pay the rest of his expenses including his

board, his journeys and his horses. I took to the arrangement none the less,
I am afraid, because Marcos was a rather well-favoured person and
attracted by me. It would not do to make many more expeditions like
that—how could I keep up my dignity with a man who has to come to my
bedroom at all times of the day, maybe when I'm sitting in my
dressing-gown of an evening?

I went back to Athens for two nights, but longed to be back in the wild,
free to lead my own unsophisticated life, away from the conventionalities of
civilization. Freedom is the crowning joy of life. Thank God there are few on
earth I really care for; I would there were none. I want to see all I can of this
beautiful world before I have to leave it, and life is so distressingly short. It
is the affections that hold us back from great enterprises, it is the affections
that tie us down to one spot on earth—if not in body, in spirit. And then at
the end of it all life is over and we have accomplished none of those great
things our soaring imaginations once led us to suppose were to be achieved.

I rejoined Marcos and we moved on to Tripolizza and then Mesolonghi,
surrounded by low damp meadows and marshes, a perfect fever-bed of
snakes and mosquitoes. Marcos didn't appreciate the snakes at all, though
he was never so vehement in his protestations that he was not afraid of them
as when he had just jumped half a foot off the ground at the sign of one. But I
wanted to get *P. Ottomanus*, so snakes and mosquitoes alike must be put up
with.

She was only a year away from the fateful meeting with Khalil Neimy
(later she changed his name to 'Charles' in the diaries). And in the
letter which, in 1978, was found to accompany the diary book, she links
their love and her wanderings for good:

> ... certainly the most interesting part of my life was spent with him, the dear
> companion, the constant and untiring friend and assistant in our
> entomological work, travelling as we did together over all the loveliest, the
> wildest and often the loneliest places of this most beautiful Earth, while the
> roving spirit and love of the wilderness drew us closely together in a bond of
> union in spite of our widely different spheres of life, race and individuality,
> in a way that was often quite inexplicable to most of those who knew us.

Pioneers

Women haven't stopped 'Beating the Boundaries' even now, when
travel has extended to the point where boundaries take some finding.
Look at Dervla Murphy *Bicycling to Coorg*, or *Castaway*, the diary Lucy
Irvine kept on Tuin. But there is another group from the past who
command our attention even more—the pioneers. They were beating
the boundaries but under a particular stress—that their adventures
were never intended to have a cosy end in a return to the life they once
knew.

Diaries from the nineteenth century show just how great that stress must have been, but also how bravely and often cheerfully it was faced. Anne Langton, with her parents, left a comfortable and cultivated 'gentlewoman's' life in England in 1837 to join her brother on a farm in Ontario. She kept a journal which, like Mrs Simcoe's, was written to be sent Home; but Anne's is considerably more informative. Just think of the 'culture shock' implied in these few words:

Thursday, October 11 [1838]

You cannot imagine how perfectly *comme il faut* rough log walls appear to us now; when we have got our striped green print up we shall feel as grand as Queen Victoria amidst the damask hangings at Buckingham Palace.

'If I say much more,' she writes in January, 'I shall frighten you on our account....'

Wednesday, January 23 [1839]

I must tell you then that the drawing-room is as warmable as ever, and the chimney does not smoke as it did last winter. When Aunt Alice and I were pasting up the wind-holes, my mother reproved us, saying it was ridiculous for people to come to Canada and not be able to bear a breath of air. She is determined not to be soft. All things are by comparison; after these frosts, when it is milder and I report the thermometer at nine or ten, my mother says, 'Oh, dear! I am afraid it is going to thaw'. You will perceive that all my thoughts run upon heat and cold to-day.

'I daresay our lakes, waterfalls, rapids, canoes, forests, Indian encampments, sound very well to you dwellers in the suburbs of a manufacturing town,' she wrote on another occasion, 'nevertheless I assure you there cannot well be a more unpoetical and anti-romantic existence than ours.'

In its very unpoetical practicality, though, Anne Langton found a moral lesson:

Saturday, October 13 [1838]

I have caught myself wishing an old long-forgotten wish that I had been born of the rougher sex. Women are very dependent here, and give a great deal of trouble; we feel our weakness more than anywhere else. This, I cannot but think, has a slight tendency to sink us, it may be, into a more natural and proper sphere than the one we occupy in over-civilized life, as the thing I mean and feel, though I do not express it well, operates, I believe, as a safeguard to our feminine virtues, such virtues, I mean, as the Apostles recommended to us, for I think here a woman must be respectable to meet with consideration and respect.

Whether or not—probably not—you want to accept the moral

conclusion, Anne Langton has raised an important point—the way in which women's experience of and attitude to pioneering must have been different from men's. It is something you rub up against from another angle in the diaries of a different set of pioneers.

More than a quarter of a million Americans crossed their continent from east to west between 1840 and 1870. More than eight hundred diaries have been published or catalogues in archives; many more are believed still to exist in family hands. They were written, according to Lillian Schlissel, author of *Women's Diaries of the Westward Journey* (not available in the UK) with one eye on history, with the full and proud consciousness that the diarist was helping to extend their continent. They were often written as a practical reference point for those who came after, rather than as a chronicle of personal thoughts and feelings—but that doesn't prevent them from being emotive enough, even so.

Helen Carpenter, in August 1857:

> When the sun was just peeping over the top of the mountain, there was suddenly heard a shot and a blood-curdling yell, and immediately the Indians we saw yesterday were seen riding at full speed directly toward the horses... father put his gun to his shoulder as though to shoot... The Indians kept... circling... and halooing... bullets came whizzing through the camp. None can know the horror of it, who have not been similarly situated... [the Indians] did not come directly toward us, but all the time in a circular way, from one side of the road to the other, each time they passed, getting a little nearer, and occasionally firing a shot... Father and Reel could stand it no longer, they must let those Indians see how far their Sharps rifles would carry. Without aiming to hit them, they made the earth fly.

The next month the party ahead of them 'found the body of a nude woman on the bank of the slough... A piece of hair rope was around her neck... From appearances it was though she had been tortured by being drawn back and forth through the slough, by this rope around her neck. The body was given the best burial that was possible under the circumstances.'

Drama apart, death was more likely to come from disease or privation than from Indian attack, but it certainly came often enough. Cecelia McMillen Adams, in 1852:

> Child's grave... smallpox... child's grave... [We] passed 7 new-made graves. One had 4 bodies in it... cholera. A man died this morning with the cholera in the company ahead of us... Another man died... Passed 6 new graves... We have passed 21 new-made graves... made 18 miles... Passed 13 graves today. Passed 10 graves....

June 25   Passed 7 graves...made 14 miles
June 26   Passed 8 graves
June 29   Passed 10 graves
June 30   Passed 10 graves...made 22 miles
July   1   Passed 8 graves...made 21 miles
July   2   One man of [our] company died. Passed 8 graves made 16 miles
July   4   Passed 2 graves...made 16 miles
July   5   Passed 9 graves...made 18 miles
July   6   Passed 6 graves...made 9 miles
July 11   Passed 15 graves...made 13 miles
July 12   Passed 5 graves...made 15 miles
July 18   Passed 4 graves...made 16 miles

and so on.

So it continues. Lillian Schlissel quotes a succession of such extracts, and notes that it was overwhelmingly the women diarists who felt the need to record each individual grave. Perhaps they had more reason to fear. '22 per cent of the married women who had reached childbearing years in this census [Schlissel writes] were in some state of pregnancy or had recently delivered. Eighteen other women wrote that they knew of or personally assisted women in neighbouring wagon-trains who gave birth on the way.' Small wonder she reaches the pessimistic conclusion she does:

> There is a kind of murderous precision in the women's recounting of mishap. Surely, the accounts must be viewed as a reflection of the continuing anxieties they felt. But the more one reads these diaries, the more one comes to feel the passionate indictment, the bitter appraisal by the women of the men's determination to make the journey. However bravely the women started, however they mustered their strength to meet the demands of each day, however they rallied to appreciate the splendors of the scenery, the women were intimately affected by the journey's dreadful toll. Their responses depended upon whether their own lives were placed within the processes of childbearing and childrearing, or whether they were still in their girlhood years. Buoyant spirits are almost always in the diaries of unmarried girls and young wives. Accounts shade and darken in the pages of women whose energies were spent nursing and caring for infants and small children.

Buoyant spirits were to be found all right. 'I like it better every day' wrote Algeline Ashley in 1852. And Lydia Allen Rudd sets out from the Missouri river in the same year 'with good courage and not one sigh of regret'. She seems to have had her own aim in Oregon: to get a land claim filed under her own name, as a new law allowed settlers to do. She didn't achieve it—her husband decided to take a job instead and 'I shall have to be poor and dependent on a man my lifetime'. But it is interesting that the idea occurred.

Perhaps the only way to look at women's diaries of the westward journey is to concentrate on a woman's diary from first to last (if only in snatches). And, in the case of Amelia Stewart Knight, in the light of a piece of information only contained in the last entry and not mentioned before....

Saturday, April 9th 1853

STARTED FROM HOME about 11 o'clock and travelled 8 miles and camped in an old house; night cold and frosty.

Saturday, April 16th

... Made our beds down in the tent in the wet and mud. Bed clothes nearly spoiled ... Husband is scolding and hurrying all hands (and the cook) and Almira says she wished she was home, and I say ditto. Home, Sweet Home....

Friday, April 29th

Cool and pleasant; saw the first Indians today.

Friday, May 6th

Here we passed a train of wagons on their way back, the head man had been drowned a few days before, in a river called Elkhorn, while getting some cattle across and his wife was lying in the wagon quite sick, and children were mourning for the father gone. With sadness and pity I passed those who perhaps a few days before had been well and happy as ourselves. Came 20 miles today.

Monday, May 16th Evening

The men and boys are all wet and muddy. Hard times but they say misery loves company. We are not alone on these bare plains, it is covered with cattle and wagons.

Tuesday, May 24th

I had the sick headache all night, some better this morning; must do a day's work.

The diary continues with sickness, the death of cattle, the crossing of rivers, a terrifying incident when one of the children was left behind and her absence not noticed until the wagon-train behind brought her on. Everything is taken as part of the 'desolate' road littered with dead animals. ('I could hardly help shedding tears when we drove round this poor ox who had helped us along thus far, and has given us his very last step.') Potatoes and salmon bought from the Indians make a welcome change in their diet, until September brings them to the last stage of the trail.

Tuesday, September 6th

Still in camp, washing and overhauling the wagons to make as light as possible cross the mountains. Evening—After throwing away a good many things and burning up most of the deck boards of our wagons so as to lighten them, got my washing and cooking done and started on again. Crossed two branches, travelled 3 miles and have camped near the gate or foot of the Cascade Mountains, (here I was sick all night, caused by my washing and working too hard).

Saturday, September 10th

It would be useless for me with my pencil to describe the awful road we have just passed over. Let fancy picture a train of wagons and cattle passing through a crooked chimney and we have Big Laurel Hill. . . . I was sick all night and not able to get out of the wagon in the morning.

Friday, Sept. 17th [sic]

In camp yet. Still raining. Noon—It has cleared off and we are all ready for a start again, for some place we don't know where. . . .

A few days later my eighth child was born. After this we picked up and ferried across the Columbia River, utilizing skiff, canoes and flatboat to get across, taking three days to complete. Here husband traded two yoke of oxen for a half section of land with one half-acre planted to potatoes and a small log cabin and lean-to with no windows. This is the journey's end.

Is it better to travel hopefully—even pregnant—or to arrive?

Part *IV*
The Life Inside

- Religion
- Despair
- Living and Dying

Chapter 12
~ Religion

'Lord, thou has been our refuge from one generation to another.'—Book of
Common Prayer

'Prayer does not change God, but it changes him who prays.'—Sören
Kierkegaard

Who does and who does not? Mention God, that is. The Bloomsbury
set do not, by and large. Liane de Pougy, writing at around the same
time, the Parisian courtesan and *'grande horizontale'* turned lay sister in
old age, does, exhaustively. The diaries kept for purposes of religious
improvement in the sixteenth and seventeenth centuries seem now to
be an odd mixture of self-abasement and stolidity; in the nineteenth
century, George Sand apostrophises Him as a way of getting at her
erring lover Alfred de Musset (to whom she planned to show the
journal) until it is a little difficult to be sure who the 'cruel Master' she
addresses really is. And in our own century, Barbara Pym passes
through a lifetime of quiet commitment to the Anglican church with
cool and half-ironical little references.

There are some surprises in store—if not too many *volte-faces* on the
Liane de Pougy scale. Queen Victoria, that emblem of an age which, we
tend to assume, took piety as the first duty of women, barely mentions
her faith. At eighty-one, on the death of her third grown-up child: 'I
pray God to help me to be patient and have trust in Him, who has never
failed me!' But the concern is all for the loss in this world: no mention of
the consolations of the next.

Duty or Devotion?

Earlier in life, Queen Victoria makes it clear that not only religious belief but religious observance can sometimes be taken, as it were, on trust:

> *22nd September 1838*
>
> Spoke for some time of church-going and Lord Melbourne said he never used to go, after he left Eton; 'My Father and Mother never went,' he said. 'People didn't use to go so much formerly; it wasn't the fashion; but it is a right thing to do.' He said Uncle, last year, wanted to go twice, but Lord M. assured him (as it is) that that was unnecessary.

How unexpected. Disconcerting even. It is almost a relief to get on to Honoria Lawrence, wife to an administrator of colonial India and exponent of what we think of as the 'Victorian' values. Soon after her marriage, in a journal addressed to her husband, she writes:

> *Sunday, 22nd October 1837*
>
> We had some discussion last night on the observance of this day, and I told you, dearest, the truth, that our Sundays had been my least happy hours since our marriage. It is our indispensable duty to make up our minds as to how the Christian Sabbath is to be observed. My beloved, seek God's teaching on the subject, follow it simply and then we shall pursue our occupations with a cheerful quiet spirit. My own view is that our rule ought to be the entire suspension of worldly business. The exceptions must be determined by circumstances. My love, I do not like to seem as if I were your teacher, but circumstances have led me to the consideration of subjects which your attention has not thus been directed to, and I now implore you to consider the matter. I should like to take some one book of Scripture for Sunday and pursue it regularly on that day, for a longer time than we give to reading in the week. Studying the New Testament in the original, reading such works as Milton, writing on matters connected with religion, all these would vary the day's occupations, and make 'the Sabbath a delight'.

Form and feeling, duty and devotion are the two sides of the religious coin. Impossible to tell, especially across a barrier of centuries, where the one began and the other ended. Take the entries of Lady Margaret Hoby, one of the earliest British diarists whose work is still preserved, and whose life appears to have been dominated by the somewhat excessive demands of her daily devotions:

> *1599*
>
> In the morninge I praied privately and wrett notes in my testament till 7 o'clock then I took order for dinner and thinges touching the house, after I had breakfast I wrought till dinner time and heard Mr Rhodes (a sort of resident chaplain) till dinner time, after dinner I walked with Mr Younge

till 2 o'clock then I went to work... after I had praied and taken order for supper walked abroad till after 5 at which time I retourned to examenation and praier at which time it pleased the Lord to give me sure testimonie of his favour in Christ his name evermore be praised who sendeth not his... away; till supper time I was busie in the granerie and after supper and praiers I went to bedd.

The other business of life is often mentioned primarily in relation to its effects on her religious duties ('I bestowed too much time in the garden and thereby was worse able to perform spirituall dutes'), but it is still more of a domestic record than the 'Diarie' (her term for it) of Viscountess Mordaunt some half century later. From 1656 to 1678 the Viscountess celebrated important events both public (the Restoration of the Monarchy, the Great Fire, the Plague) and private by writing out a prayer; the headings alone indicate the events to which they refer. The sympathy the 'Diarie' could command today might be limited were it not for a period of seven or eight weeks in 1657 when Lady Mordaunt adopted a different scheme. Each day is entered in two columns, headed 'To returne thanks for' and 'To aske perden for'. Some of the entries in the second have a familiar ring:

> Having been angry today in my house with Lady P--- and for having been dull at prayrs and for having in returne to a complement told a lye.

> I have offended my God this day by shortening my prayrs and by telling an untruthe and by being to[o] much plesed with sumthing to ete [i.e. eat].

> O forgeve derest Lord the ofences of this day, my ometing to returne thee prays for my deare Husband's returne tell now and my telling him sum things that may insence him against his mother.

Such diaries were written for purposes of religious amendment; and Lady Margaret Hoby and others must have been highly motivated to undertake such a task. We cannot deduce devotion or the lack of it from the nineteenth-century entries of a Mary Gladstone or a Lady Fanny Minto, all on the regular but automatic and apparently largely social note. ('A great party to Church today.') And we have to make an effort to come to terms with the piety of a Fanny Longfellow in the special diary she kept for her religious experience:

> *25th December 1841*
> Today, for the first time, I knelt before the altar and received the sacrament. I have often longed to partake in this touching and holy ceremony, which, if not enjoined upon us as a sacred duty, yet was addressed to our hearts in tones of thrilling entreaty to which all must hearken. A friend's dying request is sacred in our eyes, how much more then one of the last which passed the lips of Him who bestowed upon us life eternal. 'This do in remembrance of me'

has ever stirred my conscience when I have seen the Communion table spread, when I have prayed to draw nearer the well-beloved son of the Father, but I have shrunk back as too impure to handle those holy things, as not hungering and thirsting after righteousness alone, fearful of committing sacrilege should earthly appetites regain their wonted sway in my soul after it had tasted of that bread and that wine which typify the body of the blessed Redeemer. But today, this holiest Sabbath of the year, this birthday of the world, for Christ was born to bestow true life on all, in this church sombre but cheerful with boughs and wreaths from the woods of winter, beautifully in harmony with the spirit of the religion which decks the soul in its days of gloom with the never-dying garlands of hope and faith, the chanting of the Christmas anthem, with its words of healing benediction all the hopes the heavenly choir sang, the infinite love of the Creator for his children swelled my heart with irresistible emotion and drew it to the altar.

As mentioned earlier, she also kept another journal to record the progress of her children:

14th January 1849

Both chicks in study after breakfast, a pretty picture, sitting on the same cushion, looking at their little books, their rosy faces and fair locks touching. Out throwing snowballs with Uncle Stephen after dinner. Told them story of the little boy (my version of Jack and the Beanstalk) who planted bean in the garden and it began to grow, and every time he did a good thing it shot up higher and when he was generous and kind a beautiful flower bloomed on it, and when he was naughty the flower died, and it grew shorter again, and the leaves turned black and dropped off. And so it grew up and up to the sky, and he found he could climb up it, putting his feet on the leaves as steps, and when he reached the top the last flowers sprang to his shoulders and made little wings with which he flew among the clouds till he reached a lovely garden, where all good children lived and flew about, taking care of flowers, feeding little birds in nests, and doing a thousand kind and loving things, and the poor naughty children wandered outside, hearing their voices and longing to see the garden but could only peep through chinks in the wall until their beanstalk grew tall enough for them to look over the wall and the more they were good the faster it would grow, etc. etc. They listened delightedly to my moral lesson and seemed to understand it.

1st February 1849

Charley begs warmly for the story of the beanstalk and listens to it with great solemnity. If I change an accustomed phrase, or make an addition, he is in an agony, and still more if I laugh. He apologizes if he laughs himself, and says, 'I did not mean to'. It is to him too true and earnest not to be received seriously. I love this reverential spirit and am very unwilling to wound it or have it wounded. It is the best shield he can bear through life, and never, never I trust may he be ashamed of it. It is the very shadow of God's presence in his soul.

One can understand that, well enough. But it is still easier to relate to a Beatrix Potter extract:

Tuesday, 30th September 1884

It seems they will not give a child Christian burial at Hatfield unless it has been baptized. I believe it is still a common superstition that a child goes to the wrong place unless baptized. How can anyone believe that the power above us—call it Jehovah, Allah, Trinity, what they will—is a just and merciful father, seeing the end from the beginning, and will yet create a child, a little rosebud, the short-lived pain and joy of its mother's heart, only to consign it after a few days of innocence to eternal torment?

All outward forms of religion are almost useless, and are the cause of endless strife. What do Creeds matter, what possible difference does it make to anyone today whether the doctrine of the resurrection is correct or incorrect, or the miracles, they don't happen nowadays, but very queer things do that concern us much more. Believe there is a great power silently working all things for good, behave yourself and never mind the rest.

Or to housewife Nella Last, writing in the Second World War:

Wednesday, 29th November 1939

I wish sometimes I was a religious woman and could find comfort and faith in bombarding God with requests and demands... My next-door neighbour has every religious service on at all hours, and finds comfort in it. I wish I could do so—I would only find irritation at the loud noise. She says she prays God to strike Hitler dead. Cannot help thinking if God wanted to do that he would not have waited till Mrs. Helm asked him to do so.

Prayer, its efficacy or the reverse, is something that occurs to most of us, whether we think we believe or not. Beatrice Webb is unsure:

25th April 1902

The reading in which I find most relaxation is religion. It seems to rest my brain and refresh my spirit. And I am constantly pondering over the legitimacy of prayer—one's quite unaccountable faith in it, resting as it does on the good one gains from the practice of it. I enjoy the 'religious life' and it seems to enhance and not to weaken my capacity for secular work. And yet I cannot bring my faith and my practice into line with the Christian religion. I cannot acquiesce in the claims of Christianity. I should love to worship with others and to feel the support and the charm of a regular and definite ritual. But directly I hear the words in which Christians clothe their religious aspirations my intellectual sincerity takes alarm. I do not believe in their doctrine. I am not even attracted by their God, whether in the Jewish or in the Christian version. My faith is more in spiritual influence—at present being exercised by good men and good thoughts, in the communion of saints here on earth, and the relation of the good men and good thoughts to the mysterious spiritual universe which I believe surrounds us.

It is, after all, remarkably hard to get away from one's background—and everyone's background, if only in a school context, contains some degree of religious instruction. Anaïs Nin felt hers:

> Am I, at bottom, still that fervent little Spanish Catholic child who chastised herself for loving toys, who forbade herself the enjoyment of sweet foods, who practised silence, who humiliated her pride, who adored symbols, statues, burning candles, incense, the caress of nuns, organ music, for whom Communion was a great event? I was so exalted by the idea of eating Jesus's flesh and drinking His blood that I couldn't swallow the Host well, and I dreaded harming it. On my knees, lost to my surroundings, eyes closed, I visualized Christ descending into my heart so realistically (I was a realist then!) that I could see Him walking down the stairs and entering the room of my heart like a sacred visitor.... I am embalmed because a nun leaned over me, enveloped me in her veils, kissed me. The chill curse of Christianity. I do not confess any more, I have no remorse, yet am I doing penance for my enjoyments? Nobody knows what a magnificent prey I was for Christian legends, because of my compassion and my tenderness for human beings. Today it divides me from enjoyment of life.

Marian Milner, beginning her journal cum voyage of self-discovery, was surprised to find God coming into it at all—but somehow, the name turned up:

> GOD ... happiness—wrong—damnation—those who do not believe shall be damned—as soon as you are happy, enjoying yourself, something hunts you on—the hounds of heaven—you think you'll be lost—damned, if you are caught—so never stop—God is wicked, cruel—the Old Testament God, who commands whole cities to be put to the slaughter—a jealous God, visiting the sins—Oh God—what a God!—Hell—blasted, you'll be, annihilated, puffed out—pains of Hell gat hold upon me—you believed what they said and wanted to be a missionary to save your soul—God, help us—be merciful unto us, miserable sinners....

Six months later she writes:

> I BELIEVE ... in God, etc.—that's no use—God—something large up in the sky rather like a canopy—and a shrinking fear inside me—memory of pain, when I have said: 'Oh God', the ache of foreboding and fear of consequences—dread—when I have said: 'God help me'—'God, let me not be late for school'—panic, terror—unreasoning, in which only God can help—it's terror of wrong-doing, of disapproval—it seems a long time since I felt it. God—a far-away altar to a man god—Abraham on the mountain—the God of Moses with piercing eyes that burnt one's face—no, it was a burning light, the face of God, that blinded one—St Paul was also blinded—and God, no, the Lord, was not in the Fire—yet I feel he is very much fire—the queer awe and terror and excitement of watching a heath fire and fighting it, the living fury of the flames—this is as God—fierce,

destructive, beautiful, inhuman—the sun also blinds one—I cannot look upon his face—he is joyful, strong and aloof....

The American teenager 'Alice', soon to die of drug abuse, makes the same discovery. ('He' is Joel, a boyfriend):

> He's a very spiritual kind of person, not really religious, but spiritual, and he feels very deeply. I think most kids in our generation do. Even on drug trips, many kids think they see God or that they are communing with heavenly things.

She is right, of course. People of her generation—i.e. her age group—do tend to be particularly attuned to spiritual experiences. In the years of quest and exploration, the religion which was taken fairly casually on board in childhood suddenly becomes a prop (or a pose, or a passion). The question is—does the feeling last?

Youthful Ardour

Sometimes, of course, it does. Elizabeth Fry was seventeen, from a Quaker but not a particularly strict or ardent background, when she went to a London Meeting and heard William Savery preach:

> *17th March 1798*
> May I never forget the impression William Savery has made on my mind, as much as I can say is, I thank God for having sent at least a glimmering of light through him into my heart, which I hope with care, and keeping it from the many draughts and winds of this life, may not be blown out, but become a large brilliant flame, that will direct me to that haven, where will be joy without a sorrow, and all will be comfort.

So—surprisingly—it proved, as the rest of her experience was to bear out. Reviewing the London experience thirty years later, it was, she wrote, 'like the casting of a die in my life'. Not altogether easily, not at once, but, in the end, decisively. Not everyone's early religious experience, however, is so trustworthy a guide.

Written at a (somewhat precocious) twelve—and at an impatient fifteen—Marie Bashkirtseff's journal is full of passionate appeals:

> *January 1873*
> O God, give me the Duke of H...!... I'll love him and make him happy; I'll be happy too, and kind to the poor. It is sinful to believe one can purchase the grace of God by good works, but I can't express myself properly.
> I'm in love with the Duke of H---, and can't tell him so; even if I did, he would pay no heed. While he was here I had an object in going out and dressing myself, but now!... I went on the terrace in the hope of seeing him,

at least for an instant, in the distance. O God, ease my pain, I can't pray any more, but listen to my prayers! Thy grace is so infinite, thy mercy so great, thou hast done so much for me! It grieves me so not to see him on the Promenade. He looked so distinguished among the vulgar crowd of Nice.

Thursday, 20th January 1876

O God, grant my prayer! Preserve my voice; should I lose all else I shall have my voice. O God, continue to show me Thy goodness; do not let me die of grief and vexation! I long so much to go into society. Time passes and I make no progress; I am nailed to the same place, I who would live, live by steam, I who burn, who boil over, who bubble with impatience!

'I have never seen in any one such a fever of life,' said Doria of me.

If you knew me you would have some notion of my impatience, my grief.

O God, take pity on me! I have only Thee; it is to Thee I pray, Thou alone who canst comfort me!

In conjunction with Marie Bashkirtseff's age, it is hard to take her agonies that seriously—though her tragically early death was to prove her impatience better founded than she knew. But the language of these constant—not occasional—entries shows at the least an intense familiarity with the ardours of religion. As she moves out of her teens, though, the person-to-person appeals die away. The tone changes.

Sunday, 22nd August 1880

And then mamma is always talking of God: if God is willing; by God's help. They call upon God so often only to escape all sorts of little duties. It is neither faith nor even devotion, it is a mania, a weakness; the cowardice of lazy, incapable and indolent people! What can be more indelicate than to cover all one's failings with the word of God? It is indelicate; it is more, it is criminal, if one believes in God. If it is decreed that a thing is to happen, it will happen, she says, to avoid the trouble of action ... and the fear of remorse. If everything had been decreed beforehand, God would be only a constitutional president, and our wills, vices, and virtues but sinecures.

Four years later she goes further:

... this is God's punishment. But if I don't believe in God? I can't tell, and even then ... I have my conscience, and my conscience reproaches me for what I did.

And then it is impossible to say, I don't believe in God. That depends on what we understand by God. If the God we love and long for really existed, the world would be different. There is no God who hears my evening prayer, and I pray every evening in spite of my reason.

Si le ciel est desert, nous n'offensons personne; Si quelqu'un nous entend, qu'l nous prenne en pitie. Yet, how is it possible to believe?

Marie Bashkirtseff felt her way out of what you could call an automatic attitude of devotion. Anne Frank had no chance to. There is a faint echo of the gabbled, glib childhood prayer 'please God make me a good girl, amen' about the religious references in a few teenage diaries, including hers.

Saturday, 7th November 1942

Sometimes I believe that God wants to try me, both now and later on; I must become good through my own efforts, without examples and without good advice. Then later on I shall be all the stronger.

Wednesday, 29th December 1943

... I am selfish and cowardly. Why do I always dream and think of the most terrible things—my fear make me want to scream out loud sometimes. Because still, in spite of everything, I have not enough faith in God. He has given me so much—which I certainly do not deserve—and I still do so much that is wrong every day. If you think of your fellow creatures, then you only want to cry, you could really cry the whole day long. The only thing to do is to pray that God will perform a miracle and save some of them. And I hope that I am doing that enough!

A child's assumptions, or a child's expectation—up to a point—that she herself may be able to change things. A hint of the adolescent's self-consciousness? Or an adult's awareness that whether God is in His heaven or no, all is not right with the world?

The Agony...and the Ecstasy?

The impulse to turn back to childhood habits of prayer, less specifically Christian than a vague 'please, please', is common to most of those who would normally consider themelves agnostic at the very most. George Sand, born Armandine Lucile Aurore Dupin in France 1804, educated in a convent where she enjoyed, if that is the word, the intense religious experience of the teenage years, might seem in mature life, and from her public writings, to have gone beyond conventional theology. She had left her husband, changed her name, established herself in Bohemian circles as a writer. But she knew that atavistic impulse all right:

Ah, give me back my lover, and I shall be devout! My knees will wear out the pavements of the churches.

Her 'Journal to Musset', written in the hiatus of a stormy love affair with the poet Alfred de Musset, was nominally a series of letters addressed to him. But since the 'you' to whom they are addressed swings abruptly from being de Musset to being Sand's God, editor, or self, they can be taken as a journal indeed.

At the beginning of the Journal, her religious faith seems at the least in doubt:

Friday, November 1834

Liszt said to me today that God alone deserves to be loved. It may be true, but when one has loved a man it is very difficult to love God. It is so different.

A sentence later in the entry she asks God to give her back her devotion to religion. As the tone of the Journal becomes more tortured, not devotion to religion, precisely, but *something* comes flooding back:

God, thou knowest whether I could harbor such a thought and whether I ever in my life stooped to such meanness! Thou knowest whether I ever told any other lies! [than those to save Alfred from suffering] Dear God, why didst thou put me in such a horrible position, where it was necessary to lie or to kill a man by telling the truth? Why didst thou not protect me from such danger, when reason, consciousness, life itself hung in the balance? Thou knowest what we poor human beings are. Why dost thou allow us to lose ourselves and destroy ourselves? Thou alone canst absolve me from my failures and mistakes, because human understanding finds whatever it wants to find. Thou alone knowest the truth. Thou alone canst console and restore me.

Then kill me quickly, cruel Master! Have I not expiated enough? I lived through long weeks of terror and trembling. The lies I told seared my lips like a red-hot iron. Again and again I fell on my knees in those frozen churches and prayed frantically while my teeth were chattering with cold. And the other evening at Saint-Sulpice, when I cried out to thee, 'Wilt thou abandon me? Wilt thou punish me to the upmost limit? Will nothing appease thee?'—a voice in the depths of my heart answered, 'Confess, confess and die'.

Later still, in the heights of her imagination, she becomes Mary Magdalen:

Before me hangs the picture of Magdalen. She weeps and I weep with her. How magnificent her hair is! I am Magdalen shorn of her tresses but carrying her cross and her death's-head. That head at which you looked so sadly, poor sinner, did not teach so terrible a lesson as the skull on my table. You loved Jesus, who said, 'Her sins are forgiven, for she loved much'.

I also love, but I am not forgiven. How gladly I would exchange my comfortable room and warm dressing-gown for your wilderness and rags if I were permitted to carry with me the words of hope spoken by your Christ as he smiled forgiveness. Mine does not even say, 'Let the woman draw near, let her wash my feet'.

In a lesser woman, it might seem that Sand's feet were turning down a path of obsession or even delusion from which there was no safe return—especially since secure and reciprocated love with de Musset was never again to be hers. But Sand's occasional journals were in a very real sense her father confessor. Weak in the times of crisis when she turned to them, she was able to be strong again. Her life and her thoughts continued stormy. But thirteen years later, turning again to her journal to help rid herself of the depression which followed a period of ill health, she was nonetheless writing of religion in a calmer strain:

7th May 1847

I cannot say that I have ever loved life. I think I was born impatient to die. Ten years ago when I felt I was dying I was content to go. Indeed, the certainty of final death was the one comforting thought that sustained me. But I realized then that my soul was dying first, and I decided to keep my body in order to save my soul.

My soul is very well today—my body too. I am ready to go if my time has come. But, dear Lord, I do not want to die in anger, and I would rather die of almost anything than this horrid liver....

I am not afraid of nothingness. It seems restful. And rest is pleasant, and so desirable. But it is not important what I fear or desire in the so-called other life.

The one thing important is merging with God, who is goodness and love. Oh, enlighten me, infinite light! Why has death always seemed to me so beautiful? Why has death smiled at me since I was a little child?

In terms of our popular images, bohemian George Sand and saintly Florence Nightingale could hardly be further apart. But in the 'private notes' of her pre-Crimean years, Nightingale's direct appeals to her Creator are hardly less stormy than were Sand's in her worse moments. At sixteen, she was writing with conviction: 'God spoke to me and called me to His service' (7th February 1837). Unfortunately, it was fifteen years before his voice came quite that clearly again, and the long wait which saw Florence tied by her family's demands, confined to the restrictive life imposed upon a young lady, told sorely on her nerves. She was teased by addictive dreams she described as 'sin against the Holy Ghost', and the exact or the direct road to His service, was slow to appear:

5th December 1845

God has something for me to do for Him—or He would have let me die some time ago.... Oh for some great thing to sweep this loathsome life into the past.

1851

My God what am I to do?... Thou hast been teaching me all these 31 years what I am to do.... Where is the lesson? Let me read it. Oh where, where is it?

The great changes in her life when her nursing career began were reflected in her relations to her religion. 'Having been in Scutari six months today,' she wrote in a letter to her mother, 'am in sympathy with God....' At times of stress (or of the kind of stress she was least suited to bear, i.e. confinement in family surroundings) the old desperate note does reoccur, but there is another sound evocative of the public, the effective, the punishingly active Miss Nightingale. 'I must remember,' she wrote once, 'that God is not my private secretary...'.

Yes—religious fervour is a flame which doesn't always burn with the same coloured flame. But there can be few more surprising 'conversions', to use her own words, than that of Liane de Pougy, whose adventurous and, by any conventional standards, sinful career began in *fin de siècle* Paris and ended , in a religious establishment, in the days of the Second World War.

French-born Liane was raised a Catholic. One assumes that in the days of her career as a *grande horizontale*, the fact simply slipped her mind. Her diaries, the famous *Blue Notebooks*, were began in 1919, after her professional career had ended and after her second marriage to Prince Georges Ghika. Even so, there is at first a pleasurably worldly tone about her declaration of faith:

9th July 1919

I once rejected the Church to such a point that she had no choice but to reject me. But still when I remarried I wanted it to be in my Church. I was obscurely attached to it by a thousand little threads. Having been divorced, it wasn't possible, but I had been a widow since 1892. So on 8th June 1910, the civil ceremony was performed uniting Madame Marie Chassaigne (who had attained her majority—I paid them fifty francs not to say my age out loud) and Georges Gregoire Ghika (also a major). On the same day, in the little chapel of the catechism in Saint-Philippe-du-Roule, the union between Madame Pourpe, widow of Armand Pourpe, and Georges Ghika was also blessed. I had been to confession the day before.... For Liane de Pougy to make her confession must have been quite awkward, don't you think? She polished it off like this: 'Father, except for murder and robbery I've done everything.'

Her next mention is a degree less gamey, but still it manages to make religious faith sound like a matter of whim and of tradition:

1st February 1920

Salomon is not pleased with my poor little naive faith. He thinks it is a pity that a soul of my temper should be so given to nonsense. He quotes passages from the Bible and makes me put my finger on errors and contradictions. What do I care for the Bible, sermons, conventions? I draw my consoling faith from the vanquishing of my own strength. Dear Salomon, don't blow away my pathetic conviction, so frail and weak. I have had so much trouble bringing it to this point. All my family believed in God, and served Him; I choose to stand beside them.

Clearly though, we haven't heard the whole story so far:

30th December

Confession bores me, and the Mass, too, costs me an effort—I am not making progress on that road; I reproach myself for it. I am a poor soldier, at the least excuse I swing the lead. I don't rally properly to my flag, and I take the punishment for it inside myself: I am not happy. . . .

Just how much more there is to tell is revealed twenty years later:

15th October 1940

Praise the Lord, o my soul; inspire me, o Holy Spirit, to express God's goodness towards His poor, misguided, sinful creature. Great Saint Teresa who burnt with love of Him, awaken my poor heart which would be broken, bruised, bleeding if it had not been—by God's marvellous grace—recovered.

It is on my knees that I ought to be writing these lines; it is on my knees I think, that I prepare them, that I attempt to coordinate my thoughts. I never succeed. Cries break out, outbursts of feeling throw my whole being into such a turmoil that I am quite unable to write methodically about the extraordinary events which brought me here to the dear Trinitarian Ladies of Bois-Cerf, to their example, their faith and their devotion.

It was God who willed it, God who guided me. The sinner has disappeared, Liane de Pougy of the forty blue notebooks full of iniquity and scandal, lightness, frivolity, intrigue and lies—Liane de Pougy is no more. 'My God, my suffering at having offended You is extreme.'

Liane de Pougy, the notorious Liane, has become a lay sister. And the astonishing story is one she chooses in subsequent days to tell. Rambling, often repetitive, it still throws light on an amazing 'life change':

17th October 1940

After my marriage my conduct improved, but no faith, no prayer; absolute aridity: a more or less graceful, more or less charming animal drawn back into the herd by adequate emotions.

The war of 1914: our house in Saint-Germain turned into a dressing-station, devotion to the motherland, yes, but it was an unthinkable sort of excitement; Marco's [her son] departure when he volunteered with Gilbert Garros; his death . . . I fell victim to an indescribable despair, a grief made far worse by remorse at not having been a good mother, at not having loved that child enough, at having preferred Georges—that is to say myself—to my son. I became very ill, a nervous disease. . . . During this physical collapse I came to perceive the fact that I had a soul which had woken up under the pressure of suffering, a soul which was looking for the light, which was looking for something which cannot be found on earth. I began to pray to my good and powerful patron Saint Anne, mother of Mary—Mary who was so pure that my unworthiness dared not turn towards her.... I spoke to Saint Anne often, asking for forgiveness and help. In that way, bit by bit, I contrived a sort of fervent piety, a religion all my own, still very remote from the true way, but taking me—with God's help—in the right direction.... I began to resist my own inclinations and their passions. I began to go into churches. Not daring to go in further than the holy-water stoup, I stammered prayers, was present during parts of Masses, spoke to God, glimpsed Jesus on His cross, and at last I made my confession to good Abbe Duchemin at Saint-Germain. I told him everything that came into my mind and I made my act of contrition with all my heart, but I was still very far from the 'extreme suffering' which I feel today when the weight of my sins crushes me to the point of feeling dizzy as I ask how could I, how could I, when I didn't even have the excuse of liking that frivolous life of so-called pleasure.

18th October

There was the death of my son....

There was my husband's flight one July morning in 1926. That quite crushed me. That violent blow changed me completely, stripped me. Then, when my husband came back, cynical and dissolute, a wild horse trampling everything underfoot, sickly and ill—that was cruel. I took him back, I love him.

I try to set him a good example, I pray for him. There is no visible sign yet, except perhaps for a change in his language. Blasphemy, obscene words and sacrilegious irony have gradually disappeared. He is fond of the sisters and they are fond of him.

He is charming to them, gentle, friendly, doing whatever he can to please them and doing it willingly. He enjoys arranging the flowers in their pretty chapel, takes me there twice a day and waits for me near the door, in the garden. Grant me, O God, the conversion of my husband Georges, my friend, my devoted companion, my unhappy child.

And then there was the appearance in our life of the reverend Father Rzewuski.

It was Father Rzewuski who wrote the foreword to the published *Blue Notebooks*. It is his word we would have to take, if any word were needed, as to the reality of Liane's conversion. Her final lines, though, speak for themselves:

January 1941

This book will be given to Father Rzewuski. All the other notebooks have been deposited at my behest with the Dominicans at Estavayer, Monsignor Besson has given permission. I close them, I put them away, safe in this pious place. If anyone thinks that they ought to be destroyed, I approve. If anyone wants to publish them, make a selection of these memories which crush my repentant heart—if their publication either with impurities removed or in all their horror might benefit some straying soul, I approve.

But I ask above all that the presence of the divine mercy in these notebooks should be emphasized; that it should be recognized as being there, hidden for a long time between the lines as it was between the hours of my sad existence; that I repent of that existence, that I am ashamed of it, that I find it a humiliation to think today that these frightful confidences will be made public, and that it is ONLY in the spirit of humiliation that I offer them.

My God, I believe in You, I hope in You and I love You. May Your will be done.

Anne-Marie Ghika.

May those who read this say a prayer for the last of the last: A-M.G.

The Shadow of Death

When Helen Keller, even in the shadow of grief for her 'Teacher's' death, wrote of resurrection, of life beyond the grave, she wrote from a kind of personal experience:

27th March 1937

How different my last Easter and this one are from all others! Besides its own blessed message for mankind, each Easter used to bring in a new way the thrilling sense of my own resurrection when Teacher awoke me with a word, a touch, from the only death I can imagine—dark silence without language or purpose or faith. Easter, 1936, walked by me like a sad ghost. Teacher was wretchedly ill, and for the first time I feared she would never be better. Now there is no greeting from her on earth, and the vibration of the anguish still quivering in my heart muffles the joy-bells of other years. But there remains something breathtaking about Teacher's personality— the miracle that lives here and now, awes, charms and spurs me onward. This experience gives a new meaning to the Gospel of the risen Christ who shared with sorrow-laden mortals the joy of eternity interpreted by love. May His Presence drop dews of refreshment more and more, until the bondage and the strife are lifted from all souls, and the Beauty of His Peace shines in their fear-liberated lives!

But even without Keller's personal experience it is only too easy to understand why the death of someone close so often triggers an upsurge of religious feeling. It is at least a degree easier to see them pass out of our care if we can believe they are passing into the care of someone else—or Someone Else, as most of these diarists would probably put it. Elizabeth Fry is only one of many to be called upon to face the deepest chasm of all, the death of a child:

Plashet, Eleventh Month, 1815

It has pleased Almighty and Infinite Wisdom, to take from us our most dear and tenderly-beloved child, little Betsy; between four and five years old. In receiving her, as well as giving her back again, we have, I believe, been enabled to bless the Sacred Name.

On Third day, the 21st after some suffering of body from great sickness, she appeared wonderfully relieved, and I may say raised in spirit; she began by telling me how many hymns and stories she knew, with her countenance greatly animated, a flush on her cheeks, and her eyes very bright, a smile of inexpressible content, almost joy—I think she first said with a powerful voice, 'How glorious is our Heavenly King, Who reigns above the sky.'

And then expressed how beautiful it was, and how the little children that die stand before Him.... She then mentioned other hymns, and many sweet things; she spoke with delight of how she could nurse the little ones and take care of them, &c.; her heart appeared inexpressibly to overflow with love. Afterwards she told me one or two droll stories, and made clear and bright comments as she went along; then stopped a little while, and said (as in the fulness of her heart, and the joy of a little innocent child who feels very good, for she indeed appeared under the influence of her Redeemer), 'Mama, I love everybody better than myself, and I love thee better than everybody, and I love Almighty much better than thee, and I hope thee loves Almighty much better than me.' I believe my answer was, 'I hope or believe I do', which she took up and said, 'I hope thee does, if not, thee are wicked.'

Afterwards I appeared to satisfy her that it was so. This was expressed on the Third day morning, and she was a corpse on the Fifth day evening; but in her death, there was abundant cause for thanksgiving; prayer appeared indeed to be answered, as very little, if any suffering seemed to attend her, and no struggle at last; but her breath grew more and more seldom and gentle, till she ceased to breathe.

It sounds like one of those deathbed scenes beloved of Victorian novels which strike little chord in our contemporary experience, but the fact remains: it was real. And the fact that the feelings described were recorded at the time gives them an authority no one can deny. Death was something which came often to the extensive Victorian family, as one of Fry's last entries bears witness:

Walmer, Eighth Month 29th, 1844

Sorrow upon sorrow! Since I last wrote, we have lost by death first, my beloved sister, Elizabeth Fry; second, Gurney Reynolds, our sweet, good grandson; third Juliana Fry, my dearest William and Julia's second daughter; and fourth, above all, our most beloved son, William Storrs Fry, who appeared to catch the infection of his little girl, and died on Third-day of scarlet fever, the 27th of this month. A loss inexpressible—such a son, husband, friend, and brother! But I trust that he is for ever at rest in Jesus, through the fulness of His love and grace. The trial is almost inexpressible. Oh! may the Lord sustain us in this time of deep distress. Oh! dear Lord, keep the unworthy and poor sick servant in this time of unutterable trial; keep me sound in faith, and clear in mind, and be very near to us all—the poor widow and children in this time of deepest distress, and grant that this awful dispensation may be blessed to our souls. Amen.

And indeed, though this entry may be sparser in tone, the more florid, if one can use the word without disrespect, note is one which sounds again in diaries of the period. Here is one Mary Timms in 1836 recording the death of her child:

> How transient are all things here below! How soon are our hopes and prospects blasted! My babe, my dear Mary Anne is taken from me, to bloom in paradise. Ah! I fondly hoped she would have been spared to us; but God has seen good to separate us, perhaps but for a little while. O how painful to nature! my heart bleeds. I am jealous of the worms; I do not like to give my Mary Anne to them; but the mandate is, 'dust thou art, and unto dust shalt thou return'. This consoles me, it is the will of my heavenly Father. I know it is my duty to submit to be resigned.... Sweet babe! thou hast passed the bounds of time, and perhaps—O delightful thought!—thou art permitted to be thy mother's guardian angel, and wilt be the first to meet her on yon blest shore.

Here is Honoria Lawrence in 1841:

> When my darling ceased breathing I thought she said to me 'Mother, you are often afraid of this dark valley. See how easily I have passed through it.'
>
> I felt that indescribable crushing of my bodily frame under the blow, that made me think I too was dying. When my darling was gone I longed to be able to tell the poor natives around me of all that comforted me. I think it was Thursday night I awoke in tears, yet I felt very happy. When Doctor Steele on the noon of Sunday told me she was in danger it was like a thunder clap, but when he said that nothing more could be done and I took her in my lap to die, a holy calm came over me. And when my beauteous babe was stretched out in her last sleep her waxen form not the least emaciated, her lovely hair parted on her high forehead, dressed in the very clothes I had so often delighted to deck out for her, she never looked so lovely.
>
> Now the worms are spread under her and the worms over her, sown in corruption to be raised in incorruption. When I can think of her as all dissolved to dust it will be less bitter, but now only the decay and horror of death rise in my mind.
>
> *Sunday, 8th August*
> A week today since her departure. Oh, what may she in that time have learned! All that we are dearly striving to know may be unfolding itself to her unclouded faculties.

And Fanny Longfellow in 1848:

> *September 14th*
> A cold, dark day in sympathy with our gloom.... She is everywhere. In the garden I see only her merry steps and little hands grasping the flowers with

glee and shouting 'Pretty', and then I see her with them in her cold hands. But she is playing with the flowers of Paradise, I fondly trust.

Lady Frederick Cavendish heard in 1880 that her husband, sent as governor to Ireland, had been assassinated. Later, in retreat, she wrote the story out in her diary:

Uncle W. himself came in.... I saw his face, pale, sorrow-stricken, but like a prophet's in its look of faith and strength. He came up and almost took me in his arms, and his first words were, 'Father, forgive them, for they know not what they do.' Then he said to me, 'Be assured it will not be in vain,' and across all my agony there fell a bright ray of hope, and I saw in a vision Ireland at peace, and my darling's life-blood accepted as a sacrifice for Christ's sake, to help to bring this to pass.... So GOD carried me in His arms through the first terrible hours. He soothed me, even by the very exhaustion of grief, so that I could sleep; and when (as happened for the first 10 days or so) I used to wake in the early dawn, alone, clearly and vividly conscious of all that had happened (when too it is my nature to see everything on the dark side)—at those times—the most free from excitement, when there is 'deep silence in the heart, for thought to do her part'—and I should have expected a fiery trial of anguish—then there used to come over me an indescribable sense of something guarding and enfolding me. I could lie perfectly still, feeling that I was sinking deep, deep, into the depths of sorrow, so that the floods ran over me, but that beneath and around me was some mighty Protection. Or as if I was indeed falling down a precipice of grief, but with the feeling of falling soft. I knew then that it was the love of many—the prayers of thousands—which were helping me; drawing down to me in my helplessness the Boundless Love of GOD.

Coming to terms with death is obviously especially hard for the young. Canadian Henriette Dessaulles, in her convent boarding-school in 1877, has only just written 'I'm perfectly fine now that I've given up all the pious posturing' (fostered by her environment) when her piety comes up against a real trial in the illness of her little half-sister:

May 7

The news is bad. She's very sick. Dear Lord, aren't You going to make her better? Perhaps she is dying. But that's an unbearable thought, why have You given her to us if You are going to take her away again so soon. Could it be that God is capricious—like us?

May 9—In the evening

Alice and I are being kept at home for the night. The poor little thing has come out of her torpor but it's terrible. She tosses and turns, rolling from side to side, moaning all the while, it's awful. Lord! Oh Lord! Don't make her suffer; take her but don't hurt her so much. Why? Why?

In my grief there's a dreadful sense of revolt, of indignation, which tortures me because I feel it's wrong but I can't help it. Holy Mary, You are the Mother who is so gentle, so tender-hearted, please relieve her suffering.

I've just seen her. She is resting quietly. She is so pretty, so exquisitely pretty but for whom and for what? For the grave—oh, it's horrible! Yes, I know about the angels and heaven, I know about them. But all I see is the tomb and . . . the parting.

May 13—In the evening

Her moans have turned into screams. One long incessant scream! It breaks my heart . . . for she's in extreme pain. . . . This long piercing cry is harrowing and so unchildlike. Do You see, God? Do You hear? You would be able to help her and let her die without torturing her. Yet You want us to love You for Your goodness! . . . Forgive me, but I don't understand. . . .

May 15

The screams are becoming farther apart. I've just sat up with her alone for an hour and a great calm has come over me. The life of the soul in exchange for that of the body. I was guilty of doubting God's goodness and of rebelling against His will. I have glimpsed the Truth. Why did I never before think of the spiritual side of this trial which almost ceases to be a tragedy when one . . . understands.

May 19

It's all over. She is in heaven at last after so much suffering.

The conclusion she reaches is different and so is the expression, but one fear of Henriette's—'the grave—oh it's horrible!'—is echoed by American Alice a century later. She was maintaining a precarious balance after a history of drug problems when her grandfather died:

May 12

This morning I looked out the window and saw new green popping through the soil and I started crying uncontrollably again. I don't really understand the resurrection. I can't even conceive how Gramps' body which will decay and sour and mold and mildew and fall into little crumbling bits can ever come back together again. But I can't understand how brown dried-up, shrivelled little gladiola bulb can reblossom either. I guess that God can put atoms and molecules and bodies together again if a gladiola bulb without even a brain can do it.

May 14

I had a nightmare last night about Gramps' body all filled with maggots and worms, and I thought about what would happen if I should die. Worms don't make distinction under the ground. They wouldn't care that I'm young and that my flesh is solid and firm.

A month later it was another death to face:

June 16

Gran died in her sleep last night. I tried to tell myself that she's gone to Gramps, but I'm so depressed all I can think about is worms eating her body. Empty eye sockets with whole colonies of writhing maggots. I can no longer eat.

June 19

...The worst thing about today was seeing soft, frail Gran lowered into that dark, endless hole. It seemed to swallow her up and when they threw dirt on the coffin, I thought I was going to scream. But Joel [her 'spiritual' potential boyfriend] said not to think about that because that isn't what death really means and I guess he's right. I just can't think about that.

'I Shall Fear No Evil'

Four months later, Alice herself was dead. Her diary is one of those no one can read now with the taste of hindsight constantly in their mouths. The diary of Anne Frank is another such—and the diary of Etty Hillesum yet another.

A Dutch Jewess who died in Auschwitz at the age of twenty-nine, Etty's story in some ways parallels Anne Frank's. Except that she was older, more in control of her own destiny—and that the end to which she used that control was voluntarily to decide to go with a large party of her compatriots to Westerbork, the transit camp from which weekly trains left for Poland and Auschwitz.

It is impossible to read her diary now without a sense of catharsis—'the purgation of the emotions through pity and terror'. But she, who began writing of her faith at a time when menace was gathering all around, seems to have walked into the Valley of the Shadow of Death as near unafraid as it is possible to be.

Her diary begins on 9 March 1941, in quest of some kind of discovery prompted by fascination with Julius Spier, a palm-reader cum mystic, cum healer, cum psychologist. Casual references to 'God'—of the sort anyone might use—occur from the earliest pages but the path she followed led her to relate to her religion in an ever more profound way. From starting out as, in her own descriptive phrase, 'a Kneeler in training', by 18 May 1942, she is assembling her faith as a shield:

...The threat grows ever greater, and terror increases from day to day. I draw prayer round me like a dark protective wall, withdraw inside it as one might into a convent cell and then step outside again.... I can imagine times to come when I shall stay on my knees for days on end....'

When Etty prayed, she wrote once, 'I hold a silly, naive or deadly serious dialogue with what is deepest inside me, which for convenience sake I call God'. Conventional or otherwise, her faith develops into one which could take her out into the world, not keep her shut away from it:

It is sometimes hard to take in and comprehend, oh God, what those created in Your likeness do to each other in these disjointed days. But I no longer shut myself away in my room, God, I try to look things straight in the face, even the worst crimes, and to discover the small, naked human being amidst the monstrous wreckage caused by man's senseless deeds.... I am no fanciful visionary, God, no schoolgirl with a 'beautiful soul'. I try to face up to Your world, God, not to escape from reality, into beautiful dreams... and I continue to praise Your creation, God, despite everything.

'There is room for everything in a single life' she wrote later. 'For belief in God and for a miserable end.' As the miserable end came closer, her faith did not change:

11th July 1942, Saturday morning, 11 o'clock
We must only speak about the ultimate and most serious things in life when the words well up inside us as simply and as naturally as water from a spring.

And if God does not help me to go on, then I shall have to help God. The surface of the earth is gradually turning into one great prison camp and soon there will be nobody left outside. The Jews here are telling each other lovely stories: they say that the Germans are burying us alive or exterminating us with gas. But what is the point of repeating such things even if they should be true?... Many accuse me of indifference and passivity when I refuse to go into hiding; they say that I have given up. They say everyone who can must try to stay out of their clutches, it's our bounden duty to try. But that argument is specious. For while everyone tries to save himself, vast numbers are nevertheless disappearing.... I don't feel in anybody's clutches; I feel safe in God's arms, to put it rhetorically, and no matter whether I am sitting at this beloved old desk now, or in a bare room in the Jewish district or perhaps in a labour camp under SS guards in a month's time—I shall always feel safe in God's arms. They may well succeed in breaking me physically, but no more than that. I may face cruelty and deprivation the likes of which I cannot imagine in even my wildest fantasies. Yet all this is as nothing to the immeasurable expanse of my faith in God and my inner receptiveness.

Before the next extract a lot has changed in Etty's life. For a period she kept no diary. She accompanied the first group of Jews to Westerbork, but at the end of August was sent back on sick leave to Amsterdam where she remained for some weeks, leaving a legacy of these final diary notes behind her. In the silent gap, Spier had suddenly fallen ill and died. But from personal as well as public tragedy, and even more from her longing to be back at Westerbork facing the destiny she had chosen, Etty fights back to find again her own answer in complete acceptance.

Perhaps, oh God, everything happening together like that was a little hard. I am reminded daily of the fact that a human being has a body too. I had thought that my spirit and heart alone would be able to sustain me through everything. But now my body has spoken up for itself and called a halt. I now realize, God, how much You have given me. So much that was beautiful and so much that was hard to bear. Yet whenever I showed myself ready to bear it, the hard was directly transformed into the beautiful. And the beautiful was sometimes much harder to bear, so overpowering did it seem. To think that one small human heart can experience so much, oh God, so much suffering and so much love, I am so grateful to You, God, for having chosen my heart, in these times, to experience all the things it has experienced. Perhaps it is all to the good that I fell ill.... I shall follow the tried and tested old method, talking to myself now and again on these faint blue lines. And talking to You, God. Is that all right?

Saturday morning, 3rd October 1942, 6.30, in the bathroom

I am beginning to suffer from insomnia, and that's not allowed. I jumped out of bed at the crack of dawn and knelt down at my window. The tree stood motionless out there in the grey, still morning. And I prayed, 'God, grant me the great and mighty calm that pervades all nature. If it is Your wish to let me suffer, then let it be one great all consuming suffering, not the thousand petty anxieties that can break a human being. Give me peace and confidence. Let every day be something more than the thousand everyday cares. All those worries about food, about clothing, about the cold, about our health—are they not so many denials of You, my God? And don't You come down on us hard in punishment? With insomnia and with lives that have ceased to be worth living? I want to lie here quietly for another few days, but then I would wish my life to turn into one great prayer. One great peace. To carry my peace about with me once again....

It is now close on 7 o'clock. I shall go and wash from head to toe in cold water, and then I shall lie down quietly in my bed, dead still, I shall no longer write in this exercise book, I shall simply lie down and try to be a prayer. I have felt it so often, all misery for a few days and thinking I wouldn't get over it for weeks, and then suddenly the clouds were lifted from me. But now I don't live as I should, for I try to force things. If at all possible I would so much like to leave on Wednesday. But I know perfectly well I am not much good to anyone as I am now. I would so love to be just a little bit better again. But I ought not to make any demands. I must let things take their course and that's what I am trying to do with all my might. 'Not my will, but Thy will be done.'

Chapter 13
~ Despair

'Why should we honour those that die upon the field of battle? A man may show as reckless a courage in entering into the abyss of himself.'—W. B. Yeats

Despair

There is a proverb to the effect that the story of a happy life is soon told. Invented, no doubt, by the same man who said that good news is no news. This was supposed to be a chapter on 'the highs and the lows'...except for a distinct shortage of material on the former.

God forbid that the human race—or even the female half of it—should be taken to spend its days immersed in deep gloom. But it probably is true that the negative emotions are more readily recognized and acknowledged for what they are. Less pessimistically, they are the ones which cry out most urgently for verbal or written expression. Sylvia Plath described herself as writing in her journal when she was 'at wits' end, in a cul-de-sac. Never when I am happy.'

The peaks of positive emotion, moreover, tend to come under another guise—love, religion, physical well-being. Only despair and its less dramatic heralds (like extreme anxiety or depression) seem to take on a life of their own.

But even they don't come to order—don't grow in quite the places you would expect....

Clinging On

It reads like a first lesson in logic: Virginia Woolf took her own life, ergo, she must have despaired of it. But whatever the emotion she suffered, looking back on her previous bout of insanity and looking forward to the possibility of future ones, there is comparatively little indulgence of it to be found in her diaries. These—again, comparatively—uninhibited early extracts are the nearest the diaries ever get to peering down into the abyss:

Monday, October 25th 1920 (First day of winter time)
Why is life so tragic; so like a little strip of pavement over an abyss. I look down; I feel giddy; I wonder how I am ever to walk to the end. But why do I feel this: Now that I say it I don't feel it. The fire burns; we are going to hear the Beggar's Opera. Only it lies about me; I can't keep my eyes shut. It's a feeling of impotence; of cutting no ice. Here I sit at Richmond, and like a lantern stood in the middle of a field my light goes up in darkness. Melancholy diminishes as I write.

Thursday, August 18th 1921
Nothing to record; only an intolerable fit of the fidgets to write away. Here I am chained to my rock; forced to do nothing; doomed to let every worry, spite, irritation and obsession scratch and claw and come again. This is a day that I may not walk and must not work. Whatever book I read bubbles up in my mind as part of an article I want to write. No one in the whole of Sussex is so miserable as I am. . . .

'Miserable'—that's the playing down of her emotion after the brief indulgence. And more usually, Woolf adopts the practice of skating fast over the thin ice, fast and stylishly. Later, describing a much-troubled time, it is the information that 'I am not going to milk my brains for a week' which first rings alarm-bells in the brain of anyone who has read much of her diaries: deliberate inactivity usually spells trouble ahead, endured, or narrowly avoided. That, and the change from her usual diary format to a conscious procession of 'thoughts'. . . . 'the first pages of the greatest book in the world'. But in the words themselves there is a note of deliberate lightness: 'Here is a whole nervous breakdown in miniature,' she says, beginning the chronicle.

1941 was the year of her death, but you have to turn the pages back from March to January of that year before you find an entry which speaks openly of 'despair'.

Sunday, January 26th
A battle against depression, rejection (by Harpers of my story and Ellen Terry) routed today (I hope) by clearing out kitchen; by sending the article (a lame one) to *N.S.*: and by breaking into *P.H.* two days, I think, of memoir writing. This trough of despair shall not, I swear, engulf me. The solitude is great.

Ironically, that is the very extract upon which Sylvia Plath once seized: 'Just now I pick up the blessed diary of Virginia Woolf which I bought with a battery of her novels on Saturday with Ted. And she works off her depression over rejections from *Harper's* (no less!—and I can hardly believe that the Big Ones get rejected, too!) by cleaning out the kitchen. And cooks haddock & sausage. Bless her. I feel my life linked to her, somehow.'

Looking back with hindsight upon their respective journals, though, comparisons are not just odious, they are often ill-founded. It is oh so tempting—two women writers, both plagued by mental or emotional trouble, two suicides. But Plath's journals frequently sound a note unfamiliar from Woolf's: a note of naked, and often self-directed, anger:

> Saturday exhausted, nerves frayed. Sleepless. Threw you, book, down, punched with fist. Kicked, punched. Violence seethed. Joy to murder someone, pure scapegoat. But pacified during necessity to work. Work redeems.

Even her camaraderie with Woolf is undercut by that punishing spirit. After recording her admiration for *The Waves*, Plath writes: 'I shall go better than she. No children until I have done it.'

A serious depression in 1952, early on in the journal history, long before she had met Ted Hughes, foreshadowed the first suicide attempt in the summer of 1953. 'I am afraid,' she wrote on 3 November. 'I am not solid but hollow. I feel behind my eyes a numb, paralysed cavern, a pit of hell, a mimicking nothingness. I never thought. I never wrote. I never suffered. I want to kill myself, to escape from responsibility, to crawl back abjectly into the womb....' In despair, though, the anger does not diminish, nor do the ruthless demands on self:

> ...The future? God—will it get worse and worse? Will I never travel, never integrate my life, never have purpose, meaning? Never have time—long stretches, to investigate ideas, philosophy—to articulate the vague seething desires in me? Will I be a secretary—a self-rationalizing, uninspired housewife, secretly jealous of my husband's ability to grow intellectually and professionally while I am impeded? Will I submerge my embarrassing desires and aspirations, refuse to face myself, and go either mad or become neurotic?
>
> Whom can I talk to? Get advice from? No one. A psychiatrist is the god of our age. But they cost money. And I won't take advice, even if I want it. I'll kill myself. I am beyond help. No one here has time to probe, to aid me in understanding myself...so many others are worse off than I. How can I selfishly demand help, solace, guidance? No, it is my own mess, and even if now I have lost my sense of perspective, thereby my creative sense of humor, I will not let myself get sick, go mad, or retreat like a child into blubbering on someone else's shoulder. Masks are the order of the day—and the least I can do is cultivate the illusion that I am gay, serene,

not hollow and afraid. Someday, god knows when, I will stop this absurd, self-pitying, idle, futile despair. I will begin to think again, and to act according to the way I think. Attitude is a pitifully relative and capricious quality to base a faith on. Like the proverbial sand, it slides, founders, sucks me down to hell.

No one could say Plath went down without a fight. But it is like watching someone struggle in a pool of quicksand, knowing that every movement of their arms makes the final engulfment more certain.

It would be interesting to know what Plath made of the journals of Mary Shelley. If despair is an emotion which too often comes without waiting for its cue, then sometimes it seems to stay waiting in the wings long after the line has been given. This sequence of entries from 1815 reads almost like one of those competitions which challenge you to spot the deliberate mistake:

March 2

A bustle of moving—read Corinne. I and my baby go about 3—S(helley) and C(lara) do not come till six—Hogg comes in the evening.

March 3

nurse my baby—talk & read Corinne—Hogg comes in the evening.

March 5

find my baby dead—————
Send for Hogg—talk—a miserable day—in the evening read Fall of the Jesuits. Hogg sleeps here—

The next day, sandwiched in between the Fall of the Jesuits and the movements of Hogg, comes the brief note 'Not in good spirits'. Three days later: 'Still think about my little baby. 'Tis hard indeed, for a mother to lose a child.' One would have thought so, certainly...A few more days and fuller recognition does begin to come:

Monday 13th

S(helley) H(ogg) & C(lara) go to town—stay at home, net & think of my little dead baby—this is foolish I suppose yet whenever I am left alone to my own thoughts & do not read to divert them they always come back to the same point—that I was a mother & am so no longer—Fanny comes wet through—she dines & stays the evening—talk about many things—she goes at ½ 9—cut out my new gown—

Reading between the lines, the grief is there. But with every awareness of delayed shock, of the numbing effect of grief, it is still not the reaction one tends to expect from a Romantic to whom (if Marianne in Jane Austen's *Sense and Sensibility* is anything to go by!) the indulgence of emotion should surely have been a positive duty. From other sources we learn that Mary Shelley was in some ways unusually repressed, that she suffered very badly from the baby's death. But this section of the journals certainly throws into relief that other journal which follows Shelley's death. . . .

Shelley was drowned in July 1822. The journal up to that point is terse, as you see above. It breaks off to resume in October—and what a contrast. The 'Journal of Sorrow' is the repository of long lamentations—the only channel of communication, perhaps, through which she could begin to address Shelley himself? 'After a day spent in society I turn to you, my own Beloved. When in utter solitude I weep to think how alone I am—when I see others, I find myself alone—but I do not weep.'

If anything, the tone becomes more agonized as time goes on. In February 1823: 'Suffering is my Alpha and Omega.' In September 1824: 'I have little enjoyment—no hope—I have given myself ten more years of life—God grant that they may not be augmented—I should be glad that they were curtailed.' The tone of lamentation, of looking back to the past, is a recurring theme.

It becomes less continual of course. From the first, in fact, there are moments when Mary Shelley can be seen setting her face forward, though any stress of sadness seems to throw her back yet again on the thought of what is gone. But it is a long wait for the kind of acceptance we find in June 1840—'though I no longer soar, I do not repine—though I no longer deem all things attainable, I enjoy what is.' Significantly, the journal itself now nears its end. Has its purpose been served?

Swimming Against the Tide

Sometimes, reading women's diaries, you find an entry—or a chain of them—which seem to have found their way into the 'wrong' book. The primary-school picture of Florence Nightingale is one of sweetness, light and calm strength, a graceful statue whose head is haloed in the steady radiance of her famous lamp. Many of us know a bit better than that—are dimly aware that not only did she face massive and exhausting opposition in the war zone, but she had a family battle to fight on the home front which prevented her beginning her career until a comparatively late age. But you would have to know quite a lot more not to be surprised by the depths of this note:

December 31 1850
My present life is suicide. Slowly, I have opened my eyes to the fact that I cannot now deliver myself from the habit of dreaming which, like gin drinking, is eating out my vital strength. Now I have let myself go

entirely ... I have no desire but to die. There is not a night that I do not lie down on my bed, wishing that I may leave it no more. Unconsciousness is all I desire.

Or by the vehemence of this, a few weeks later:

Oh, how am I to get through this day. To talk all through this day, is the thought of every morning. ... In my thirty-first year I see nothing desirable but death ... Why, oh my God, can I not be satisfied with the life that satisfies so many people? ... My God, what am I to do?

'The plough goes over the soul,' she had written earlier. 'I cannot live—forgive me, oh Lord, and let me die, this day let me die.' The note of extremity, almost of hysteria, was to be sounded in letters as well as 'private notes' throughout Nightingale's life, though often with good cause. It did not cease to sound forever when her working life began in 1853. But during those long years of enforced young ladyhood, when only dreams offered escape from an intolerably unrewarding life, it is fair to say that her despair was the direct result of external circumstances, i.e. the conventions of the time and the demands of her family.

Nella Last's reaction to the son who spoke of her as 'always gay and kind and firm' may be due to the fact that she was writing near the start of a war which could only hit hard at a woman with a son of fighting age. Or, again, it may not:

I must be a very good actress, for I don't feel gay often. Perhaps, though, I'm like the kid who whistled as he went past the churchyard to keep his spirits up, for down in my heart there is a sadness which never lifts and, if I did not work and work till I was too tired to do anything but sleep when I went to bed, would master me. Like the little Holland boy who put his hand in the hole in the dyke and kept back the trickle of water that would have quickly grown to a flood, I *must* keep my dykes strong enough—or else at times I'd go under.

Stress outside oneself can often confuse the issue of the stress inside, and how many of us can always trace the roots of our own emotions? Although Ellen Newton, trapped in an appalling 'old people's home', as mentioned earlier, knew the cause of hers:

Thursday

There can't be many places better equipped than Haddon for you to graduate in loneliness and rejection. The days are long, and though the staff are friendly they simply haven't time to talk. Perhaps this sense of being a castaway comes from being indefinitely confined to this kind of room. Oh to walk to the gate and collect a letter from the box, or perhaps have a word with a passer-by.

The emotions produced are sometimes close on overwhelming:

Saturday, July

Beside me, on the locker, is a little bottle of tablets. It's always beside me. In red letters its label says, 'CAUTION. To be used strictly as directed by a physician'. I hold it in my hand. 'Two sublingually every four hours.' Yes, *two*. But eight—twelve—twenty—all at once...?

Helen—Veronica—David—the other children . . . They would have to know I'd let thought dig my grave. Most deliberately I stretch my arm till that small bottle of mortality is pushed well out of easy reach.

Not many years ago I told someone that I would never 'go gentle into the dark night'. But where else is there to go? Where in all this world?

With the resilience someone a third of Ellen Newton's age might envy, she repeatedly pulls herself back and moves firmly away from the brink.

For Katherine Mansfield a specific, tragic event proved the focus for what—she thought then—she had long been feeling:

November 1915, Bandol, France

I think I have known for a long time that life was over for me, but I never realized it or acknowledged it until my brother died. Yes, though he is lying in the middle of a little wood in France and I am still walking upright and feeling the sun and the wind from the sea, I am just as much dead as he is. The present and the future mean nothing to me. I am no longer 'curious' about people; I do not wish to go anywhere; and the only possible value that anything can have for me is that it should put me in mind of something that happened or was when we were alive. 'Do you remember, Katie?' I hear his voice in the trees and flowers, in scents and light and shadow. Have people, apart from these far-away people, ever existed for me? Or have they always failed me and faded because I denied them reality? Supposing I were to die as I sit at this table, playing with my Indian paper knife, what would be the difference? No difference at all. Then why don't I commit suicide? Because I feel I have a duty to perform to the lovely time when we were both alive. I want to write about it, and he wanted me to. We talked it over in my little top room in London. I said: I will just put on the front page: To my brother, Leslie Heron Beauchamp. Very well: it shall be done.

It is a cliché that at times of great present distress one reads the same emotions into past and future. But events, in the shape of the tuberculosis which killed her, were to give Mansfield no chance to bounce back.

14 October 1922

My spirit is nearly dead. My spring of life is so starved that it's just not dry. Nearly all my improved health is pretence—acting. What does it amount to? Can I walk? Only creep. Can I do anything with my hands or body? Nothing at all. I am an absolutely hopeless invalid. What is my life? It is the existence of a parasite. And five years have passed now, and I am in straiter bonds than ever.

Katherine Mansfield's depressions and despair were, as she obviously felt, an imposition from the outside, which bestowed a fatal illness upon her, a cloud without trace of any visible lining. There is no echo of May Sarton's experience that: 'Sometimes one has simply to endure a period of depression for what it may hold of illumination if one can live through it, attentive to what it exposes or demands....':

> The reasons for depression are not so interesting as the way one handles it, simply to stay alive. This morning I woke at four and lay awake for an hour or so in a bad state. It is raining again. I got up finally and went about the daily chores, waiting for the sense of doom to lift—and what did it was watering the house plants. Suddenly joy came back because I was fulfilling a simple need, a living one. Dusting never has this effect (and that may be why I am such a poor housekeeper!), but feeding the cats when they are hungry, giving Punch clean water, makes me suddenly feel calm and happy.
>
> Whatever peace I know rests in the natural world, in feeling myself a part of it, even in a small way. Maybe the gaiety of the Warner family, their wisdom, comes from this, that they work close to nature all the time. As simple as that? But it is not simple. Their life requires patient understanding, imagination, the power to endure constant adversity—the weather, for example! To go with, not against the elements, an inexhaustible vitality summoned back each day to do the same tasks, to feed the animals, clean out barns and pens, keep that complex world alive.

With George Sand's pragmatic recipe for the control of extreme emotional states, we are back in 'cloud with a silver lining' territory. There is not so much as a nod forwards to modern ideas about the therapeutic value of 'letting it all hang out' in this note to herself:

> When mental sickness increases until it reaches the danger point, do not exhaust yourself by efforts to trace back to original causes. Better accept them as inevitable and save your strength to fight against the effects.
>
> Try to find the immediate daily causes of these crises. Observe what you are doing or thinking to bring them on. In that way you may prevent them, or at least diminish their force.
>
> When your mental state is normal, try to realize that the delirium is bound to recur. Then when you are delirious, strengthen yourself by the certainty that you will recover your mental poise.
>
> Do not allow yourself to be the dupe of your sick state of mind.
>
> Take care of your bodily health. Eat little at a time and eat often. If your body is accustomed to tonics, take them faithfully. If you are not used to them, do not acquire the habit.

Do not allow yourself to cry. Tears are debilitating. They are followed by exhaustion and other extreme reactions. The only tears that should not be restrained are those of tenderness and compassion.

Above all, above everything, never give way to feelings of anger and vengeance. They are wasteful expenditures of strength.

But a glance at any of her more turbulent entries (under 'Religion' or 'Love') shows that this is a case of 'Do what I say, not what I do'. Sand preserved the fragment, she wrote a year later, 'to remind me of one of the most unhappy phases of my life. I was on the border line of madness but I had ceased to brood on the thought of suicide.'

Not Waving But Drowning

Beatrice Webb did not think of suicide, but for years on end her diary expressed the repeated hope that her life would not last much longer. Her grief was an unrequited passion: she lived, loved again, found work, and prospered into a ripe old age. Sylvia Plath attempted suicide once and succeeded a second time, but her husband Ted Hughes destroyed the journals of her last months so that their children should never read them: she went, in effect, silent to the grave. Other diaries trace every step.

Lytton Strachey, writer and familiar of the Bloomsbury circle, died on 21 January 1932. On 12 February the diary of his lover, the painter Dora Carrington, reflects her grief:

February 12th 1932

I can think of nothing but the past, everything reminds me of Lytton. There is no one to tell one's thoughts to now. And the loneliness is unbearable. No one can be what Lytton was. He had the power of altering me. So that I was never unhappy as long as he was with me. I keep on trying to forget it is true. At Fryern I almost pretended it was a holiday and things weren't all altered but the pressure to keep these thoughts out of my head is almost as much of a strain as the pain of thinking of Lytton dead. Then I have a longing to enmesh myself in his relics. That craving for death which I know he disapproved of and would have disliked. If I could sit here alone just holding his clothes in my arms on the sofa with that handkerchief over my face I feel I would get comfort, but I know these feelings are bad. And if I became bad then I should feel he would disapprove and all would be worse. So I must and cannot go backwards to his grave.... What can I do. For no future interests me. I do not care about anything now. Everything was for you. I loved life just because you made it so perfect, and now there is no one left to make jokes with, or to talk about Racine and Molière and talk of plans and work and people.

Everything I look at brings back a memory of you. Your brown writing case that I bought you in Aix. Your clothes that I chose with you at Carpentier and Packer. All our pictures and furniture that we chose together. Oh darling did you know how I adored you. I feared often to tell you because I thought you might feel encumbered by your 'incubus'. I knew you didn't want to feel me dependent on you. I pretended so often I didn't mind staying alone. When I was utterly miserable as the train went out and your face vanished. You were the kindest dearest man who ever lived on this earth. No one can ever be your equal for wit and gaiety. And you transported me by your magical conversations and teaching into a world which no one could have dreamt of; it was so fantastically happy and amusing. What does anything mean to me now without you. I see my paints and think it is no use, for Lytton will never see my pictures now, and I cry.

On the 16th her focus on the dead was if anything more intense: 'At last I am alone. At last there is nothing between us. I have been reading my letters to you in the library this evening. You are so engraved on my brain that I think of nothing. . . .' On the 17th, 'Every day I find it *harder* to bear. . . . It is impossible to think that I shall never sit with you again and hear your laugh. *That every day for the rest of my life you will be away.*'

On the 19th there is an ironic entry: 'Yesterday at Biddesden suddenly I came face to face with Death.' Her horse bolted and threw her, she was unhurt. It seemed, indeed, as if Death had finally passed by, on the other side of the street. Looking back, a few days later, on the darkness of her thoughts ten years before: 'In ten years perhaps I'll be just as prosy and wise about myself now!'

Instead, on 11 March, she shot herself with a gun she had borrowed on the pretext of shooting rabbits. Letters she wrote in the preceding weeks sound calm, on the road to recovery. But the lines from a seventeenth-century poem by Sir Henry Wotton, found copied in her handwriting, wipe the anomaly away:

> He first deceased, she for a little tried
> To live without him, liked it not and died.

Actress Rachel Roberts' depression, unlike Dora Carrington's, was not triggered by any single event. It is a long story, one in which alcohol played its part, and it had unrolled itself almost to the end when she began to write the diary-cum-memoir which her biographer Alexander Walker has described as a downward spiral, one which by its very recapitulation of her life-story helped sweep her towards the end. By the time her notebooks assumed the character of a daily record, that end was not far away:

Rex just called from America, in control of himself, looking forward to watching *Face the Nation* on television, shaved and bathed, active and interested in things. It's very sweet of him to call me. But no one gets through any more, I'm submerged by it all, not wanting to do anything, see anybody... convinced it's just over for me. Simply find the way out. No tears today. My great faults have won over the nice little virtues. I just seek obliteration.

'How do they do it, these other human beings?' she asked on 16 October. On the 20th, 'The game is up... I don't know how to fill the endless hours... Everyone I know has his or her niche planned out and are living. I'm flapping terrified wings at life... My speck of flesh feels gargantuan; my sufferings are immense; my problems insurmountable.' The reiteration becomes almost unbearable. On 22 October: 'It is 10.37 am, in California, with a beautiful day outside. A day I just can't face.' On the 28th: 'Let me able to live again, God, let me be nourished by tomorrow.'

She can't quite have given up hope, but she must have been terribly afraid of reaching that final barrier. A month later, she was there:

November 24, 1980

I never expected this total despair. Even as I look back on it, I remember days of vitality and happiness and hope. And now faced with hopelessness, I can't believe what is happening to me, to Ray, to Rachel Roberts....

November 25, 1980

I can't control it any more and I've been trying with all my failing strength. I'm paralysed. I can't do anything and there seems to be no help anywhere. What has happened to me? Is it that my dependence over the years on alcohol has so severely debilitated me that now, without it, I just cannot function at all? Or is it that my nervous system from birth has always been so very frail that life for me is too much to cope with? That I was the hopelessly dependent little girl who found everything too hard to handle, so that my intelligence and talent have been overcome now that I'm in my fifties and I can't withstand it? Day after day and night after night, I'm in this shaking fear. What am I so terribly frightened of?

Life itself, I think.

The next day, she was dead.

Chapter 14
~ Living and Dying

'...death (like life) is too serious a subject to be taken solemnly.'—from
C. Murray Parkes' foreword to *On Death and Dying*
by Elisabeth Kübler-Ross

'To die will be an awfully big adventure.'—J. M. Barrie, *Peter Pan*

Living and Dying

It's a grandiose title and one which could, accurately enough, encompass the whole book. But it is a fact that besides enjoying or enduring the various experiences which make up life with a small 'l', those of a certain cast of mind also feel impelled to comment upon LIFE—in capitals. And all of us have been forced—at one time or another—to develop some attitude towards its inevitable sequel, Death. To discover, or to invent, some handle which enables us to grasp (understand? rationalize? accept?) what looks at first like the senseless end to all experience.

Historically, of course, the answers have come ready-made, in the shape of conventional religion. Chapter 12 is full of women who found in their religion an answer convincing enough, in the face of tragedy, to stifle the great question 'Why?'

Happily, perhaps, it still leaves some other questioning voices, at least in the present century. It may or may not be coincidence that every extract in this present chapter (the only one of which this is true) dates from the last seventy-five years. It would seem that even those who profess some degree of religious faith, who have presumably discovered their 'why?', still feel the need to develop and to test their own recipe for *how* to live.

Learning To Live

'How to?' No, not quite. There is a kind of dogmatism, of self-confidence, about the phrase which rings with an assurance not belonging to our doubting days. For modern writer May Sarton, consciously using a period of solitude and creativity to come to terms with her life (and her depression), the discoveries come in a far more tenuous form than that:

February 4th

I woke to the sun on a daffodil. I had put a bunch of daffodils and purple tulips on the bureau and when I woke the sun hit just one daffodil, a single beam on the yellow frilled-up and outer petals. After a bad night that sight got me up and going.

Jung says, 'The serious problems in life are never fully solved. If ever they should appear to be so it is a sure sign that something has been lost. The meaning and purpose of a problem seem to lie not in its solution but in our working at it incessantly. This alone preserves us from stultification and petrefaction.' And so, no doubt, with the problems of a solitary life.

After I had looked for a while at that daffodil before I got up, I asked myself the question, 'What do you want of your life?' and I realized with a start of recognition and terror, 'Exactly what I have—but to be commensurate, to handle it all better.'

'Yet it is not those fits of weeping that are destructive. They clear the air, as Herbert says so beautifully: 'Poets have wronged poor storms: such days are best; They purge the air without, within the breast.'

What is destructive is impatience, haste, expecting too much too fast.

Perpetual movement, in order to stand still? Constancy, to be found only in a state of flux? Yes, fatiguing though it sounds, it strikes chords in the 1980s' sensibility. Liane de Pougy's recipe has a very different flavour, but it still has the authority of the very basic, and basically true.

July 4 1919

Friday, market day. I love to go shopping with my little Fatoum. [Her favourite little Negro maid.] The noise, the bustle, the hurly-burly—all of it delights me. I love buying and choosing. I love carrying my booty back to the house. I am greedy; I try to be a good housewife. Things which might well bore me, which I have to do whether I like it or not—those things I really concentrate on enjoying. I got this from Reynaldo Hahn. One evening, when we were having dinner together, I hardly deigned to look at the menu. Reynaldo took it gravely, consulted it with much care, ordered some substantial and delicious food, then said to me: 'Look Liane, the way to live is to bring all the enthusiasm you can muster to everything: studying, talking, eating, everything.' I understood him so well that I made it a rule of conduct.

With a different vocabulary and a different emphasis, writing from a standpoint worlds away in intellectual experience, Frances Partridge is saying almost the same thing:

March 19th 1940

We talked of the varying intensities at which people required to live. I said, thinking it was axiomatic, that my great—almost my only—object in life was to be as intensely conscious as possible. To my surprise, neither Ralph nor David agreed in the least. What I most dread is that life should slip by unnoticed, like a scene half glimpsed from a railway-carriage window. What I want most is to be always reacting to something in my surroundings, whether a complex of visual sensations, a physical activity like skating or making love, or a concentrated process of thought; but nothing must be passively accepted, everything modified by passing it through my consciousness as a worm does earth. Here too comes in my theory that pleasure can be extracted from experiences which are in themselves neutral or actually unpleasant, with the help of drama and curiosity, and by drama I mean the aesthetic aspect of the shape of events. The exceptions are physical pain and anxiety, the two most stultifying states; I can't hold intensity of experience to be desirable in them.

Anne Frank says much the same, in different language again. Even if we do feel inclined to laugh, very kindly, at her youth endeavouring to instruct her Peter in the way he should go:

Thursday, 6th July, 1944

... We all live, but we don't know the why or the wherefor. We all live with the object of being happy; our lives are all different and yet the same. We three have been brought up in good homes, we have the chance to learn, the possibility of attaining something, we have all reason to hope for much happiness, but ... we must earn it for ourselves. And that is never easy. You must work and do good, not be lazy and gamble, if you wish to earn happiness. Laziness may *appear* attractive, but work *gives* satisfaction.

In The Midst of Life...

It is a little difficult to know what to make of Frances Partridge's next extract on the subject of 'life', written several years later in 1945:

January 30th

The excitement of hearing about the advance into Germany puts us into a frenzy of impatience, and I am well aware of wanting to forge along through time as quickly as possible, looking forward each day to evening, and then to the start of a new day, and so on. I said to R. [Ralph, her husband] how much I deplored this scrabbling through our lives.

'Yes, I want to get on to the end of the story,' he said. F.: 'What? to old age, decrepitude—the tomb?' R.: 'Yes' (in a serio-comic voice), 'the

236

tomb—that's where I want to get.' 'And separation from me!' I cried. 'Don't you realize that's what it'll be, even if we are lucky enough to die at the same moment—the end of all our happiness together!' *'Don't,'* said R., 'that's something I keep trying to shove out of sight, like Burgo and the *Flat Iron for a Farthing* [their son and a book he hid because it was "too sad"]. And he rushed from the room leaving me in tears.'

You could dismiss it as one of those serio-comic maudlin moments into which everyone falls. You could take it as a reflection of Ralph's bent of mind, Frances' being reflected in the earlier, more positive extract. You could put it down to the debilitating effect of five years of war on two committed pacifists, or choose to concentrate on the strength of a relationship which alone makes death a thing to be feared. Or, simply, accept the fact as true. Explanations are not something Frances herself chooses to make. Perhaps, when we get on to talking about 'life', none of us are really that sure just what we are trying to say. Barbara Pym's expression is one of bafflement. She uses the comparison of a story:

October 1st 1979

As I am not feeling well at the moment (more fluid) I find myself reflecting on the mystery of life and death and the way we all pass through this world in a kind of procession. The whole business as inexplicable and mysterious as the John Le Carré TV serial, *Tinker, Tailor, Soldier, Spy*, which we are all finding so baffling.

For Rachel Roberts, nearing her suicide, a woman (as Edna O'Brien told Alexander Walker) full of anger, life was something actual, something which must surely exist, if only for other people:

August 23 1980

This August Bank Holiday week-end normal people are living life. Neil away for the week-end with friends. Hazel and her husband watching television. Rex no doubt out to dinner with Mercia....

October 10 1980

Life must be something else, not just taking clothes to the cleaners or giving 'dinner parties' to suspicious friends.

November 14 1980

I wish I could have lived a proper life. But I was the fourth wife of a difficult and egocentric actor and I drink too much. I never had children and I never grew up. Alan and I had a grim little marriage. Acting was all once, but I was never Rosemary. And now it doesn't feed me at all.... It's my life, I know, and looking back there don't seem to have been many alternatives to the path I chose. I wish there had, or that I'd been different....

Grow up, Cinderella!,

she told herself.

Life isn't the Connaught. No, it isn't. Nor is it your life. But it's a hell of a lot nicer then most of what 'life' is about!

...we are in Death

Writing in the years of the Second World War, it is, appropriately enough, the mindlessness of death that Frances Partridge most dreads:

April 3 1941

Opening *The Times* this morning I read with astonishment: 'We regret to announce that the death of Mrs Virginia Woolf, missing since last Friday, must now be presumed.' From the discreet notice that followed it seems that she is presumed to have drowned herself in the river near Rodmell. An attack of her recurring madness I suppose; the thought of self-destruction is terrible, dramatic and pathetic, and yet (because it is the product of the human will) has an Aristotelian inevitability about it, making it very different from all the other sudden deaths we have to contemplate.

In an earlier war, it was precisely such mindlessness with which Vera Brittain had to come to terms when her fiancé was killed at the front. The news came at the cruellest moment—on a day when she had left the hospital where she was working and travelled down to Brighton in the expectation of spending a late Christmas leave with him. At a time when, although an adult who professed no religious faith, she had just attended Christmas service because, 'I felt that I must thank whatever God there be for Roland and for all my love and joy. So I knelt in the little chapel, and looked dreamily at the Latin inscription on its walls of "I am the Resurrection and the Life. He that believeth in Me, though he were dead, yet shall he live, and whosoever liveth and believeth in Me shall never die".'

The next day, Monday, 27 December 1915, she received the following telegram:

T223. Regret to inform you that Lieut. R. A. Leighton 7th Worcesters died of wounds December 23rd. Lord Kitchener sends his sympathy.
Colonel of Territorial Force, Records, Warwick.

A few days later she wrote:

New Year's Eve 11.55

2 *The Crescent, Keymer, Hassocks, Sussex*
This time last year He was seeing me off on Charing Cross Station after *David Copperfield*—and I had just begun to realise I loved Him. To-day He is lying in the military cemetery at Louvencourt—because a week ago He was wounded in action, and had just 24 hours of consciousness more and then went 'to sleep in France'. And I, who in impatience felt a fortnight ago that I

could not wait another minute to see Him, must wait till all Eternity. All has been given me, and all taken away again—in one year.

So I wonder where we shall be—what we shall all be doing—if we all still *shall* be—this time next year.

Over the next few months, the diary shows her trying to accept the unacceptable—or seeking a position in which it might be possible to bear the load. You can almost hear her trying out different attitudes here:

January [1916]

It seems more than probable He went out of life without knowing it. He would almost certainly have sent some message had he known—and to have received some message to inspire the long dreary years ahead would of course have made it easier for us. . . .

. . . And yet—he would perhaps have suffered exceedingly if he had fully realized all he would never have any more—if he had known he would never see sunset and dawn again, never go back to his Mother or Uppingham or 'Life and Love and'—me. As it was, he must just have gone to sleep, glad to be at rest after the weariness of 4 months in the trenches in the worst possible weather, thinking he would wake to the light of day next morning, possibly seeing dreamily in his mind (as one does in quiet after long stress) scenes of the past at school, or at home when he was a child, or with me in later years, & probably rejoicing that he was wounded at last as he was always meant to be, & thinking he would have a long happy time at home, seeing much of the people he loved. . . .

In my mind I have lived through his death so many times that now it has really happened it seems scarcely any different from the many other occasions in which the only difference was that it was not an actual fact. In fact I don't believe even now that I have felt such an utter desperation of renunciation as I did the first time he went to the front. I think my subconscious self must have told me then that I should not have him for long, in spite of my apparent belief, originated I suppose by my desire that I should. Into my diary of that time, and into all my letters, there seems to have crept in spite of myself a quite unmistakable prescience of death. I was always writing to him about it, & facing it with him from all points of view. I remember writing once, before he came home on leave, 'If only Fate will let me see him once again, I feel I could forgive it anything it may have in store for me.' Have I forgiven it? I wonder.

When the beauty of sunrise at the end of night-duty, or a glimpse of very pure sky behind bare tree-branches, takes me for a minute out of myself, I get sudden shocks which shake me to the very depths . . . And then, although I have often wished I was dead, it seems so unfair that I should be left to enjoy these things, & he not. And I feel as if I am taking an unfair advantage of him, & can never enjoy them again because he cannot—or because *perhaps* he cannot. . . . It is strange to think that into the things we speculated about so much—he & I—he has entered, passed over what seems such an impassable barrier until it comes, and he *knows*—while I am left here, speculating still.

Like every other bereaved person, a day later, she is groping after contact with the elusive lost one, taking up the most tenuous thread:

Tuesday January 25th-Wednesday January 26th

On Sunday night at 11.0—the day of the month and hour of His death— I knelt before the window in my ward & prayed, not to God but to Him. For if the Dead are their own subconscious selves they can surely hear us and know that we are thinking of them even though we cannot know that they know or are thinking of us. Always at 11 pm on the 23rd day of the month I mean to pause in whatever I am doing & let my spirit go out to His. Always at that hour I will turn to Him, just as the Mohammedans always turn to Mecca at sunrise.

Thursday, March 23rd, Camberwell

I leaned out of the window to-night and prayed to Him (Roland)—at 11.00 o'clock. I always believe that there is something beforehand about the hour at which one is going to die which marks it out from all the rest, & perhaps there is after too. So perhaps He heard—even though I am a sceptic still. I looked out at the dark trees & houses & the distant lights & the black cypress tree in the garden & felt perhaps he was there in the midst of them all. And I asked Him to look after me—for I don't seem able to look after myself after all.

Like many other bereaved people, she found one special circumstance to twist the knife in the wound. Several, in fact. The first was the formal return of Roland's officer's kit—the photograph, the letters, the scented soap, the hair-brush and the clothes... 'Everything was damp, & worn & simply caked with mud. All the sepulchres and catacombs of Rome could not make me realize mortality & decay & corruption as vividly as did the smell of those clothes.' A few days later, she was to write of 'that distilled Death, the mud of France'.

The second blow was a letter from Roland's soldier servant, innocently implying that his death may have been due to his stepping out at night in the bright moon light, clear to a sniper's view: 'And I ask myself in anguish of mind was it heroism entirely—or was it partly folly? Certainly at points the two qualities come close.' The third was another letter, arriving a crucial few weeks too late, offering Roland a tempting—and safe—post on the staff at Salonika:

'Oh! if—if—if...! One begins to feel that if there be a God or Fate (call it what you will) it is after all not infallible, & that this was one of its mistakes.'

A few lines later she is back to finding refuge in the elevated note:

For when one thinks of his strong honourable character, his influence, immense & pure, over all ranks of men, his school record, his Army record, his prizes, his poems, the many who adored him, & the fullness and crowdedness of the life that was so very brief, viewed in this light does it not seem wonderful that this Perfect thing was allowed to exist at all, rather than that it was not permitted to last?

Making the difficult decision to stay at the hospital rather than give up her work and go home, she writes:

Now, at any rate, I can say His poems to myself, say the War Sonnets of Rupert Brooke, without feeling afraid of them, without feeling so bitterly unworthy that I dare not face the thought and meaning of them.

The romanticism of Rupert Brooke and his 'one corner of a foreign field that is forever England' is out of fashion now. We have more sympathy with Frances Partridge, writing in the next 'war to end all wars': 'I wish I had kept a collection of the more imbecile letters in *The Times*, all saying in their different ways, "just see me die, how dashingly I'll do it". Or the balderdash uttered by politicans. Lord M says, "If we must die let's die *gaily*", and Lord C that we must do it "On our toes". "Go to it", and "keep a high heart" and millions of other parrot phrases.' But Vera Brittain has occasion to quote Brooke again:

May 1st [1917]
Had two cables—one to say that Victor's eyesight was hopelessly gone, the other—an hour later—that Geoffrey was killed in action on April 23rd. . . .
  Sat out on the rocks' edge in front of Night Quarters & suddenly something seemed to tell me to go home. Nothing much doing in Malta—& chances of Salonika seemed further off than ever; decided to go home for Edward's sake & Victor's, & if he wishes it, to devote my life to the service of Victor, the only one (apart from Edward, who is different) left of the three men I loved. For I loved Geoffrey . . . I spent the rest of that day on the rocks, feeling all the time that I was not alone, but that Geoffrey was there & if I looked up I should see him standing beside me. . . .
  His last letter to me—dated April 20th—arrived that evening. He told me they were going up 'for a stunt' in two or three days, & said his only fear was that he should fail at the critical moment, & that he would like to do well, for the School's sake. Often, he said, he had watched the splendour of the sunset from the school-field. And then, perhaps seeing the end in sight, he turned as usual to his beloved Rupert Brooke for comfort & finished with

War knows no power. Safe shall be my going . . .
Safe though all safety's lost; safe where men fall;
And if these poor limbs die, safest of all.

241

My dear dear Geoffrey!
He leaves a white
   Unbroken glory, a gathered radiance,
   A width, a shining peace, under the night.

On 9 June 1917 Victor, too, died of his wounds. A year later Edward, Vera Brittain's dearly beloved brother, was killed in action.

Last Words

'Nothing is certain except death and taxes.' That's how the saying goes, isn't it? Something could be written about the very sparse mention of money affairs in women's diaries, but there is no shortage of material on the other great inevitability. And the authors aren't chronicling only the deaths of others, either. They are giving a step by step, stumble by stumble, account of their own progression down into the grave.

In the last chapter, Dora Carrington and Rachel Roberts, Sylvia Plath and Virginia Woolf chose the moment of their own goodbye. Marie Bashkirtseff—young, passionate, and famished for life and fame—is trying to come to terms with the fact that she can't choose hers:

Monday, May 5th 1884

To die is a word which is easily said and written, but to think, to *believe* that one is going to die soon? Do I really *believe it?* No, but I *fear it.*

It is of no use trying to hide the fact; I am consumptive. The right lung is much damaged, and the left one has also become slightly diseased in the last year. In short, both sides are impaired, and with another kind of frame I should be almost wasted.

'I am too wretched,' she writes, 'I must believe in God... God must be just; and if He is, how can it be?... Death at least offers this advantage—that you will learn the truth about this famous other life.'

'These horrible fears...' she writes three months later. 'All these years—these many years; so little—then nothing!' But it takes the state of a fellow victim to bring what one has to call despair:

Wednesday, October 1st 1884

Such disgust and such sadness.
   What is the good of writing?
   My aunt has left for Russia on Monday; she will arrive at one o'clock in the morning.
   Bastien grows from bad to worse.
   And I can't work.
   My picture will not be done.
   There, there, there!

He is sinking, and suffers terribly. When I am there I feel detached from the earth, he floats above us already; there are days when I, too, feel like that. You see people, they speak to you, you answer them, but you are no longer of the earth; it is a tranquil but painless indifference, a little like an opium-eater's dream. In a word, he is dying. I only go there from habit; it is his shadow, I also am half a shadow; what's the use?

He does not particularly feel my presence, I am useless; I have not the gift to rekindle his eyes. He is glad to see me. That's all.

Yes, he is dying, and I don't care; I don't realize it; it is something which is passing away. Besides, all is over.

All is over.

I shall be buried in 1885.

She was, in fact, buried in 1884, days after that entry. It might possibly have given her some consolation to know that her journals live on and that she is above all others the diarist other diarists quote.

Fifty years earlier, Emily Shore, aged eighteen, speaks with a quieter spirit. In December 1837 she is writing: 'Well it is no use to go on always struggling with weakness and incapability of exertion. I cannot hold out for ever; and now I begin to feel thoroughly ill.' In July of the next year: 'I have been addicted of late to growing faint after breakfast. I do not mind it myself, only that it alarms papa and mama...I suppose I am never to be strong again.'

July, 1838

Here is a query, which I shall be able to answer decidedly at the end of this volume, most likely before. What is indicated by all these symptoms—this constant shortness of breath, now tinged with blood, this quick pulse, this painfully craving appetite, which a very little satisfies even to disgust, these restless, feverish nights, continual palpitations of the heart, and deep, circumscribed flushes? Is it consumption really come at last, after so many threatenings? I am not taken by surprise, for I have had it steadily, almost daily, in view for two years, and have always known that my lungs were delicate. I feel no uneasiness on the subject, even if my ideas (I cannot call them fears) prove right. It must be my business to prepare for another world; may God give me grace to do so.

July 1838

What share the weakness of my bodily health has in it I cannot exactly say, but I feel myself sinking into a gloom and melancholy I cannot describe. I have a sort of hermit-like misanthropic feeling. I am quite pining for entire quiet. I have more constant depression of spirits that I have ever known before, and seem to have lost all interest in my occupations. I feel almost as if I shall soon have done with this world, as if my studying days were quite over, and as if I had no longer any interest in the busy scenes of life.

April 1839

On the 4th April I broke a blood-vessel, and am now dying of consumption, in great suffering, and may not live many weeks. God be merciful to me a sinner.

That was dying without modern anaesthetics. Dying with the aid of them, Barbara Pym puts it this way:

5 August 1979

Perhaps what one fears about dying won't be the actual moment—one hopes—but what you have to go through beforehand—in my case this uncomfortable swollen body and feeling sick and no interest in food or drink.

Is the news from the last front all bad? Not necessarily. Witness Alice James, an invalid most of her adult life, whose 'tragic health' was, in the opinion of her brother Henry the novelist, 'the only solution for her of the practical problem of life'.

She may or may not have agreed with Henry's analysis of her. (8 July 1890: 'How well one has to be, to be ill!') But there is no doubt at all something was happening there which made ill-health, to her, more than the conventional matter of misfortune. After decades of inexplicable sickness, breast cancer was diagnosed; then, a death sentence. Here is how she took it:

May 31st 1891

To him who waits, all things come! My aspirations may have been eccentric, but I cannot complain now, that they have not been brilliantly fulfilled. Ever since I have been ill, I have longed and longed for some palpable disease, no matter how conventionally dreadful a label it might have, but I was always driven back to stagger alone under the monstrous mass of subjective sensations, which that sympathetic being 'the medical man' had no higher inspiration than to assure me I was personally responsible for, washing his hands of me with a graceful complacency under my very nose. Dr Torry was the only man who ever treated me like a rational being, who didn't assume, because I was victim to many pains, that I was, of necessity, an arrested mental development too.

Notwithstanding all the happiness and comfort here, I have Andrew Clark four days ago, and the blessed being has endowed me not only with cardiac complications, but says that a lump that I have had in one of my breasts for three months, which has given me a great deal of pain, is a tumour, that nothing can be done for me but to alleviate pain, that it is only a question of time, etc....

To any one who has not been there, it will be hard to understand the enormous relief of Sir A. C.'s verdict, lifting us out of the formless vague and setting us down in the very heart of the sustaining concrete. One would naturally not choose such an ugly and gruesome method of progression down the dark Valley of the Shadow of Death, and of course many of the moral sinews will snap by the way, but we shall gird up our loins and the blessed peace of the end will have no shadow cast upon it.

... things couldn't always continue on that elevated note, of course. Not when the pain got worse and, six months after the diagnosis, 'the treacherous fiend Morphia, which while murdering pain, destroys sleep and opens the door to all hideous nervous distresses, disclosed its iniquities to us and K. [her companion/nurse] and I touched bottom more nearly than ever before'. But testing that original relief she had felt at Sir A.C.'s verdict, Alice James found it sincere:

February 2nd 1892

A little while ago we had rather an amusing episode with the kind and usually understanding (Dr) Tuckey, who was led away into assuring me that I would live a good bit still—I was terribly shocked and when he saw the havoc that he wrought, he reassuringly said: 'but you'll be comfortable, too,' at which I exclaimed: 'Oh I don't care about that, but boo-hoo, it's so *inconvenient!*' and the poor man burst into a roar of laughter. I was glad afterwards that it happened, as I was taken quite by surprise, and was able to test the sincerity of my mortuary inclinations. I have always *thought* that I wanted to die, but I felt quite uncertain as to what my muscular demonstrations might be at the moment of transition, for I occasionally have a quiver as of an moment. But my substance seemed equally outraged with my mind at Tuckey's dictum, so mayhap I shall be able to maintain a calm befitting so sublimated a spirit!—at any rate there is no humbuggy 'strength of mind' about it, 'tis simply physical debility, 'twould be such a bore to be perturbed.

She dictated her journal to within what proved to be hours of her death:

March 4th

I am being ground slowly on the grim grindstone of physical pain, and on two nights I had almost asked for K's lethal dose, but one steps hesitantly along such unaccustomed ways and endures from second to second; and I feel sure that it can't be possible but that the bewildered little hammer that keeps me going will shortly see the decency of ending this distracted career; however this may be, physical pain however great, ends in itself and falls away like dry husks from the mind, whilst moral discords and nervous horrors sear the soul. These last, Katherine has completely under the control of her rhythmic hand, so I go no longer in dread. Oh the wonderful moment when I felt myself floated for the first time into the deep sea of divine *cessation*, and saw all the dear old mysteries and miracles vanish into vapour! That might became a seduction.

It took Katherine Mansfield a long time to win through to any concept of 'the blessed peace of the end'. Like Marie Bashkirtseff, her instinct was to fight it. But finally:

December 15th 1919

All these two years I have been obsessed by the fear of death. This grew and grew and grew *gigantic*, and this it was that made me cling so, I think. Ten days ago it went, I care no more. It leaves me perfectly cold.

I must put down here a dream. The first night I was in bed here, i.e. after my first day in bed, I went to sleep. And suddenly I felt my whole body *breaking up*. It broke up with a violent shock—an earthquake—and it broke like glass. A long terrible shiver, you understand—and the spinal cord and the bones and every bit and particle quaking. It sounded in my ears—a low, confused din, and there was a sense of flashing greenish brilliance, like broken glass. When I woke up I thought there had been a violent earthquake. But all was still. It slowly dawned upon me—the conviction that in that dream I died. I shall go on living now—it may be for months, or for weeks or days or hours. Time is not. In that dream I died. The *spirit* that is the enemy of death and quakes so and is so tenacious was shaken out of me. I am (December 15th, 1919) a dead woman, and *I don't care*. It might comfort others to know that one gives up caring; but they'd not believe any more than I did until it happened. And, oh, how strong was its hold upon me! How I *adored* life and *dreaded* death!

I'd like to write my books and spend some happy time with Jack (not very much faith withal) and see Lawrence in a sunny place and pick violets—all kinds of flowers. Oh, I'd like to do heaps of things, really. But I don't mind if I do not do them.

But two months later, she is writing with passion of a moment of intense experience, watching the waves break on the seashore:

In that moment (what *do* I mean?) the whole life of the soul is contained. One is flung up—out of life—one is 'held', and then—down, bright, broken, glittering on to the rocks, tossed back, part of the ebb and flow.

There are, you could almost say, two forces contending through Mansfield's emotions at the time. Life and death. Sometimes, they meet head on:

December 1920

Oh Life! accept me—make me worthy—teach me.

I write that. I look up. The leaves move in the garden, the sky is pale, and I catch myself weeping. It is hard—it is hard to make a good death....

And this is Etty Hillesum, facing death not from sickness, but from the Nazi concentration camps:

3 July 1942

By 'coming to terms with life' I mean: the reality of death has become a definite part of my life; my life has, so to speak, been extended by death, by my looking death in the eye and accepting it, by accepting destruction as part of life and no longer wasting my energies on fear of death or the refusal to acknowledge its inevitability. It sounds paradoxical: by excluding death from our life we cannot live a full life, and by admitting death into our life we enlarge and enrich it. This has been my first real confrontation with death. I never knew what to make of it before. I had such a virginal attitude towards it. I have never seen a dead person. Just imagine: a world sown with a million corpses, and in twenty-seven years I have never seen a single one. I have often wondered what my attitude to death really is. I never delved deeply into the question: there was no need for that. And now death has come as large as life and I greet him as an old acquaintance. Everything is so simple. You don't have to have any profound thoughts on the subject. There death suddenly stands, large as life and part of it.

*　　*　　*

The last words on the subject none of us can every really forget? Not really. Not while the diaries live on. . . .

I want to go on living after my death. And therefore I am grateful to God for giving me this gift . . . of expressing all that is in me.

—Anne Frank

To the reader, maybe yet unborn, I leave this record of the wild and fearless life of one of the 'South Acre children' who never grew up and who enjoyed greatly and suffered much.

—Margaret Fountaine

And Marguerite Duras, prefacing *La Douleur:*

I found this diary in a couple of exercise books in the blue cupboards at Neauphle-le-Château.
I have no recollection of having written it.
I know I did, I know it was I who wrote it. I recognize my own handwriting and the details of the story. I can see the place, the Gare d'Orsay, and the various comings and goings. But I can't see myself writing the diary. When I would have done so, in what year, at what times of day, in what house? I can't remember.

La Douleur is one of the most important things in my life. It can't really be called 'writing'. I found myself looking at pages regularly filled with small, calm, extraordinarily even handwriting. I found myself confronted with a tremendous chaos of thought and feeling that I couldn't bring myself to tamper with, and beside which literature was something of which I felt ashamed.

Postscript

April, 1988

Another woman's life arrived on my desk this morning, one book which could stand as the epitome of so many. *A Victorian Household*, by Shirley Nicholson, is based on the diaries found lurking in a back drawer of one Marion Sambourne, a real-life Carrie Pooter, Victorian wife and mother. She touched the great world—her great-grandson was to be Lord Snowdon, she met William Morris and Oscar Wilde—but her entries are more likely to centre on the small domestic world of her own. Written without thought of publication, her diaries are often quite mind-bogglingly banal. That, of course, is their charm. 'To Harrods, dirty place though cheap. Bitten horribly by fleas.'

She loved her husband but was often maddened by him: she couldn't quite cope with her luxuriously crowded house and gave up the attempt to control her son. She lived, in fact, on the perpetual cycle of swings and roundabout, small vexations and satisfactions, that we all do. And there, if anywhere, lies the lesson that a year's steady diet of women's diaries has taught me.

Women's experience, people's experience, doesn't change that much. A Tudor lady (Anne Clifford) discusses her marital problems and a Georgian one (Betsy Sheridan) seeks status independent from that of her family. A Victorian Beatrice Webb talks work ethics and a steady stream of today's teenagers have one thing—boys—on their mind. What above all else *Recording Angels* has given me is a sense of community, of continuity, with the generations that have gone before. And if ever anyone dares doubt the Sisterhood of Women, the proofs are there in the form of their diaries—in the libraries, the junk-shops, the bookshelves... even lurking in a back drawer.

Index

This index is confined to contributors only –
see Contents Page for thematic entries.